CONTENTS

The Things That Dreams Are Made Of

by Roi de Lune

Demystifying dreams in a no-nonsense, straightforward and practical way, this book examines the things that dreams are made of, and tries to make some sort of sense of it all, whilst hopefully being a bit easier to digest than the often impenetrable and sometimes misleading majority of books on dream analysis can be. A book on dream analysis, then, full of lots of suggestions for what the things we dream of *might* mean, together with plenty of curious, strange and interesting facts about dreams and and sleep, for people like me, and maybe like you.

This is not in any way supposed to be some sort of high-handed 'ultimate guide' to what dreams mean, shrouded in

'New Age' vagaries and lofty, pseudo-mysterious metaphys-ical bobbins. Nor is it a dry, academic tome of Psychobab-ble-based clinical observations, designed to appeal to, er, I assume, dry academic types. It's also not supposed to be an exhaustive presentation of inflexible definitions, nor a need-lessly complex collection of spurious information and inter-pretations. The possible meanings of the 1,000 plus dream symbols I've included in the A to Z 'dictionary' section are there by way of example, a guide, only, to examine what such things could mean.

And it definitely cannot help you to see into the future, nor the past, or enable you to cunningly choose the winning lot-tery numbers!

What this book is, however, is a guaranteed no-nonsense and bullshit-free look at the subject of dreams, and sleep, in a hopefully useful and entertaining way which can be applied to most of us. Being that I am also a musician, I naturally have a somewhat musically related slant on the way I look at things, so to me this is kind of like a 'punk' book on dream-ing, in the truest sense of that old but still loaded, powerful word. Punk, replete with all its beautifully life-affirming con-notations of liberality, freedom of self-expression, disrespect for many of the questionable established norms of society, experimentalism, and a suitable amount of naughtiness, com-bined with a unique, individual spirit.

Remember: reading about dream analysis is good food for thought, but only YOU can really ever truly know, and in-stinctively sense, what a dream you've had might possibly be about.

Essentially, to me, rather than TELL you what you what your dreams mean in a rigidly defined, fixed way, the role of a dream analyst should be to help *you* to to see and understand the *potential* symbolism in your dreams, in order to try and assist you in making sense of the relevant issues in your life. I hope I can help you to spot the hidden messages or meanings, *if any*, regarding the product of your subconscious mind, be it a recurring dream, or in relation to you at any given point in time when you had a particular dream.

And all I'm telling you is how things seem to me, from my own perspective. It's just my individual opinion of course, my interpretation of things, my viewpoint... call it what you like.

As I say, only you can know, ultimately, what your own dreams might truly represent to you, as the unique expression of human life that you are, with your own experiences to draw from. However it's good, helpful even, to get someone else's opinion too, whether that be a friend, a relative, or someone like me, who spends a large amount of time looking at people's dreams, trying to make some sense out of all the weird, wonderful, and often obtuse, difficult to fathom riddles that our dreams regularly present us with.

And, like at the Doctors, you are entitled to a second opinion... or a third, a fourth, or an umpteen-billionth opinion if you like, it doesn't really matter. It's all merely food for thought. That's what this book is: a hopefully nourishing psychological and/or spiritual meal, with which to help sustain you on your way through this funny old life. Something like that, anyway.

The possibilities of a dream's meaning are technically as infinite as life itself; in fact, even more so, as in dreams, wonderfully, unfathomably, amazingly, sometimes even horrendously, ANYTHING can happen, regardless of the supposed 'laws' or apparent restrictions of the universe which surrounds us.

So, I hope that this book might help you to understand what your dreams could possibly be about, to decipher the messages your subconscious mind is sending you as you sleep. That in some way it could assist you in analysing what your own dreams are saying to you, as a fully formed, individual human being. This book is intended only as a sort of signpost - albeit a rather longer and more complex signpost than the ones you might see at the end of your road, admittedly - which I hope might point you in a few interesting directions, and help you explore some of the different avenues, paths or, if you prefer, beautiful meandering country lanes, that you can take when it comes to interpreting dreams.

What IS dreaming, and why do we do it?

We humans are obsessed, it seems, with trying to understand the purpose and meaning of our dreams - but why? What are they, really? What are they for?

Our dreams let us 'experience' all manner of emotional, interesting, amazing, frightening, delightful, funny, fascinating and powerful things, many of which we may never get the chance to do in our waking lives, or are quite simply impossible. Beyond just providing us with our own, fascinating 'private cinema', they can present us with so much more than just seemingly random images, sounds and events. They uncover our secret desires, lift the lid on what's really going on in our lives, especially 'behind the scenes', and illustrate to us a plethora of deeply hidden fears and anxieties. And we've always been fascinated by them, from as long ago as we can practically measure, since any written or pictorial records of such things began.

Messages from the Gods? A potted history of dream analysis

Dating back as far as 4000 BC, dream analysis is at least as old as recorded human history, and practically goes hand in hand with the invention of writing. In ancient times our ancestors believed that dreams were actually messages from their supposed 'Gods.' They thought that their gods 'kept an eye out' for them throughout their lives to the degree that they would send people strange messages as they slept, in order to help them understand what life was really all about. The Assyrians and Babylonians god of dreaming was called An-Za-Oar. They believed he ruled over an underworld which they called The Great Land and that he had lots of helpers whose job it was to deliver his wise instructions to us when we slept.

The King of Babylon, Nebuchadnezzar, was obsessed with dreams. According to the Bible, he was immensely disturbed by them, and had trouble remembering them clearly. To attempt to understand their meaning, he sent for magicians and sorcerers, whom he expected to explain not only the meanings of the dreams, but also the exact details of those dreams which eluded his memory too - unsurprisingly, their failure rate was rather high!

The ancient Greeks had Zeus as the father of all their gods, assisted by his son Morpheus, the god of dreaming, and Hypnos, the god of sleep. Morpheus would send their messages to us sleepy mortals by the winged messenger Hermes. Morpheus is the basis for the famous graphic novel character invented by Neil Gaiman called The Sandman - a character I am regularly compared to by my best friend Susannah, as not only do I work in the realm of dream-related shenanigans, but because my hair-do is somewhat reminiscent of his too! Anyway, I digress... The Greeks also had Aristotle, the famous philosopher, who tried to palm everyone off with the notion that dreams were merely the result of certain of our physiological - ie. bodily - functions.

In the Hellenistic period before the Roman Empire fully emerged, dreaming was seen as a very healing process. In fact, there were even specially built temples where people who were sick could go to be treated, and as an important part of their treatment, to dream too. These temples were called Asclepieions - the name derived from the Greek god Asclepius, the god of medicine. Some of the sick there were given Opium in order to actually induce dreaming, especially if they were in great pain.

The Egyptians were greatly in awe of anyone who could allegedly interpret dreams, and also of anyone who even had any portentous or meaningful dreams in the first place!

In China, they believe that when we dream we leave our earthly bodies behind and our 'souls' go and visit another realm entirely from the physical world. Mexican and native Americans have a similar idea, and claim that this other dimension is where you can go to visit your ancestors.

As times wore on in the western world, in the middle ages, dreams eventually developed rather a bad reputation for themselves thanks to religion's stifling grip on many people and the immense power of the church. They were viewed as evil manifestations conducted by the devil himself, sent to tempt us into sin! Good heavens. Thank goodness for the appearance of Sigmund Freud and Carl Jung in the late 1800s then, as they realised the reality of the possible significance of our dreams, and instilled in humans all over the world a newly rekindled desire to attempt to analyse and understand them again. And so, here we are: and here I am, and there are you, reading this. Hello there! Hope it's going well so far? I'd best crack on and write the rest of this really though, so ta-ta for now.

But what ARE dreams? And what are they FOR?

Well, believe it or not, we STILL don't really have a clue what dreams actually, really, truly are. Nor what they're definitely for either. We know much more than we ever did in the past about them though (probably) and people have made countless observations, and written very thorough, academic notes and books and things, and measured all kinds of scientific type stuff pertaining to sleep and dreaming - but, what are they, and what are they *for*?

Despite a plethora of theories, everyone is basically, utterly stumped, when it really comes down to it. "Erm, we're still trying to work that out, but perhaps come back in a decade or two, we might have a better idea then, maybe. Um, possibly...".

Some claim, however, that the true purpose of sleeping, is actually to allow us to dream in the first place. This is because dreaming plays a very significant and important role in maintaining our emotional stability and mental health. When we are asleep, our brains get busy sorting through the events of the day and all the stimuli we've been subjected to along the way, which seems to correlate somehow with how much and how long we actually dream. What's interesting though, is that researchers have discovered the less stimuli our brains receive whilst we're awake, the less sleep we need, and so the less likely it is we'll sleep, or dream, for quite so long. Hmm, curious indeed.

It's all about the subconscious - well, a bit

What we know is this: dreams are the result of strange, inexplicable interactions between the conscious and the subconscious/unconscious mind. When we sleep, our conscious awareness takes a back seat, and it's when that elusive, sneaky, subconscious part takes the reigns that things start getting really interesting.

One way of looking at how the subconscious mind works is imagining it to be made up of four different levels or layers, each one deeper than the previous one; these levels/layers are where our dreams generate, where they appear, at least, to come from.

Imagine a layer cake with light, plain, fluffy sponge at the top, and as you eat it each layer you get to is more and more rich, full of all kinds of amazing flavours and unexpected, interesting ingredients and textures.

Depending on which of these layers our dream is coming from, we get certain types of dreams as a result. Although our dreams can contain elements from each and every one of the layers at any given time, there's usually one particular layer that tends to dominate in any given dream.

First Layer

Dreams associated with this initial layer come from the area of thought known as the 'Preconscious', which is the most easily accessed part of the mind. The preconscious mind holds all the things most easily related to our 'normal' conscious life, everyday sort of things like work, home, family, our friends, what we normally do in our daily lives. These kinds of dreams never feel very important to us when we have them and usually leave us wondering what the point was in having such an 'ordinary' dream at all! The truth is, it's really just the mind unburdening itself of the events of the day, almost as if it wants to 'make room' for more interesting thoughts and experiences.

Second Layer

This is where it starts to get more interesting, as dreams that come from this layer are directly from your own personal 'Subconscious' mind. These are the dreams that can give us insights and understanding beyond what we find during our normal, conscious, waking lives. They include our dearest wishes that we keep to ourselves or sometimes have got so used to hiding away that we've buried them so deep down we've forgotten what they are. Our fears surface in these dreams too, as well as all our true, often unacknowledged emotions, feelings and personal symbols that are important to us. The events and scenarios of these dreams are usually very different to anything we've experienced, or could even imagine experiencing, and can affect us really strongly when we remember them.

Third Layer

Much less common are the dreams that come from what's called the 'Collective Unconscious'. These are dreams that represent the deepest desires, fears and issues surrounding human nature that we can all relate to, such as the meaning of life, love, death and spirituality. In fact all the archetypal symbols and themes of life as we know it, what we imagine it could mean and would like it to be.

Fourth Layer

Although rarely, we can sometimes experience dreams that are truly life changing and feel extremely significant to us indeed. They go much further than all the others and are hard to explain in normal ways, as usually they're made up of feelings, situations and forms we can't easily define, but nevertheless affect us the most of all. These dreams are attempts by our deepest unconscious mind to explain the universe and our whole existence, and often represent our search for the ultimate meaning to life and everything. Phew! Thankfully most of us can expect to experience these momentous kinds of dreams only once or twice in our lives, or we'd all be meandering miasmas of mindful thought and reflection, and have little time for anything more earthbound or 'trivial'.

Don't keep it all in...

Our dreams are also affected by how freely or honestly we express ourselves in everyday life. We can often find ourselves at various times, for one reason or another, withholding or suppressing our true feelings. Maybe we don't want to upset someone with our opinion or honest reaction, perhaps we're concerned that we could feel embarrassed or silly to let on how we really feel about something, or it could be that it just wasn't the time nor the place for us to react in the way our heart and mind is telling us to. Whatever the reason, when we hold back like this, we stand a strong chance of experiencing the results of doing so in our own private dream worlds as we sleep. These feelings will, whether directly or, more likely, symbolically speaking, manifest via your subconscious in your dreams, and can often be the root of unpleasant, or downright horrible nightmares, too. So the lesson here, if you're having such troubled dreams, might be to try simply your best to express your true feelings as often as you can - you seriously might well find that you get a much more restful sleep, and a better night's dreaming by doing so.

I NEVER dream... is there something wrong with me?

The amount of people who have said this to me is amazingly high! Some people quite simply feel that they never, ever have dreams, and, even worse than this, think that there could be some kind of mental or physical problem causing this situation to happen to them. Well, I'm here to tell you that this is absolutely and totally untrue! Every single human being, and most mammals for that matter, will have on average anything up to seven or eight dreams a night. Scientists have proved beyond reasonable doubt that in every human subject they've monitored during periods of sleep there are always very significant amounts of brain activity, indicating of course that all kinds of thoughts and feelings are affecting them. Just because you don't remember your dreams doesn't mean you don't have them! Things that can often make us unlikely to remember our dreams include drinking alcohol, having a fever, over-tiredness from lack of sleep, certain kinds of antibiotics and very high levels of stress too.

Types of Dreams

Although we all enjoy thinking and talking about what our dreams mean, have you ever wondered exactly why we have the types of dreams we do? Broadly speaking, dreams usually tend to fall into one of the following categories, but just to confuse things further for you, they can also be a mixture of several of these at the same time! Oh gawd 'elp us...

- Amplification
- Anticipation
- Cathartic
- Compensation
- Daydreams
- Desire or Wish-fulfillment
- Everyday or Factual Processing
- Inspiring
- Lucid
- Nightmares
- Precognitive
- Problem Solving
- Recurring
- Re-enactment
- Symbolic

- Telepathic

Amplification

Essentially, an amplification dream is one where a situation you might have had, could have one day, or a tendency or character trait of yours, features in your dream in an exaggerated fashion. This is usually a result of your subconscious highlighting something to you to make you more conscious of said thing/s, so that you might pay more attention to it/them. This is especially true of situations or behaviour patterns etc that are causing, or could possibly one day cause you, trouble or grief in some way.

Anticipation

These kinds of dreams are your subconscious mulling over the prospects of certain results or scenarios materialising in our lives, due to a certain situation or other which is happening currently, or seems likely to occur. It's almost like practising or rehearsing, sort of testing the water beforehand, which as we all know can be most useful indeed sometimes.

Cathartic

When there are things we haven't done or said that we'd like to, because we feel we either can't, won't, are too scared to, or just don't get the opportunity to in life, then we sometimes experience these kinds of dreams. It's like a pressure valve bursting, and all that backed-up desire or bottled up feelings can come rushing out all at once. This is when we have dreams of doing things exactly like that which, for whatever reason, we haven't, or things which give us some sense of relief, catharsis, pleasure, gratification and pleasure from the frustrations of our daily life. I know I've definitely found myself having such dreams, where I've told someone exactly what I think of them, or done something I've been dying to do but couldn't, finding myself suddenly being able to in some blissful, though sadly far too short, dream...

Compensation

This is where your subconscious whisks you away to, more often than not, much greener and pleasant lands than the one you feel you're inhabiting in your conscious, everyday waking existence. They're most likely to occur at times of real stress, sadness, displeasure, unhappiness, misery and so on, such as a relationship ending, being made redundant from work, or the death of someone close to us. So rather than perpetuate or otherwise continue the unpleasantness of the day's events, our subconscious tends to like to treat us to a little holiday whilst our conscious mind is asleep, to help restore some sense of equilibrium in us. It takes us somewhere lovely instead, like the seaside, a city we love, or to a tropical country. It also has us doing things we might love to do, or behaving in ways we don't find ourselves doing normally, things that are fun, exciting, happy and joyous, and the opposite to such horrors of the mundane and often all too real world around us.

Daydreams

Did you know that we humans daydream on average between one to two hours each day? I wonder how many minutes of that are when we're supposed to be working? Not that I do it of course, no I'm far too busy... yes that's right, mmm... er, what, sorry where was I... aah yes, writing about daydreaming. Actually, I do this all the bloomin' time. My Drama teacher in school, Miss Walters, used to call me Dicky Dormouse, because I was always daydreaming, rather than paying much attention to what was going on in class! I still managed to get my Drama GCSE though, against the odds somewhat.

So, as I was saying, for anything up to two whole hours a day we spend our time drifting away to far off imagined climes, painting all manner of wonderful, illusory scenarios in our minds, making vague, idealistic plans and such like. Daydreaming is a state of semi-consciousness between being awake and asleep, where our general awareness of what might be happening around us is considerably less than normal.

Far from being simply 'fantasies' or merely whimsical thoughts, the symbolism and subsequent meanings of what happens in our daydreams is not really any different to that of our night-time dreams. One big difference however, is that we can normally exercise a great deal more 'control' over what happens in them than when we're asleep. We can even use this to help us achieve our goals in life. For example, by 'visualising' positive outcomes to whatever scenario we want to succeed in whilst we daydream, we greatly increase our chances of succeeding. Daydreams are a lovely way to temporarily escape reality too, and serve to creatively refresh and revitalize our spirit throughout the day.

Desire or Wish fulfillment

These dreams contain things you might like to happen, or are even subconsciously curious about, but are just fantasies, eg. snogging your favourite rock star or your boyfriend's best mate, or being a princess, or that you have super-powers, or are taller, or more beautiful and/or powerful than you really are, and so on. They're unlikely to happen, and you know that, but they are fun dreams to have, and frequently the result of your brain simply entertaining itself. It's like when you day-dream to amuse yourself, for nothing more than the distraction from everyday circumstances.

Everyday/Factual processing

Really, such dreams as this are just your subconscious processing or going over the events of the day. They're normally the very ordinary things that happened, and often the more boring or repetitive things at that. Not a great deal of real meaning to these dreams, but they're so dull aren't they? You wake up from them and just think "well what the bloody hell was the point in that; I've just been dreaming all night (it's never ALL night, but can seem like it I know) of being at work, and now I've got to get up, and go BACK to work again! Cheers, Brain. You bastard." Oh well. What can I say? They're a part of living though, and likely to happen many times whilst you have the (let's face it) privilege of being alive - sorry!

Inspiring

There are so many accounts of artists, writers, musicians, poets and all kinds of wonderfully creative people all over the world having had inspiration come directly from one of their dreams. The subconscious can be so immensely creative, it's a real mystery how these things happen, and once again, no one really understands how or why dreams like this occur, but happen they certainly do. Some of the most famous examples of dream inspired creations are Samuel Taylor Coleridge's poem Kubla Khan, the Beatles song Yesterday written by Paul McCartney, the novels Jekyll And Hyde by Robert Louis Stevenson and Frankenstein by Mary Shelley, paintings such as The Nightmare by Henry Fuseli and much of Salvador Dali's surrealist artwork. Even I've had this happen to me, where I once had the entire music for a song come to me fully formed in a dream, which upon awakening I made sure I wrote down sharpish I can tell you, and it ended up being recorded and will soon be released on my next album.

Lucid

Tricky to manage, but by no means impossible to do. To have a lucid dream means that you've managed to become fully aware that you're dreaming whilst you are doing so, and are somehow able to actually control or direct events in your own dream. Some people can do this quite easily, but although I've had this happen a little bit to me, just a few times, it wasn't on purpose and I woke up fairly soon after realising it was happening! There are many books on the subject, and it's fascinating to research if you've any inclination to.

Nightmares

These can fit into all the previous categories, but obviously the difference is that these kinds of dream are very unpleasant, and tend to represent our fears and anxieties. People often have nightmares when going through big, or stressful changes in their life, such as getting a divorce or having a hard time with a partner, moving house, changing job, etc. Most children go through phases of having lots of nightmares, because their lives are so full of change as they grow and develop - their young minds can't quite take it all in fast enough, or process so much new information, so everything ends up being a really big deal to them, and can be the cause of much fretting or anxiety.

Precognitive

I often get asked about supposedly 'Predictive' dreams, which are in fact something we are ALL capable of having, believe it or not. You don't need any 'special powers' to have them, beyond those which you possess already, as the already incredibly special, magnificent and mysterious product of Nature known as a Human Being you are.

Such dreams are referred to in dream analysis as Precognitive dreams, which means they are dreams which occur prior to a certain event or experience happening, yet contain specific details, sensations and circumstances which appear to resonate with those which eventually actually occur or take place. You can't possibly know if a dream is Precognitive in advance of something happening though, or even until such events transpire which appear, with hindsight, to be particularly relevant to the dream in question.

And do you know what, to this very day, absolutely nobody claiming to be an 'expert', 'researcher' or any other such knowledgeable clever-clogs in the scientific, unexplained or spiritual realms can convincingly explain precisely how or why they occur. But occur they most assuredly do, and are one of the greatest mysteries of dream analysis, and, to my mind at least, of life generally. Strange indeed... but it's absolutely fantastic that they can even happen at all isn't it?

These can be loosely defined as when you dream an event beyond your control is going to happen, and it does. This is normally on a very basic level such as, say, you have a dream you are going to have a conversation with your Mum about a kettle and you do - in fact, mothers and daughters often have precognitive dreams involving each other, as there is a strong psychic bond between such close family relations. There are times though, when individuals dream about big events or circumstances that they couldn't possibly foresee. These instances are rare, but they do happen, and can have a very significant effect on the dreamer too. Sometimes, what's known as a 'collective precognitive dream' can occur. For example, when Princess Diana died there were many reports of people dreaming about this event before it actually happened. This kind of phenomena occurs when something significant, which is going to affect many people's lives, is going to happen. The reason people have this kind of dream could well be because we, the past, present and future, are all connected together in ways we don't yet comprehend.

Problem Solving

'Sleep on it' they so often say, don't they? People, I mean, well meaning ones usually, when they're trying to be helpful and you have a problem to solve. But you know what, rather than just being one of those cliches in life that people so often throw around as 'advice' without much real thought behind it, it's actually true in many cases - once we're asleep our subconscious minds are able to explore our waking life problems and to express themselves unhindered, and very often solve whatever is troubling us, without the pesky conscious mind getting in the way and causing even more jip. Some claim, and it could well be true, that this is because our unconscious has already solved the problem in the background, as it were, whilst we were awake. This is a bit like when your computer downloads updates unbeknownst to you whilst you're messing about on social media, or photoshopping a cat's face onto your own or whatever you prefer to get up to on your computer, without you realising it's done so, until you switch it off and then suddenly as if from nowhere it tells you it's installing them - and when you go to sleep and 'switch off' your conscious mind, your subconscious can then (finally) get a word in edgeways and tell you exactly how to solve your problem!

Recurring

This is how we refer to dreams you've had more than once - and more often than not, quite a few times in your life - that contains similar or identical events and details. Whatever we dream about, most of the time we experience a particular dream only once, but we can also experience dreams which recur too. This means that there can be more than one occasion, at different points in time, where we have a dream with either the same, or similar, content as a dream we've had before. And girls have more of them than boys too, with up to

70% of women experiencing recurring dreams compared to 65% of men!

These dreams usually recur because there is a particular aspect of your personality or life, which the subconscious mind finds especially important and needs to deal with in some way. This could be anything, like a previous significant event that happened in your life (especially if the event was stressful), something about you or your nature that you are unhappy about, or perhaps something you're afraid of happening. They're very common however, and nothing to worry about, although if you are having recurring nightmares they can certainly be quite unpleasant.

Re-enactment

These are dreams that represent actual events in your life, and their effects on you. They usually involve pretty ordinary, day to day kinds of scenarios, such being at work, visiting friends, or driving your car. Although the themes and content of these kinds of dreams are quite mundane, they symbolise things you might be anxious about, or that you're subconsciously aware of the need to work through or deal with, in order to be happier or more successful in your life.

Symbolic

The dreams you might have which fall into this category involve things your subconscious mind hasn't revealed to you as yet, things that it's trying to make some sense of, understand, or cope with. They can involve anything at all, and these dreams can require quite a bit of detective work to fathom out. That said, the content of these dreams also often contains universally understood symbols, as generally speaking a good deal of our cultural references tend to be similar across the world - for example most people are afraid of large spiders, know that boats float, or see elephants as wise. Although the elements within these dreams could be seen as seemingly random, to really work out what they might mean, you also need to examine what the essential, significant elements of these dreams might mean to you specifically, too.

Telepathic

These are dreams where you and another 'appear' to be actually communicating, sometimes even when the other person is no longer alive. From the kind of dream where a deceased loved one seems to come back from the dead, dreaming of the face of the person you one day end up marrying, or just talking with someone you know well... these dreams are the kind people tend to remember all their lives, as they feel so significant. The reasons behind such dreams are hard to define, and as variable as humans are. It's likely that we have these dreams because they contain a hidden message unique to us, or a lesson we need to learn, that for some reason is vitally important for us to know.

Trouble with sleeping and dreaming?

Most of us at some time or another have had trouble getting to sleep, or sleeping for long enough periods of time. As an example of what you can do to help with such nocturnal troubles, here's a case I had a few years ago of a lady called Kate, who write to me on my Facebook page - she had dreadful problems with sleeping, including nightmares, sleep paralysis and more. This is what she wrote to me, and my written response to her problems, including advice on what to do to help counteract her symptoms...

"Dear Roi de Lune,

When I fall asleep, my body is asleep but my mind immediately goes into a dreamlike state, yet I am consciously aware that I'm dreaming. In my mind it's like I'm falling and I can hear people talking to me. I'm not always sure what its about. Its very frightening and I do suffer with nightmares or odd dreams every night. I told the doctor who says it may be stress but its getting to the point where I can only go to bed after a lot of red wine. If I go to bed completely sober I suffer with this ten times worse. I don't wish to become reliant on alcohol. I also suffer from night paralysis. It's becoming a nightly event and I don't know how to stop this... I didn't want to write this sleep problem on your wall as I don't want my Facebook friends knowing something that I find a bit too personal and I think it's a private thing. I know you're busy but I'm so desperate to get a natural nights sleep without the interruptions of these horrific nightmares... I will do anything to help myself sleep well without aids or alcohol. I don't want to depend on anything. Please can you help?"

Kate

Dear Kate,

It certainly sounds to me like you've been having a right royal time of it, trying to get to sleep without having such terrifying nightmares. As you quite rightly say though, drinking alcohol, although it can seem to help to some degree, is really not a good way to attempt to alleviate your predicament, and it's definitely a quick route to developing a dependency on it, as well as all the subsequent problems which go hand in hand with that. What you really need is to find a healthy, practical, and natural way to get a sound night's sleep, without so many, or hopefully any, unwelcome disturbances.

In the interest of honesty, transparency, and my own integrity, as well as your personal health and safety, and the pennies in your purse, I'm going to avoid recommending any specific 'off the shelf' sleeping aids, of which there are many available in the 'Health' food stores around the country, as I'm sure you're aware.

Perhaps they may indeed provide some semblance of help to some individuals, and not so much for certain others, but as each of us have our own unique and personal chemical and biological make-up, it's hardly surprising that these food supplements and magical potions and lotions can be so variable in their success rate and effectiveness. It's entirely up to you whether or not you wish to try any of these Kate, but if you do decide to try any of them, I would strongly recommend that you first at least consult the people in the store selling such things, who should be able to help you avoid making any potentially costly mistakes, in more ways than one.

In my years of studying and researching Dream Analysis, I've (perhaps obviously) become rather well aware of how the nature of our personal circumstances, and all manner of internal and external factors, can have a great effect of the content and quality of not only our dreams, but indeed on our sleeping patterns, and our lives generally, in many ways. I'm not in a position to be able to sufficiently appraise you psychologically, or to gain any real grasp of the nature of your personal life, nor of course could I possibly be aware of all the specific factors and influences around you, which uniquely comprise what you know and recognise to be your daily existence. But, all of these elements could, would, and certainly do, have some bearing and effect upon your unconscious/subconscious mind, and therefore also the quality of your sleep, the nature and content of your dreams, and also without a doubt have some part to play regarding the nightmares you're experiencing. Also, as your Doctor told you, stress is usually a major contributing factor in these regards, frequently disturbing our sleep patterns, and our dream lives.

Firstly, what you're experiencing when you initially try to go to sleep, and the sleep paralysis you've experienced too, belongs to a common group of sleep disorders known as 'parasomnias'. Parasomnia involves movement during sleep, like sleepwalking, as well as a person seeing, hearing, and feeling things, which are not actually there... that are essentially not real. And Nightmares are a frequent factor with this group of disorders, too.

Now, the thing is here, is that what you're experiencing during your initial falling asleep stage is so *vivid* that it all really and truly *feels* real, but it is in fact only a type of hallucination. It falls into the category known as 'Vestibular' hallucinations, which is the word given to sleep hallucinations including sensations of acceleration like floating, flying and indeed, falling, like you're experiencing. Please don't worry about this though, you're not going bonkers and it doesn't mean you're ill, or anything of the sort! It's actually incredibly common for people to experience these 'sleep hallucinations', which, although me telling you this doesn't take them away, is hopefully at least some comfort for you to understand and realise.

Something which may help you, is to know that the likelihood of sleep paralysis occurring is much greater if you sleep on your back. Try to sleep on your side if you can help it, from the word go as soon as you get into bed preferably. It could very well lessen the frequency of it happening at all, and it may even help you temper the almost lucid dream-like experiences you're getting when you initially try to drop off.

Another contributing factor which triggers this disorder occurring in the first place, is in fact drinking alcohol. That red wine you mentioned, or that little night cap, or whatever your evening's tipple of choice was, prevents you getting into the regenerative 'deep sleep' mode, and frequently does (and usually will) give you unpleasantly disturbed sleep in the middle of the night - and, if you're prone to it, as you appear to be, this can manifest as sleep paralysis. It will trigger strange, alarming, or disturbing, dreams and nightmares, as it interferes with your physical systems, including your breathing, cell reproduction, and your bladder too of course! We often feel worse if we wake up from sleeping after drinking, mainly due to the extra stress we've put our bodies and brains under. So I would recommend that you try to avoid booze completely, on most days at the very least, or even entirely, if you can manage that?

Additionally, don't drink any Coffee, Tea, or other caffeine containing beverages in the evening, and if you smoke, I'd recommend you think about stopping - caffeine and nicotine both increase your heart rate, and release adrenaline into your bloodstream, which will definitely have a major effect on your ability to relax and get to sleep, increasing your chances of your parasomnia recurring. And lastly, before I finish, rather than list just a few token examples here for you, I'd seriously advise that you read a few good books or websites on relaxation and de-stressing techniques, and try to incorporate some of what they advise into your daily routine, as they may well help you sleep better too. I would highly recommend you get into some sort of relaxational routine, ideally lasting a full hour before you go to bed, for example involving such things as having a long soak in a scented bath with low lighting, turning the TV off, listening to relaxing music, reading a book, anything which helps you unwind and calm down at the end of the day, basically. Hope that all helps...

Common Dream Themes

S ome of the most frequently occuring dream themes we have as a species generally seem to involve such things as death, flying, nudity, teeth troubles and work. Here I take a look at some of these, and what the devil they might mean is going on in our lives when we have them.

Flying

To dream of flying, unaided, is an especially wonderful experience for most of us that have had such dreams. It tends most usually to signify a much needed or hoped for freeing up of your spirit, or a sense of liberation from daily life, normality, and the humdrum routines we have to endure so often. We are literally rising up and soaring above our problems.

Flying in an Airplane often symbolises that you have an increasing sense of freedom, and more mental, spiritual, or psychic energy than usual. Essentially, it's that things are becoming seemingly easier for you to handle in life. If your dream flying happens in a helicopter, this can indicate that you sense you have, or perhaps want to have, more freedom than ever, regarding the direction you can take in whatever situation you might have on your plate currently.

Falling

Falling in your dreams is something which tends to happen very early on in your sleep cycle, when you've just nodded off and are in the first stage of going to sleep. Very frequently, such dreams are accompanied by those familiar spasmodic 'hypnic jerks' we often get when we're drifting away, which although perfectly normal, can sometimes wake us right back up again, rather irritatingly!

Falling generally symbolises some kind of lack of control in your life, which is making you feel especially ungrounded and uneasy. It might even be that your position is seemingly downright precarious in some way and you don't know, right now, anyway, what to do to stop it or change things.

Unfortunately, some very silly people, over the years, have put about the nonsensical, and potentially psychologically damaging to some, 'myth' (ie. utter bollocks) that if you dream of falling, and you end up hitting the ground in said dream, then you will actually die in real life. This is absolutely unmitigated rubbish and total tosh, I can promise you! In fact, dreaming about getting up off the ground unharmed after a long fall can represent you overcoming your present troubles and strife in so-called 'real life'. So there.

Being Chased

Curiously enough, such dreams as these tend to symbolise a determination to succeed, indicating a strong motivation is lurking within the subconscious in pursuit of something significant to you. These kinds of dreams are even more likely to occur if you're struck by an urgent desire, which needs satiating and quickly too.

Now that said, of course there are also dreams like this which rather more directly represent a longing to avoid troublesome issues, situations, or indeed people. They can indicate that a person isn't accepting responsibility for their own actions, or that they're attempting to escape their fears and insecurities.

Teeth

Here's an interesting fact to get your teeth into; almost everyone has at some point had a dream involving their gnashers. No wonder - they feature very prominently in our daily lives don't they, so most of us place rather a lot of importance on our teeth, and especially if something goes wrong with them. When teeth feature in your dreams, you'll find all sorts of potent, hidden meanings behind your smile/grimace/Grrr-face. Here's a good selection-box type collection of some of them.

Teeth Falling out

Lack of faith in your own decisions, feeling undervalued or ignored by others, being in no-win situations

Loose teeth

Indecision, fear, trepidation, insecurity, lack of self-confidence, non-assertiveness

White and bright

Joyfulness, success in endeavours, confidence, happiness

Missing

Inability to attain things, lack of success, desire for the unobtainable

Decay/Cavities

Unacknowledged mental health issues, bad business ideas, poor abilities for planning ahead

Too big

Boastfulness, egoistic tendencies, overconfidence

Too small

Overwhelming burdens, unmanageable situations, unrealistic goals

Vampire fangs

Aggressiveness, selfish thoughts and actions, exploiting others for your own ends

New Teeth coming through

New ventures, ideas forming, breakthroughs, learning something new

Soft teeth

Difficulties, hard work situations, ineffective actions

Dentures

Dishonesty, not speaking your true thoughts, deceitfulness

Braces

Need for emotional support, seeking guidance, looking for help

Teeth being pulled out

Being prevented from progressing, blocked paths, feeling deliberately persecuted or attacked

Almost dying

We don't half get ourselves into some tricky situations in life don't we? The majority of which, mercifully, we manage to either escape from, or avoid, relatively unscathed and without experiencing too many negative effects. Here's a choice selection of some scary scrapes and nasty near misses which, when they appear in our dreams, symbolise what's actually going on beneath the surface in our waking lives.

Airplane crash-landing

Setting unrealistic goals for yourself, experiencing a debilitating lack of self-confidence, fear of losing respect or position of power.

Nearly drowning

A relationship is undergoing emotional stress, emotional issues are getting you down generally, or you might be falling back into old bad habits.

Knife attack

Something needs to be cut out of your life for your own good, a bad relationship needs to end, someone is feeling sexually frustrated with you

Escaping from a building on fire

You're in a dangerous but passionate affair of the heart, times of intense personal introspection, family problems are coming to a head

Surviving a car accident

Time to change direction, altering your approach to things, slow down, rethink plans

Being crushed

Outside pressure to behave a certain way is building up in your life, oppressive tendencies from people in positions of authority above you, something is limiting your experience of life

Poisoned

Negativity is adversely affecting you and your life, you're allowing something or someone into your life which you know could be bad for you, someone has been saying unpleasant or hurtful things about you

Narrowly avoiding being blown up

People with angry feelings or volatile emotions surround you, an unpleasant situation is coming to a head and you need to get away from it immediately

Surviving a firing squad

A confrontation with authority can work in your favour, your individuality and single-mindedness will help you through a particularly trying time

Being electrocuted

Fear of the consequences of your actions, feeling extremely on edge about something you're doing, an exciting but dangerous sexual desire or involvement

Almost suffocating

Being stifled by a relationship, feeling increasingly unable to express yourself or say what you want

Death

Don't worry if you dream of yourself coming to the ultimate end though - that is to say of course, dreaming of actually dying. This is in fact a positive thing, as it reflects the fact that not only do you recognize the fact that something in your life is in need of a change, but you are trying to change that something as you feel it has outlived its useful purpose for you. This is a very common and important occurrence in most people's dreams at one time or another, and mainly shows that you are going through a very transitional phase you're willing to go through, whatever it takes now to make your life more how you'd like it to be. You're becoming more and more enlightened, maybe even spiritual, in your approach to existence, and are likely about to enter into a new, far more productive time.

Nakedness, nudity, finding yourself with absolutely no clothes on at all!

It happens to us every day at one point or another, but sometimes it happens to us in our dreams too. Dreaming of finding yourself apparently nude, naked as the day you were born, especially in front of other people, is a very common dream indeed. It can symbolise many things to us as individuals but there are some generally held opinions about its significance to our subconscious. Mainly, it represents feelings of insecurity, of being 'found out' in some way. It's usually that we're worrying we're not really what or how others may think we are, especially in work situations or potentially significant social occasions – ultimately, a fear of being mortally embarrassed forever and ever, if anyone actually found us out as the 'frauds' we fear we might be.

Water

When we have dreams involving water, this symbolises different aspects of our emotional state of being at the time of having them. Seeing as our bodies are 80% water and it's almost impossible to 'switch off' our emotions for any length of time, perhaps our subconscious minds are already programmed to associate our emotions with water, as both things are so important in our lives that they practically rule our very existence. So, water in our dreams generally represents our emotional lives, our unconscious, spiritual, and psychic states of mind.

Calm, smooth surfaced water shows that you're feeling serene, that your life is on a very even keel with plenty of ways or reasons for achieving peace of mind around you. Spiritually, this signifies that you're feeling absolutely 'at one' with life and your inner psychic processes are aligned well with your desires.

The more movement in the water in your dream, then the

more 'movement' there also is in these areas of your life. If it really starts seeming like quite a 'choppy' scene then this indicates you're feeling emotionally unbalanced, and that things are generally suffering from a degree of upset somehow.

Boiling water means that previously hidden feelings and thoughts from our unconscious are coming to the forefront of our minds and need attention.

Dirty water represents clouded thoughts or feelings, and even negative emotions about a situation or person close to you. It's time to start clearing out these murky, negative thoughts and issues, to clear your psychic and spiritual 'waters' again.

When it's raining in your dreams, this signifies fertile situations. If you dream of seeing rain fall around you, then this symbolises your own feelings of forgiveness towards someone. If you're getting rained upon yourself specifically, then your forgiveness is being directed towards yourself instead.

Work

At some point most of us will have had a dream or several about being in work. Such dreams are very common to most of us, and we can even experience what seems like an entire day at work in our dreams, only then to wake up and finds ourselves having to actually go and do it all over again for real - not often an especially favourite dream memory for some people, that one! To have dreams involving work in some way can suggest other things to us too, aside from the fact that it features so much in all our lives.

The most common reason we dream of our jobs or being at work somehow, is simply that we're working a lot, maybe even too much or too hard. If you find yourself having dreams of being at work very often, perhaps you need to consider whether you're working more overtime than you can cope with comfortably, or that you're maybe taking on too much during your working day. If any of this is the case, try to aim to be more realistic with your workload somehow, and take a well earned break or holiday as soon as you can.

All work and no play can really have a negative effect on you and your life, and will of course affect the quality of your work in the end, too, so you end up becoming less productive by stressing yourself trying to do so much. If we aren't happy in our work, then most of us end up dreaming about our current jobs an awful lot, which certainly would suggest that it's time to start looking at what it is that you might be happier doing for a job.

We dream about doing work that isn't what we normally do for a living too. It's quite interesting to look at the nature of the work you are doing in your dream when it's something other than your usual job, to see what the differences are between them, and then think about whether there is some aspect of your real-life job that you perhaps might want to change or could improve upon, that your dream-life job is showing you in some way.

Sometimes we dream about being in an old job, or doing some kind of work that we used to do a long time ago. What this suggests is that there's an old lesson or approach we once learned that we may have perhaps forgotten, which we need to apply to our life or a current situation somehow. It could be helpful to you, if you have a dream like this, to think back to the time when you were doing that particular job. Think about what abilities or qualities you discovered, learned or found in yourself back then, whether regarding work or other aspects of life, to see if doing this could have any kind of positive use to you now – it may trigger off a memory or two that could be just the thing to help you on your way!

We can sometimes even find ourselves dreaming of doing the dreaded housework, with a duster in one hand and the Hoover in the other, frantically making the place all spick and span! This can actually represent to us that we are making some significant changes in our lifestyle, perhaps breaking with old habits, doing away with a previous way of thinking or living, and moving on to better ways that will serve us much better.

Although it could also possibly be a very literal kind of a dream, and that you really do need to get scrubbing and polishing at home very soon indeed, but surely that couldn't be the case at all... could it?

Strange Stories, Interesting Facts & Other Amazing things About Dreams & Sleep

A cornucopia of odd, amazing, weird, funny and curious facts, useful hints and tips, & various other bits and bobbins I've come across along the way, during my extensive research of dreams and sleep.

Oneirology

This is the word given to the scientific study of Dreaming. This word dates all the way back to 1653 when its use was first documented, but there wasn't much in the way of progress in the field of scientific Dream research until the mid-20th century. Nathaniel Kleitman, the Russian born Professor Emiritus in Physiology, is recognised as the Father of modern Dream research who, along with his student Eugene Asirinsky at the University of Chicago, discovered Rapid Eye Movement (REM) in the 1950s with the aid of a machine called an Electroencephalograph (EEG). It was they who discovered, and successfully demonstrated, that REM recorded during certain cycles of sleep correlated directly with periods of Dreaming and brain activity!

What the Dickens?

On his travels around the world, Charles Dickens carried a compass at all times to check his bed was always facing the right direction. He believed, as many did, that his head should point due north, with his feet south, so the flow of magnetic current would go straight through him, thus benefiting his body and mind whilst he slept! Well, it didn't seem to do him any harm, anyway.

Real or rubbish?

The early fathers of philosophy had very different views on dreaming. Plato argued strongly in favour of dreams being the way through which we could communicate with a world way beyond that of our physical existence. Aristotle, on the other hand, thought that dreams were simply the inevitable results of leading a busy, stressful, or exciting lifestyle. Well... what do YOU think?

Sail away...

Record breaking Yachtswoman Ellen MacArthur sailed around the world single handed, surviving on just five and a half hours sleep a day - but never all in one go. To maximise the benefits she divided it into short, regular naps averaging at 36 minutes long, throughout her entire 94 day voyage. She totalled 891 naps, and became the fastest ever woman sailor! Bet she slept for a week when she got home.

The Collective Unconscious

In the early 20th century, Carl Jung, a psychologist from Switzerland and a contemporary of Sigmund Freud, formulated the idea of the 'collective unconscious'. This is based on his theory of a virtual 'reservoir' of shared memories and experiences, which we all subconsciously identify with, providing us with the archetypes, symbolism, themes, and reference points for modern day dream analysis. The most common dream themes are; water, being trapped, death, travelling, running, falling, houses, flying, nudity, being late, and sex!

A bit of Feng Shui for your Boudoir

Feng Shui is a system of thought originating in the Far East, concerning the practice of living in harmony with our environment, and manipulating our Chi (energy levels) by the art of arranging the things around us. Accordingly, the layout of your bedroom has a very strong effect on your sleep. For a healthy life, and to encourage dreaming, a good night's sleep is essential. There are many positive effects to be gained by following some of the rules of Feng Shui - but in some cases, for troubled sleepers, the effect of bad Feng Shui could be negative, and seriously affect the quality of their sleep, and their lives in general!

• In an ideal world, your bedroom should be as far away from your front door as possible

• Don't have a ceiling light or a lamp directly above your bed. Use soft, deflected lighting instead, it's much less harsh (and it's much more flattering to our features too!)

• Get a strong headboard to help regenerate and protect your Chi whilst you sleep

• To enhance feelings of inner security, make sure that you can see your bedroom door from your bed, but that your bed is nowhere near the door

• Pastel colours encourage restful sleep - surround yourself with pillows, bed linen, wall hangings coloured in delicate shades

• Avoid having your bed positioned between the bedroom door and your windows

• Prevent yourself from sleeping with your head too close to a window. Your Chi (energy) will just fly out the window and you'll feel much more tired than you should do when you awake

• If you have a bedside table, make sure it has rounded corners instead of square ones. This prevents 'cutting' Chi from being directed at you in bed

• Got a bathroom, toilet or shower room leading off from

your bedroom? Make sure the door is shut when you sleep

- Beams on the ceiling can look nice, but above the bed? Very poor Feng Shui, that is... paint them so they blend in with the ceiling, or perhaps drape or pin up some nice material over them instead

- Here's possibly the worst Chi depleting sleep related thing of all time - you must absolutely avoid ever sleeping with your image visible in a mirror! Especially if said mirror is at the bottom end of your bed - yikes!

Write it down!

After just five minutes of waking up half of your dream will have been forgotten, and after ten minutes more than ninety five percent of it will have disappeared. For the most part, unless we write our dreams down, we don't remember them - but when we do so, the results can sometimes be amazing. Samuel Taylor Coleridge famously wrote his poetic masterpiece 'Kubla Khan' after a dream he'd just had. After furiously scribbling down over fifty lines, somebody interrupted his recollection by knocking at his door! When he returned to attempt to finish his poem off, he found he couldn't remember any more whatsoever of his wondrous dream, and so it was to remain unfinished forever. Mary Shelley's 'Frankenstein' was also the result of a dream she had, and Robert Louis Stevenson was inspired to write his nightmarish tale of 'Doctor Jekyll and Mr. Hyde' by a dream, too. More on these famous examples later...

Hindu consciousness

An ancient Hindu story describes three states of mind in humans relating to dreams and consciousness: Vaiswanara, the state of wakefulness, when we perceive things by our senses; Taijasa, the state of dreaming sleep, that 'reflects in the mind what's happened in a person's past'; and Prajna - the state of dreamless sleep, when 'the veil of unconsciousness envelops thought and knowledge, and subtle impressions of the mind apparently vanish'. Well, fancy that.

Shocking news-flash!

Ever been asleep and experienced a flash of brilliant light, or heard a shot, or sensed something akin to an explosion in your dreams? These startling experiences result from electrical stimulation of the brain's occipital lobe, where dreams physically originate, due to a build-up of static electricity in the larger muscles. It discharges as a self-induced electric shock into the head, and is reputedly responsible for having beneficial healing effects.

Do we sleep differently when we're old?

Sleeping patterns do indeed alter as we age. Older people tend to get less night-time sleep, as they often can wake frequently throughout the night, but they make up for this lack of nocturnal sleep by snoozing more during the day instead. This is known as Biphasic, or, if there are more than two periods of sleep within a 24 hour period, Polyphasic sleep.

How low [G.I.] can you go?

Eating low G.I. (Glycaemic Index) food before bedtime helps you get the most from your night's sleep and promotes dreaming. This is as a result of the slow energy release which occurs after eating such foods, which prevents glucose and insulin levels from dipping during the night. Foods include: Oats, Apples, Peanuts, Pumpkin Seeds, Rye bread, Bran, Chickpeas, Cherries, Grapefruit, Carrots and perhaps surprisingly, Spaghetti!

The wandering Somnambulist

Somnambulism, also known as Sleepwalking, is one of the most common sleep disorders occurring during deep sleep. This is a general term though, referring to people who perform any kind of movement during their sleep, not just walking about. Somnambulists are usually totally amnesic about their behaviour, so they never remember what they did or where they went. Factors which may trigger an episode of somnambulism are the consumption prior to sleeping of alcohol or caffeine, as well as experiencing excessive fatigue or stress, and even taking sleeping pills can cause it.

Dreaming of the future

Although dreams are almost exclusively products of our sub-conscious mind, very rarely they can actually turn out to be prophetic in nature. For example, in 1947 Sugar Ray Robinson dreamt that one of his punches would kill Jimmy Doyle in their forthcoming welterweight title fight. He warned his manager and a priest, who both dismissed his fears, only for his prophetic dream to sadly come true in the 8th round.

How important is dreaming and sleeping?

The third of our lives that we spend dreaming and sleeping is a very important time. During these periods we not only re-generate our bodies, but also reconnect with the very source of life itself. From this life-source comes our energy, encouragement, hope, and inspiration which we could never hope to generate or discover purely from just our intellect, or our waking 'conscious' minds.

Dear Diary...

Keeping a Dream Diary is a great way of getting a good old peek into your subconscious! Here's a few pointers on keeping one.
- Keep your pen and paper near the bed
- Try using a voice recorder of some sort to record your dreams the moment you wake up. Most phones have one built in these days.
- Make a note of the date of each of your dreams
- Don't wait until later to write your dreams down - you normally forget 95% of your dream after 5 minutes of waking
- Write every dream down - No dream is too silly or trivial

- Write as much detail as possible
- Give each dream a title - be descriptive!

B-serious

Nutritionists recommend eating plenty of B-vitamin rich food in order to help promote healthy sleep. B-vitamins are associated with sleep due to their involvement in the control of Tryptophan, and other helpful sleep inducing amino-acids. To maintain your daily supply of B-vits, try eating more turkey, dairy, soy, oats, kidney beans, wheat, poultry, cabbage, eggs, red meat, and almonds!

R.E.M.=S.E.X. [sort of]

Around 25% of the time we spend asleep is spent in the REM period; REM stands for Rapid Eye Movement, which is where the band REM got their name, fact-fans. During REM sleep a strange physiological phenomenon occurs - we all experience significantly increased blood flow to our nether regions. Those erotic midnight episodes which happen to blokes in their sleep, happen to women as well - and it's nothing to do with whether or not we've been having 'sexy' dreams, either!

Smokey stuff

A research project, conducted by the Health Behaviour Unit at the Institute of Psychiatry in London, which involved 300 cigarette smokers who'd recently quit, produced some interesting results.

- As a direct effect of tobacco withdrawal, nearly all recent quitters regularly dreamt of themselves enjoying smoking a cigarette.

- The dreams they had were incredibly vivid, far more than usual, with the strongest dreams occurring during the first few weeks of withdrawal.

- Over a third reported dreaming about actually catching themselves in the act of smoking - and feeling guilty or panic-stricken as a result!

- Even in subjects who hadn't smoked for a whole year, 63% still reported dreaming of smoking sometimes, albeit only occasionally

It just goes to show doesn't it; smoking is such a powerful habit to break that the addiction even enters the world of dreams.

Sleepless nights

What's the longest time you've gone without having any sleep? Researchers at the British Ministry of Defence have discovered how to 'reset' the body clocks of soldiers, enabling them to remain fully alert and on duty for up to 36 hours at a time! They make them wear glasses with special optical fibres built into them, which project a ring of white light the same spectrum frequency as a sunrise around the retina of their eyes. This fools their brains into reacting as though they've 'just woken up' and keeps them awake for 50% longer!

To sleep, perchance to Dream

Here are some of the major issues today which can affect our sleep - and our dreamtime.

● 24 hour accessibility to the Internet is one of the major factors in society today distracting people from getting a good night's sleep

● Even the faint light from a digital alarm clock display can be enough to negatively affect your sleep - the light turns off a neural switch in the brain that regulates the sleep cycle

● After a Boozy night out you might well get to sleep alright, but it will be a very light sleep that you experience, which inhibits your body's ability to maintain itself, and means you're unlikely to dream very much at all.

● Some sleeping tablets suppress REM sleep, which can be dangerous to our mental health if taken long term

● In 'pre-light bulb' Victorian times, the time adults went to bed and awoke changed seasonally in accordance with sunset and sunrise times, and slept on average 9-10 hours per night, in contrast to the present average of 7-8 hours

- A new baby in your life typically deprives both parents of anywhere between 400 and 750 hours of sleep within the first year

Sleep more, Live longer!

Not getting enough sleep could seriously affect your health. Recent studies by Dr David Johnson show that if you regularly get less than 6 hours sleep a night, then you are directly risking a life-threatening increase in your own mortality. Consistently lacking enough sleep means we're up to four times more likely to become obese, or develop diabetes, heart disease, osteoporosis, memory loss, or even to suffer a stroke. Dr Johnson says 'We need to open up our eyes to the value of closing them'! Some people is the US are even turning to such new methods as cranial electrotherapy stimulation, to help them increase the alpha-waves in their brains, to help them relax and and get a better quality of sleep.

How long do YOU sleep?

Bats sleep 18-20 hours a day

Cats sleep about 12 hours a day.

Dogs sleep between 10 and 11 hours daily.

Giraffes sleep only about 2 hours each day.

Some birds and aquatic creatures sleep uni-hemispherically - which means they send one half of their brain to sleep whilst the other is still awake!

Killer whales and Dolphins don't sleep at all for the first month of their lives.

Some fish never sleep.

Newborn babies will sleep anything up to 18 hours.

Young children sleep around 12-15 hours a day.

Teenagers need around 9 hours sleep - despite claims to the contrary from many of them of course

Adult humans *who live the longest* tend to sleep on average between 6 to 8 hours each night, and *regularly* sleeping for more or less than this in a 24 hour period significantly increases the risk of serious illness. You have been warned! (And so have I... Must set my alarm tomorrow.)

Where do we go when we dream?

Well the Chinese used to believe that the dream-world is an actual place that our spirits go to visit each night. They think that our souls leave our physical bodies entirely whilst we sleep, in order to go off to Dreamland for all manner of adventures, and that if we're suddenly woken up, our spirit might not make it back to our bodies in time and we could die. And believe it or not, because of this belief even to this day some Chinese people are afraid to even have an Alarm Clock in the house to wake them so unceremoniously in the mornings.

The Sensual Dream-world

When we dream, many people make the mistake of assuming they're just 'visual' experiences - in fact, our dream-worlds are made up of all kinds of different combinations of information and feelings from all our other senses too. For blind people who've been deprived of that particular sense from birth and have no concept of sight, their dream-worlds are based entirely on their other senses - imagine that.

What a jerk!

It happens to us all, and no one really knows why. A Hypnagogic or Hypnic jerk is the name given to the inexplicable 'jumping' or 'jerking' sensation, which most of us experience on a regular basis when we're either falling asleep or waking up. Although we do have several weaker ones which we normally sleep through, we tend to experience these stronger ones around once or twice a night, and are often accompanied by feelings of 'falling' in our dreams, frequently ending rather abruptly with us jerking ourselves awake.

Recording Dreams?

Scientists at ATR Computational Neuroscience Laboratories in Kyoto, Japan say they might one day be able to 'record' our Dreams! They've succeeded in replicating an image that someone was looking at by just using the information they got from scanning the person's brain with an 'MRI scanner' whilst they looked at the image. The next stage is to see if this will work just as well on an image that someone is only thinking of... if that works, which seems likely by all accounts, then as they improve their technique, one day we could be able to actually record our Dreams.

Jekyll and Hyde

First published in 1886, the hugely successful best selling novella by Robert Louis Stevenson 'The Strange Case of Dr Jekyll and Mr Hyde' was inspired by a dream Stevenson had, which gave him the initial idea for the story. Often better known as simply 'Dr Jekyll and Mr Hyde' it details the investigations of a lawyer from London, looking into a very odd situation which involves his old friend Dr Henry Jekyll, and a very unpleasant and anti-social fellow known as Edward Hyde, whom, it turns out, are in fact one and the same person. It has become so popular around the world, that the phrase 'Jekyll and Hyde' entered the English language, and is most commonly used when talking about two contrasting aspects of a person's personality or behaviour.

Tangerine Dreaming

Strongly influenced by Surrealist literature, painting, and music, German 'New Age' electronic group Tangerine Dream were formed in the 60s by Edgar Froese. Like their heroes the Surrealists, they were hugely inspired by the strange imagery and feelings which come from the world of Dreams. They took their name from the surrealist influenced song 'Lucy in the Sky with Diamonds' by The Beatles. As the band themselves put it: "In the absurd often lies what is artistically possible".

When in Rome...

In Roman times, dream interpretation was taken extremely seriously. Dreams were thought of as direct messages from the

Gods themselves, and the dreams of members of the senate were frequently and openly discussed and analysed amongst its members. Dream interpreters were often in fact sent into battle, to give the military leaders council on their dreams in relation to their bloody campaigns.

Dream sculpture

'Dream' is a huge public art sculpture standing in St. Helens, Merseyside at the old Sutton Manor Colliery site. It was made by artist Jaume Plensa, at a cost of £1.8 Million, and funded by The Big Arts Project. The 20m high, 500 ton sculpture is made of glimmering, twinkling white Spanish Dolomite, to deliberately contrast the coal which used to be mined there, and depicts a 9 year old girl's head with her eyes closed in meditation, as though she might be dreaming.

A Dream Within A Dream

'A Dream Within A Dream' is a wonderful, especially culturally significant poem written by the 19th Century American poet and writer, Edgar Allan Poe. Widely held to be one of his finest, it is in fact a revised version of a poem he originally wrote in the 1820s, and was published for the first time in 1849 by the Boston based 'story paper' The Flag Of Our Union, which featured stories by notable writers of the day, as well as the news. The poem looks poignantly at how we comprehend and understand the difference between the things which are real in our lives, and the things which are not, and only fantasy. Poe philosophically questions whether 'real life' as we apparently perceive it, is in fact no more than exactly what the name of the poem implies: that life is simply a dream, and a dream which we're experiencing within yet *another* 'waking' dream. He was particularly well regarded for his ingeniously creepy tales of darkly romantic horror, including stories of murder, revenge and insanity, which many modern day books and movies have been greatly influenced by.

Jet-lagged but Lucid

Jet-lag can cause lucid dreams. Crossing time zones whilst jet setting across the world causes our body's internal Circadian clock to become out of sync with the actual time of day of our present environment. This brings on the effects of sleep deprivation, & significantly a lack of deep REM sleep. When you start to catch up on your REM sleep, this is when you are very likely to experience that wild but fascinating phenomenon known as a lucid dream.

The Wizard of Oz

I'll get you my pretty! Poor Dorothy. Who can ever forget The Wizard of Oz, and the role of Dorothy, beautifully portrayed by the wonderful Judy Garland in this timeless film, packed to the rafters with intentional symbolism and archetypes? Or indeed any of the other larger than life characters who featured prominently too, such as the infamous Wicked Witch of the West, the Good Witch of the North, the Munchkins, Scarecrow, Tin Man and Cowardly Lion, and of course the 'great' Wizard of Oz himself! When the twister struck, and Dorothy found herself and her little dog Toto in the Land of Oz, her world transformed from ordinary black and white into a land of phantasmagorical technicolour glory, replete with amazing landscapes, unbelievable magical creatures, and outlandish adventures... only for us all to discover at the end of the film that it was all in fact really just a dream Dorothy had experienced whilst she was asleep. This 'oh it was all just a dream after all' thing became a 'device' nicked I mean used by many subsequent TV shows and movies thereafter.

The Sandman

The wonderful, critically acclaimed series of fantasy/horror graphic novels by Neil Gaiman, entitled The Sandman, was all about the adventures of the main character, Sandman, who was a living personification of Dreams. He went by many different names and guises, all ultimately the same character;

Morpheus, Lord L'Zoril, The Shaper, Dream, Oneiros, Kai'ckul, and the Lord of Dreaming. The story was based upon many elements of classical and contemporary mythology, with events mainly taking place in the present day, both in the world of dreams and the 'real' world.

Mamma Mia... not another song about dreams?

Can you guess which top pop hit about dreaming, from 1979, was written by Bjorn Ulvaeus and Benny Andersson, with vocals by Anni-Frid Lyngstad and Agnetha Fältskog. Released on the album "Voulez-Vous"? Also released in Spanish as the single "Estoy Soñando"? Featuring rather prominently in the film/musical "Mamma Mia"? The answer is of course 'I Have A Dream' by the internationally renowned Swedish pop sensation, with 357 million record sales to date and counting, the almighty ABBA!

Elephant's Dream

The 2006 computer-generated short film 'Elephant's Dream' is a strange, dream like, surreal story. The film's producers wanted the film to illustrate the abstract nature of the world of computers, which they saw as being comparable to the equally abstract world of dreams. The story centers on two men, Proog and Emo, who find themselves living in something known as The Machine. Emo is new to this peculiar world, so Proog tries to introduce him to it as best he can, but Emo is confused as to what the real purpose of it is, in a similar way to how most people view their dreams. It was produced almost exclusively using free 'open source' software, by many different artists and animators from around the world, to show just what can be done with such free software.

Nightmare on Elm Street

Originally a 1984 'slasher' film, featuring Johnny Depp in his film debut, 'Nightmare On Elm Street' is about a group of hapless teenagers who fall prey to a weird, unexplained phenomenon - if they fall asleep, they get 'killed' in their dreams by the star villain of the film Freddie Krueger, who then subsequently goes on to *actually* kill each one of them, for real. The film was the start of a huge franchise of course, with many further films, TV series, and remakes which have come along since. Although essentially a very graphic and entertaining horror film, the underlying premise is that it plays with our understanding and conception of the differences between what we *perceive* to be 'real' life, and that of the events which occur within the world of our dreams and imagination.

BFG

The BFG', or to give the main character his full name 'The Big Friendly Giant', is a prize-winning book written by Roald Dahl, published in 1982. It's the story of the only nice, kind giant in the world, who secretly collects good dreams, which he finds floating about in a place called Dream Country, and then distributes them to sleeping children. If he catches a nightmare though, he blows it up, or uses them to cause havoc amongst the other, nasty giants, who like to eat children instead of helping them have lovely dreams, like the BFG does. It's so well loved by kids and grown-ups alike, that it's even been adapted as a theatrical production.

Yesterday

Did you know that one of the most famous songs in the world was composed in a dream? The entire melody for the 1965 Beatles hit 'Yesterday' came to Paul McCartney in a dream he had one night, whilst staying with girlfriend at the time, Jane Asher. As soon as he awoke, he ran to a piano to play it so he wouldn't forget it. It came to him so completely in his dream, that he was initially worried that he might have accidentally plagiarised it from someone else; a genuine psychological phenomenon, by the way, called Cryptomnesia. When he was eventually convinced that the tune was his, and after a short time being known as 'Scrambled Eggs' before the proper lyrics were written, it was to become one of the most loved and re-spected songs The Beatles were ever to record.

Remember... in dreams, as in life, size isn't everything

It's worth remembering that even the most seemingly insig-nificant detail in a dream can have a lot of symbolic mean-ing. Despite how epic or overwhelming the main events in your dream might be, it's often what's going on in the back-ground, almost unnoticed, which can provide a key to what your dream could *really* be about. So if you like to analyse your dreams, make sure you write down as much detail as you can remember.

Inception

One of the biggest box-office smash hit films ever is 2010's dream-influenced science fiction epic 'Inception' which was written by, co-produced, and even directed by, the rather multi-talented Christopher Nolan. For his multiple Academy Award winning film, he took direct inspiration from the ideas of 'lucid dreaming' where a dreamer is aware they're dreaming, and can control what happens, and 'dream incubation', a technique whereby someone can learn to plant a 'seed' in their mind to introduce a specific topic into their dreams, often to try to solve a problem, or even just to see what might happen! It stars Leonardo DiCaprio and Michael Caine, and worldwide has grossed over $800 Million so far.

How much sleep do we need?

According to Dr Chris Idzikowski, once the chairman of the British Sleep Society, to ask the question 'how much sleep do we actually need each day?' is as impossible to answer as 'how many breaths do we need?'. He claims that the amount of sleep we need isn't something we should try to control, ideally, as it depends entirely on what we've been up to during the day when we're awake, and everyone has different physiological and psychological needs.

DMT

DMT is a naturally occurring, very powerful psychedelic compound, which is found worldwide in plants, mammals, and even includes humans. Medical researcher J. C. Callaway suggests that the DMT produced in the human brain is particularly responsible for the strange, often other-worldly visual effects we experience in our dreams. Plant-based DMT is collected and used in some cultures as a psychedelic drug, such as in the Amazonian 'tea' Ayahuasca, which they brew for healing and divination purposes. When ingested, DMT's effects range from powerful psychedelic trips, near-death experiences, 'religious visions', and can even temporarily cause loss of connection to conventional reality, similar to the kinds of experiences we can have in our dreams.

The Science of Sleep

'The Science of Sleep' is an incredible film from 2007 by Michel Gondry, director of the box office hit movie 'Eternal Sunshine of the Spotless Mind'. He takes us on a wild and crazy dream-filled journey, through the waking and sleeping life of a shy, retiring man, played by Gael Garca Bernal, who attempts to reconcile his amazingly vivid and creative dream-life, with the rather more lacklustre circumstances of 'reality'. He meets a beautiful woman, played by Charlotte Gainsbourg, and romance blossoms between them, helping him to build his personal confidence and happiness to the levels he's used to only experiencing when he sleeps, and come to terms with the fact that his life can be just as wonderful as that of his dreams.

Sleeping Pills

Sleeping pills, whilst a popular 'quick fix' for the troubled sleep patterns of many people, are potentially addictive and seriously interfere with the beneficial qualities of the sleep you get. They lessen the proportion of healing 'REM' and 'deep sleep', when we normally dream, to levels as low as just 5% of what we would normally experience, lessening time spent dreaming. Sudden withdrawal from sleeping pills has the reverse effect, creating vivid, anxiety filled dreams.

The Nightmare

Painted in 1781, 'The Nightmare' is the most famous, and arguably most disturbing, dream-based oil painting by the Swiss/English artist Henry Fuseli. It depicts a woman asleep experiencing the effects of a bad dream, with the very subject of her nightmare sitting squarely on her, symbolising the 'weight on the chest' breathless feeling commonly associated with sleep paralysis and sleep-related dyspnea. Fuseli painted many sleep or dream related paintings, including 'The Shepherd's Dream', 'Joseph Interpreting the Dreams of the Butler and Baker of Pharaoh', and 'Richard III Visited by Ghosts'. First exhibited in 1782, it swiftly became so famous that Fuseli painted a further 3 versions of it!

Sunny snoozing

Did you know that a good healthy dose of sunlight can help you to sleep more soundly at night? Light helps regulate our internal biological clock, which governs when we need sleep, and when we wake up. People deprived of natural sunlight will experience all sorts of drastic changes in their sleep patterns, as well as their hormone cycles, and even body temperature. Get out and about in the fresh air for even just an hour or two a day, and see what a positive difference it makes to the quality of your sleep!

Stephen King's dreams

Acclaimed horror author Stephen King frequently finds inspiration for his grisly novels in his dreams. He came up with the fully formed story for Misery whilst dreaming, as he slept on Concorde travelling at supersonic speed to the UK, writing the first 40 pages in one go as soon as he arrived at his hotel! When he was writing 'It' and experiencing writer's block, he dreamt of Leeches inside discarded refrigerators, woke up, and decided that was exactly where the story should go next. In an interview with Naomi Epel in her book 'Writers Dreaming' King says: "I've always used dreams the way you'd use mirrors to look at something you couldn't see head-on, the way that you use a mirror to look at your hair in the back. To me that's what dreams are supposed to do. I think that dreams are a way that people's minds illustrate the nature of their problems. Or maybe even illustrate the answers to their problems in symbolic language."

Pillow Talk

The quality and condition of your pillow really affects the quality of your sleep and your health. Old, worn out pillows harbour increasing amounts of harmful bacteria, dust, dust-mites, and fungus, and provide poor support for your head. This can all end up seriously disrupting your comfort and sleep patterns, and cause health issues especially with your neck and spine. Is your pillow beginning to lose its shape? Time to replace it.

Ladysmith Black Mambazo

Ladysmith Black Mambazo, the world famous South African all-male vocal group, were reformed from their original incarnation in the early 1960s, directly because of dreams experienced by founding member Joseph Shabalala! Over a 6 month period, Shabalala had a series of recurring dreams featuring a choir singing incredibly beautifully, in the traditional

Zulu form of harmony known as "isicathamiya". His dreams prompted him to reform the group, originally made up of Shabalala's older cousins and brothers, from younger members of his family. He trained them hard, the group eventually winning practically every one of the local isicathamiya singing competitions, resulting in them actually being banned from entering competitions in the 1970s, as they would always win! They're perhaps best known for singing on Paul Simon's 1986 Graceland album, which went on to sell 16 million copies worldwide.

Bedroom Colour Etiquette

The colour of your bedroom seriously affects the quality of your sleep. The more restful shades and colour schemes really do promote a better night's sleeping and dreaming. Warm pinks and peach tones are the best for rest, but pale greens can be soothing, and lilacs can be calming. Avoid reds though - unless you prefer to feel all vibrant and stimulated when trying to go to sleep!

Anne Rice

The authoress Anne Rice, now world famous for her tales of Vampires, found her route to literary success via a sadly precognitive dream she had. She experienced a horrifying dream that her daughter was dying, due to a problem she had with her blood. Months later the dream's prophecy became reality: her daughter had a very rare form of leukemia, which was to eventually claim her life, just before her sixth birthday. Her daughter's death prompted Anne to write her now legendary first novel 'Interview With a Vampire' in just five weeks - a story featuring a 5 year old vampire who desperately hungers for blood to keep themselves alive.

Exercise yourself to sleep

Did you know that people who exercise regularly have a much sounder sleep than those who don't do much in the way of physical activity? Experts believe this is because of the rise in body temperature that exercise promotes, thus aiding a deeper sleep. So, if you want to sleep more healthily at night, get up and about, and be as physically active as you can in the day.

Icelandic Dreamers

Most people in Iceland believe very strongly in dreams and dream analysis. In 2003 a Gallup survey showed that more than 70% of Icelanders thought their dreams were full of hidden meaning, and 40% had experienced precognitive dreams, which feature future events before they happen, known locally as 'Berdreymi'. It's also believed that the dead visit them in their dreams in order to provide them with names for their babies.

Jorge Luis Borges

Jorge Luis Borges was an Argentine writer and poet, born in Buenos Aires in 1899. Much of what Borges wrote was heavily based on his dreams, and ideas of 'unreality' and surrealism. His most successful books were compilations of his short stories; 'Ficciones' written in 1944 during the Second World War, and 'The Aleph' written in 1949, which both feature a lot of dream symbolism, as well as poignant references to philosophy, religion and God. He died in 1986.

Electric Dreams

Fancy being able to make yourself have happier dreams? Well the technology to do it might be nearer than you think. Using magnetic impulses, applied via non-invasive electrodes on the skin, scientists can now alter brain activity in specific areas to alleviate depression, and stop seizures. Some researchers claim to be able to use just such devices to positively affect the content of a person's dreams whilst they're asleep, just by electronically stimulating certain areas of the brain.

Roseanne's Dream

The last episode of incredibly long running No.1 US TV sitcom 'Roseanne' - about the daily life of Roseanne Conner's family - revealed that the events of the entire final season were all in fact just a dream she had (sound familiar?). Starring the inimitable Roseanne Barr and John Goodman, in contrast to much of the series' usual, and rather more ordinary, everyday occurrences, the ninth and final season featured many fantastical scenarios. The family won the lottery, met celebs like Debbie Reynolds, Hugh Hefner, Jerry Springer, Joanna Lumley, and George Clooney, even battling a group of terrorists single-handed... only for it to be revealed in that final 2-part episode that all these things were just figments of Roseanne's imagination after all.

Sleep Hallucinations

Sleep Hallucinations are something that usually accompany sleep paralysis, a common phenomenon experienced during the onset of sleep by many people. They're different from most dreams, in that they normally feature extremely vivid visual experiences, like symmetrical patterns and shapes, or formless waves of colour, and auditory effects such as loud bangs, explosions, bells ringing and nonsensical words being shouted! Well with all that going on it's a wonder anyone gets any sleep at all sometimes, isn't it?

Wynken, Blynken, and Nod

Wynken, Blynken, and Nod is a delightful poem by the American poet Eugene Field, featuring dream-like imagery, intended as a bedtime story for children - it's original title was in fact 'Dutch Lullaby'. First published in 1889, it's a beautifully written story of three little children, Wynken, Blynken and Nod, sailing in a wooden shoe, and fishing amongst a sea of silvery stars. In the end, it becomes clear that all these images come in reality from a mother, telling her child this enchanting bedtime story - Wynken and Blynken being the child's sleepy eyes, and Nod is its tired, nodding little head. The poem has grown to be hugely influential, very well loved, and widely respected throughout the entire world.

Leonardo Da Vinci

Perhaps the greatest, most creative dreamer of all time, is the visionary genius Leonardo Da Vinci, who lived from 1452 until 1519. Leonardo was the archetypal Renaissance Man, with an incredibly inventive imagination, and helped to shape our current way of life through his work and his vision. Although internationally renowned primarily as an inspirational painter, he was also a world-class original sculptor, anatomist, mathematician, musician, writer and architect, and most notably, a dream-inspired inventor like no other that had ever been before. He actually dreamt up and designed the aeroplane and the helicopter, a submarine, the tank, the calculator, and solar power, 500 years before these things would eventually become reality. Now THAT'S what I call a dreamer!

Napoleon

French political and military leader Napoleon Bonaparte used to base and plan all his military maneuvers and campaigns on his own dreams. He kept a dream diary by his bed, and upon waking would immediately write his dreams down in it. Then, he would go to a special box of sand he kept, which had hundreds of tin toy soldiers in it, and he'd painstakingly work out the French army's next moves with them, according to the visions which appeared to him in his sleep. And he's now regarded as one of the greatest military commanders of all time.

Kate Bush - The Dreaming

In 1982 the rather wonderful Kate Bush released her fourth studio album, which was entitled *The Dreaming*. She produced it entirely herself, and eventually went on to call it her 'I've gone mad' album! She deals with complex personal issues in the lyrics, referring specifically to her own demons, and the darker side of our personalities, and other more worldly ones, such as the plight of indigenous Australians on the title track. Combined with the unusual soundscapes she created with the newly emerging digital sampling technology of the time, such as the Fairlight, the songs on the album evoke much of the strange nature of the subconscious mind, and the world of

Dreams... hence the title. It went on to reach number 3 in the UK album chart, and has been cited by Bjork as being one of her favourite albums of all time.

Does Counting Sheep actually help you get to sleep?

This stereotypical method of allegedly inducing sleep is deeply ingrained into the popular culture of the western world, but it's effectiveness in actually sending you off to the land of nod is negligible to say the least. All kinds of repetitive, rhythmic exercises, both physical and mental, have been proven to help us drop off, but imagining sheep jumping over a fence is not very high on the list of tried and tested methods! Anything which helps you expend mental or physical energy can help you get to sleep really... in India, for example, rather than sheep, they count stars in the sky instead.

Terry Gilliam

Dreams is the name of the incredibly popular fan website dedicated to the fantastical, magical, and especially dream inspired work of Monty Python co-creator, screenwriter, director, actor and animator, Terry Gilliam. Almost everything Terry has ever created has been heavily influenced by the strange, impossible world of dreams and the imagination, especially his animations for Python, and of course his films. The most notable movies amongst his huge body of work include Jabberwocky, Brazil, The Adventures Of Baron Munchausen, The Fisher King, Fear And Loathing in Las Vegas, The Brothers Grimm, and The Imaginarium of Dr Parnassus.

Cicero

Dreams are a natural outlet for the weird, strange and downright bizarre thoughts that lurk within us, otherwise unseen. The Roman author Cicero (106-143) said " Nothing can be so silly, so impossible, or so unnatural that it cannot happen in a dream." However crazy or bonkers your dream may be, rest assured things are just as they should be in the private world of your subconscious. In fact, research has shown that if we were to be deprived of our dreams - our inbuilt facility enabling our minds to run riot, and go a little bit 'insane' - then there is a very real danger that we may end up attempting to act out some of these somewhat more 'psychotic' tendencies whilst we're awake.

The Sleep of Reason Produces Monsters

Spanish artist Francisco Goya's famous etching from 1799, 'The Sleep of Reason Produces Monsters' is a wonderfully powerful image, depicting nightmarish creatures, including Owls and Bats, besieging an artist, who sleeps at his drawing table. He chose these creatures as, according to Spanish folk tradition, they symbolise mystery and evil. Some believe he was making a proclamation about society; that without Reason, evil and corruption prevail. However, despite Goya's alleged views on Spanish society by some as being 'demented and ripe for ridicule', a more likely explanation, is that Goya was making a comment about both life and art: that imagination should never be totally ignored in favour of merely rational thought, which only ever produces abominable results - things tend to be, although perhaps arguably, much more interesting, when the two are combined.

Depression Difficulties

In a country-wide study of Depression, conducted by the UK's Office of National Statistics, they found that the most common symptoms people experienced were sleep-related. Well, the lack of, to be more precise: amongst those unfortunately affected by depression and anxiety, over 30% of sufferers in the UK's population stated that despite having problems to varying degrees with fatigue, they also had considerable difficulty sleeping.

In Dreams

The beautiful song 'In Dreams' written by my [half]namesake Roy Orbison, is a very singular, special song indeed. It reflects the process of The Sandman sending Roy to sleep, then subsequently becoming lost in a fantasy world of dreams involving his lover, only to then awake to find, to his horror, that she's gone. The song's progression doesn't follow the standard Verse/Chorus/Verse etc. 'Rock 'n Roll' song format: it constantly changes, very uniquely, from one movement to another, in all seven times! It was released as a single in 1963 by Monument Records, and spent 5 months in the British charts. Rolling Stone even list it at No. 319 of their 500 Greatest Songs Of All Time.

A Dream Caused by the Flight of a Bee around a Pomegranate One Second Before Awakening

"At night I always dream of extremely agreeable things, and it is precisely when I am perfectly wide-awake, in broad daylight and in contact with practical life, that my most hallucinatory nightmares have always occurred"
- Salvador Dali

One of the most famous paintings by incredible, surrealist artist Salvador Dali, is 'Dream Caused by the Flight of a Bee around a Pomegranate One Second Before Awakening'. Painted in 1944 whilst he lived in America, this extraordinary work was directly the result of a dream which his wife Gala, the voluptuous female nude in the painting, had experienced. Her dream had involved many unusual, bizarre images, which she claimed originated via the flight of a bee around a pomegranate, whilst she slept. Dali left nothing out in his depiction of his wife's vivid dream-image, and ended up creating one of his most arresting, fascinating paintings.

Ready for bed?

Ever wondered if what you'd done before going to bed might have affected your dreams? In 1988, scientists at the College of William and Mary Psychology Department, in Williams-burg, USA, conducted a study on precisely that: they wanted to find out if whatever we do before sleep had any significant effect on the quality of our dreams. They got a class of students to keep dream diaries for several weeks, during which time they were all given differing positive, neutral or negative imagery to look at before sleeping. When they examined the responses, they eventually concluded that whatever we do before sleeping *does* influence the *kind* of dreams we have - but *not* the specific elements or the 'physical' content.

'The Dreams' by The Eccentronic Research Council

Sheffield electronic music duo The Eccentronic Research Council, together with British actress Maxine Peake, have re-corded a tribute to the BBC Radiophonic Workshop's Delia Derbyshire, one of the female pioneers of electronic music, who famously helped create the Doctor Who theme in the 60's. In 1964 she recorded a collaborative piece with Barry Bermange entitled 'The Dreams'. This combined clips of people recalling their dreams with strange, electronic sounds, to create a 'journey' through the subconscious mind. In the ERC's version of Delia's creation, Maxine talks about a dream she has, recounting a last minute trip to infamous party island Ibiza. The single was released on the Desolate Spools label, and is available to to buy with a bundle that includes a hand-made cassette *Dreamcatcher Tapes* featuring recordings of 10 other dreamers, all with soundtracks created by the ERC.

Midnight Snacking

You know those midnight trips to the fridge where you decide to scoff all the leftovers, and then feel guilty in the morning? Well for some people, they really can't help themselves, and it happens almost every night - they're actually suffering from a recognised 'Parasomnia' known as SERD: Sleep-Related Eating Disorder. The condition consists of repeat episodes of compulsive binge eating/drinking, after waking up in the middle of the night, often leaving them with partial or no memory of what they've done. These episodes are usually very short, around ten minutes or so, during which time sufferers mainly consume foods they wouldn't normally eat, often very high in calories, leading many to have issues with weight gain.

Moon and Sun breath

People who practice Hatha Yoga are known as Yogis. Hatha comes from the word Ha which means 'Sun' and Tha, meaning 'Moon', and refers to the regulation of the flow of our breath through each nostril, which is central to Hatha yoga. The left nostrils breath is known as 'moon breath' and the right one 'sun breath', which is characteristically slower by comparison. They believe that regulation of the flow of our breath brings about a harmonic balance of the forces between the Sun and Moon. They even sleep on their left side too, to leave their right nostril with a clearer path to ventilation, to help make their sleep more refreshing.

Eyes Wide Shut

Directed, produced, and co-written by Stanley Kubrick, this film was based on the 1926 novel by Arthur Schnitzler called Dream Story. The film has a very dreamlike quality, and examines the overwhelming power of people's dreams and fantasies, along with the lengths they will go to, to fulfil them. It centers around the experiences of the central character, played by Tom Cruise, amid a crowd of masked strangers at a huge, bizarre, and potentially dangerous orgy held by a secret society, and the adulterous fantasies of his wife, played by Nicole Kidman. It was to be Kubrick's final film in the end though, as he died only days after completing it.

Smart Dreams

A smart-phone app called Sigmund, developed by Harvard in conjunction with MIT graduate students, claims to be able to influence the content, and even what actually happens, in your dreams. It 'works' by repeating words to you, which you pre-select from a database, during the REM cycle of your sleep pattern.The creators of this technological marvel believe that one day dreams will become the ultimate in 'virtual reality' style controllable entertainment.

Too dark to dream?

Being afraid of the dark is surprisingly common. It's sometimes known as Nyctophobia, from the Greek 'Nyktos' meaning night, and 'phobos' meaning fear. Nobody really knows what causes it, even after all these years, as there has been surprisingly little research into it. Around 60% of us go through a stage of experiencing this in our lives, usually during childhood, and it can be very severe in some cases. Some claim it stems from a built-in evolutionary fear we have, of being stalked and subsequently attacked by prehistoric creatures of the night.

Dream Dieting

The more time you spend asleep, dreaming, the less hungry you'll be for fatty, calorific foods. In a study by St Luke's Hospital in America, published November 1st 2012, they found that compared to those getting a decent night's sleep, the less dreamtime participating volunteers had, the slower their metabolism got, and the more they craved foods high in carbohydrates and fats too. And here's another thing that's good to know: Dreaming is in fact quite demanding on the calorie front, so if you want to help yourself lose weight, just get yourself to bed and start dreaming it all off!

Do we dream in Monochrome or Colour?

The sort of TV and films you watched as a child may have taught you what colour scheme to dream in, according to a study conducted by psychologist Eva Murzyn of Dundee University in 2008. Studies from 1915 onwards show that up until the 60s, when colour TV was introduced, the majority of people's dreams were in black and white, but colour dreams increased for 83% of the population after colour TV and film really took over. She found that pretty much everyone under the age of 25 these days dreamed in colour, but those aged around 50 and older frequently still dream in good old black and white! It's possible this goes some way to show that there's a critical time growing up, that watching TV or films has a powerful effect on the way we go on to visualise things in our dreams.

The Atomic Dream

World-famous Dutch physicist Niels Bohr quite literally dreamt up the definitive, now iconic image of atomic science - the eponymously named Bohr model of what an Atom actually looks like. The image came to him in a dream one night; he had a vision in his dream where the nucleus of an atom was stationary, in the middle, with its electrons spinning all around it on steady, fixed orbits, just like the planets in our Solar system do with our Sun. Upon testing his theoretical 'discovery' it turned out that he was absolutely right - so his dream was a true vision! He was involved with the creation of CERN (the European Organisation For Nuclear Research) in Switzerland, and went on to win the Nobel prize for physics in 1922.

Dream Lag

The day's events frequently re-emerge and feature in our dreams when we go to sleep that night. Sometimes, however, there can be a delay in this happening of anything up to a whole week, for certain 'special' memories, things which stood out for us, usually in a positive way, in our life. This 'dream-lag' happens during deep REM sleep, because of the way the brain's hippocampus transfers these special memories to the neocortex, taking from five to seven days to complete the transference. In a study conducted by The Sleep Laboratory collective, at Swansea University, who specialise in investigating what happens to us during sleep and when we dream, they also found that due to the way we process positive emotional responses to events, when these events appear in our dreams they're normally even more positive and exaggerated than the original events.

Man Ray

The prolific and wonderfully talented artist Man Ray (born Emmanuel Radnitzky 1890 - 1976) has been named one of the most influential artists of the 20th Century. Originally from the US, he lived mainly in Paris, France, and became best known for his groundbreaking photography. However, he also worked in all kinds of experimental media, often very unusual ones, and significantly based most of his painted work on dream imagery, producing some fantastical, strange and highly striking images indeed. As the man himself said in an interview in the 1970s, *"I paint what cannot be photographed, that which comes from the imagination or from dreams, or from an unconscious drive."*

The Devil In The Room

Produced as part of 'The Sleep Paralysis Project' Carla MacKinnon's 2013 short film 'Devil In The Room' is based on the fascinating subject of Sleep Paralysis. The film uses methods such as stop motion animation, live action film and projection mapping techniques, to explore the strange things people can experience during sleep paralysis. Sleep paralysis is a general term which covers quite a variety of symptoms, but usually describes the experience of a person waking up or going to sleep who experiences temporary, inexplicable paralysis of their physical body. It's frequently accompanied by hallucinations, intense fear and a feeling of being 'crushed', usually on the chest area, and has been the subject of a great deal of study, and even been inspiration for several major works of art, for many years. Via live events, film and online resources, The Sleep Paralysis Project explores this troubling phenomenon, and attempts to offer support and information to sufferers of this condition or those interested in the subject.

Nightmares are good for you

Psychologist Rosalind Cartwright of Rush University undertook a study of the dreams people were having, when they were experiencing immense degrees of stress in their lives, such as divorce. There was a perhaps surprising and paradoxical twist to what you might expect she found regarding their dreams: stressed and depressed folk frequently experience dreams that are generally more enjoyable and pleasurable! It was the more well-adjusted, happier and resilient people who had more nightmares. She claims that subconsciously dreaming of conflicts and other troubling scenarios helps us to sort ourselves out and deal with emotional problems better in our waking lives.

Dream Inspiration

Legendary artist Frida Kahlo may have exclaimed *"I don't paint my dreams or nightmares, I paint my own reality"* but many world-renowned, famous creative people throughout the course of history - artists, poets, musicians and writers - have turned to their own dreams as a seemingly never ending source of imagery and inspiration for their life's work. Van Gogh claimed "I dream my painting and I paint my dream", whilst Francis Bacon said "If I sit and daydream, the images rush by like a succession of colored slides". Writer and founder of the Surrealist movement, Andre Breton, is famous for stating *"Objects seen in dreams should be manufactured and put on sale"*, and as Mr Walt Disney put it *"If you can dream it, you can do it!"*.

Getting All Emotional

Dreams seem to help us process emotions by encoding and constructing memories of them. What we see and experience in our dreams might not necessarily be real, but the emotions attached to these experiences certainly are. Our dream stories essentially try to strip the emotion out of a certain experience by creating a memory of it. This way, the emotion itself is no longer active. This mechanism fulfils an important role because when we don't process our emotions, especially negative ones, this increases personal worry and anxiety. In fact, severe REM sleep-deprivation is increasingly correlated to the development of mental disorders. In short, dreams help regulate traffic on that fragile bridge which connects our experiences with our emotions and memories.

Do You Have The Sleep Pattern of A Genius?

Ever wonder what the sleeping patterns of a creative genius might be? If your own matches any of these, perhaps YOU might be a genius too - but maybe you just don't know it yet.

Maya Angelou, Author and Poet; 10pm til 5.30am

Gustave Flaubert, Author; 3am til 10am

Ludwig Van Beethoven, Composer; 10pm til 6am

Sigmund Freud, Father of Dream Analysis and Psychoanalysis; 1am til 7am

Victor Hugo, Novelist and Poet; 10pm til 6am

Honore De Balzac, Playwright; 6pm til 1am, then a nap from 8am til 9.30am

John Milton, Poet; 9pm til 4am

Marina Abramovic, Performance Artist; 10pm til 6.30am

Charles Dickens, Author; 12am til 7am

Charles Darwin, Naturalist and Geologist ; 12am til 7am then a nap from 3pm til 4pm

Pyotr Tchaikovsky, Composer; 12am til 8am

Mary Flannery O'Connor, Writer; 9pm til 6am

F. Scott Fitzgerald, Author; 3.30am til 11am

Albert Einstein, Physicist; Old Albert had one of the most strange sleep patterns of all... categorised as Polyphasic sleep, he trained himself to only sleep for short periods at a time, from 2 to 6 hours on average, which he did several times throughout the day!

Max Ernst

German painter Max Ernst lived from 1891 until 1976, and was one of the most prolific and leading exponents of the Dada movement and Surrealism in the 20th century. Originally inspired by Van Gogh, it was paintings by Chirico which originally sparked his interest in fantastical, dream-like images, and whilst studying Psychology he visited several asylums, becoming fascinated with the art of the mentally ill. These interests lead to him creating his own astonishing artworks, famously containing highly irrational combinations, remarkably strange scenes, and almost hallucinatory visions - as though the world of dreams had been directly transferred to the wonderful canvases he created.

All Mammals Dream

Dreaming is something many animals do. In fact, scientists claim that ALL Mammals experience REM sleep, which is the kind of sleep you need to have for dreaming to occur. From monkeys, polecats, dogs and cats, to elephants, giraffes and lions... they all dream. Dolphins experience the least amount of REM, while humans are around the middle mark, but for some reason it's the Possum and the Armadillo who dream the most!

Binaural Beats

The experimental sound-manipulation technique known as Binaural beats, and how its auditory effects can literally alter our brain-waves, was discovered in 1839 by Heinrich Wilhelm Dove, but took over 130 years to gain any significant public awareness. This is due mainly to recent advances in 'alternative medicine', particularly since the 1970's. Practitioners in the field have finally acknowledged the potentially relaxing, creative, and fascinating effects such sound experiments can have on us, which aid such practices as meditation, sleep, and even lucid dreaming.

In Dreams, the movie

The movie 'In Dreams' starring Robert Downey Jr. was released in 1999, directed by Neil Jordan, and its screenplay was written by the notorious Bruce Robinson of 'Withnail And I' fame. It's all about an ordinary mother who has weird nightmares about a stranger kidnapping and killing a little girl, only for it to actually happen to her very own child, by the hand of the character played by Robert Downey. She has more visions of his murders, and senses her mind and the killer's are linked in the world of dreams, that she knows exactly what the killer's next moves are going to be... but despite her precognitive dreams about her little girl, no one believes her and they lock her away.

Artificial Light is Stealing our Night

Due to the fact that our cities and towns are getting brighter, with more and more artificial lights being added every day, our precious Night, so essential to our lives, is disappearing fast. 'Skyglow' is something caused by light pollution from buildings, street lamps and vehicles and on some nights, it even outshines the poor old Moon. Scientific research has shown that this is NOT a good thing for us humans, nor in fact for any organic being, animal or plant. The American Medical Association has confirmed that all this night-lighting badly affects our circadian rhythms. It can exacerbate or even cause Diabetes, Obesity, Depression and reproductive issues, disrupts growth cycles in plant life, and changes activity routines, mating and migration behaviour in animals too. So, switch that light off!

The Cult - Dreamtime

The first album released by world famous Goth rockers The Cult is called 'Dreamtime'. Lead singer Ian Astbury was heavily influenced by indigenous tribal cultures, including Native American and Australian Aboriginal beliefs. The title of the album Dreamtime comes from their song of the same name, which was inspired by the Aborigines concept of 'dreamtime'. The idea is that there's an alternate Universe that people can find and enter through dreaming, or by seeking out deliberately induced altered states, even death - it's a place which is beyond time and space, where the past, present, and future exist altogether as one unified thing.

Boozy Snoozes

Drinking alcohol regularly has a pretty detrimental effect on you and your sleeping patterns, even affecting ex-drinkers for months after they stopped. A drink or two certainly can help reduce the time it takes to nod off, but after 3 or 4 hours the alcohol in your system really disturbs your sleep. Some of the reasons for this are the often very strange, and frequently highly disturbing dreams and nightmares it can cause. Also, being a diuretic, it fills up your bladder fairly often in the night, so trips to the loo prevent you getting much real rest. It affects your breathing too, making you snore or even temporarily stop breathing altogether, leaving you feeling woolly-headed and still tired after waking. For ex-drinkers still suffering from disrupted sleep, having a drink in order to help them finally catch some much missed Zs is a major cause of relapse.

In Clouds Descending, In Midnight Sleep

Along with Emily Dickinson, Walt Whitman [1819-1892] is considered one of America's most important poets. One his anti-war poems, published in 1867, details the harrowing life in the trenches of warfare at the time, and specifically how his dreams were filled with the faces of the fallen, in stark contrast to the beauty of nature surrounding him. He goes on to tell us how their faces haunt him still years later, in the world of his dreams and nightmares.

Dream baby, dream

Dream Researchers tell us that babies spend a huge amount of time in the REM [Rapid Eye Movement] phase of sleep; the time when we dream the most. In fact, unborn babies at 30 weeks spend almost 24 hrs a day in REM sleep! As they mature and develop, this decreases to 50% in newborns, and 35% in a one year old. They also claim that REM sleep is directly linked to brain development. The question is though: what do they dream about?

Dream & Live Harmoniously

If you want to live a harmonious, happy existence with everyone around you, get enough sleep. Dreams, and the quality of our sleep, are strongly linked to our emotions, as discovered in a study published by Matthew Walker and his colleagues of the Sleep and Neuroimaging Lab, based at US Berkeley. They found that if we have poor or interrupted sleep, which causes a reduction of the time we spend in REM sleep - the time we experience dreams - it can impact heavily on our ability to understand complex emotions in our waking lives. This causes all sorts of problems, as we rely on this kind of emotional awareness to aid us in our normal social interaction with others.

E-Books

Reading e-books at bedtime (er... just like this one) instead of 'paper' books is damaging our sleep and our health too, American doctors warn. After conducting tests, they've found that 'blue light' - the name given to the wavelength of light emitted by most e-readers, phones and tablets - disrupts your body clock and inhibits the production of sleep hormone melatonin, causing poorer quality sleep overall, leading to a variety of related illnesses and conditions. Sticking to normal books is fine though, and so is the original Kindle with its unique 'paper' effect screen.

Dick Van Dyke

The episode called 'It May Look Like A Walnut' of 1963 TV series 'The Dick Van Dyke Show', is based almost entirely on a strange dream experienced by lead character Rob Petrie, played by Dick himself. After watching a Sci Fi movie, he goes to bed and dreams Aliens are taking over the planet, and have removed his thumbs, together with his sense of humour. Walnuts also feature heavily in this peculiar storyline, culminating in him opening a cupboard door to a veritable flood of walnuts, ridden by his screen wife, who has been possessed by aliens! Well; they don't make 'em like that anymore do they?

Don't Dream It, Be it!

The cult musical Rocky Horror Show, originally written as a play by Richard O'Brien in the early 1970's, is an affectionate tribute to Science Fiction and Horror B-movies. Made into a film in 1975, The Rocky Horror Picture Show went on to become the longest running movie of all time in cinemas. One of the key songs, sung by the lead, transvestite scientist Dr. Frank N. Furter, is 'Don't Dream It, Be it' which rather sums up the ethos of O'Brien's inspired creation: rather than shy away from our dreams, we should embrace and realise them instead. And quite right too, don't you agree?

Sleep On it!

A team of researchers at the University of Sheffield suggest that if you want to help yourself learn new things, and make lessons and information stay in your brain better, get some sleep soon afterwards. Highlighting reading at bedtime as a key to improved learning, they say the best time to learn is right before going to bed. This is especially important in earlier years, growing up, but still works at any age.

The Matrix

Starring Hollywood stars Laurence Fishburne, Keanu Reeves and Hugo Weaving, 1999's The Matrix, written by The Wachowski Brothers, is a stunning sci-fi movie with a mind-bending twist and a half! Set sometime in the near future, reality as we know it turns out to be an ultra-complex 'dream-world' constructed by sentient machines, intent on subduing the unsuspecting human race, and harvesting our electrical energy and body heat for their own ends. The film went on to win BAFTA and Saturn awards, and features truly stunning, innovative visual effects. It's been deemed so significant a movie, it has now been added to the National Film registry for preservation.

TST: the evolutionary function of dreaming?

Some scientists claim that encountering threatening events in real life actually increases the likelihood of experiencing an ancient, evolutionary self-defence mechanism: bad dreams and nightmares. Researchers of TST, or Threat Simulation Theory, say that higher incidents of real life threat proportionately triggers this 'nightmare-mechanism' giving us all manner of imaginary threatening situations to cope with as we dream. They tell us it's developed in us gradually, via evolution, to improve our self-preservation abilities, leading to higher survival rates, and ultimately, better odds of our reproductive success.

Is It A Dream?

Is It A Dream? by Classix Nouveaux was a Top 20 hit in the UK 1982, featuring charismatic, bald-headed lead singer and songwriter of this hit, Sal Solo. It demonstrates his peculiar ability for singing in a somewhat schizoid style; Sal would alternate between singing in a tremulously deep voice, and then switch to a piercing falsetto, alerting the ears of many a canine in the process no doubt. He uses his rather OTT, bombastic technique to great effect in this song, to illustrate the difference between the dream world and the real world, in his dramatic lyrics. Is It A Dream?, their most successful single, reached No.1 in many countries across the Globe.

Emotional Dream Training

According to recent dream research, one of the purposes of dreams appears to be to help us deal with our emotions more effectively. What we do in our dreams isn't 'real' but our emotions regarding such imagined experiences certainly are! Dreams create 'memories' of such emotions experienced as we sleep, which help us deal with such possible eventualities if and when they might actually occur. They say the brain does this in order to help reduce worry and anxiety in our waking lives.

Vitaly Samarin Alexius

Born in Novokuznetsk in Russia, now living in Toronto, Vitaly is an illustrator and artist with a very special style and unique vision all of his own, which he's named 'Dreaminism'. You only have to look at a few of his paintings to see why this is quite the perfect name for his art. The strange, the familiar, and often unlikely elements, all come together in Vitaly's mind and are depicted in his stunning creations. Using photography, computers and whatever other medium he may choose, he makes dramatic, beautiful, striking although sometimes rather unnerving, impossible scenes, rendered in absolutely meticulous detail.Themes are often romantic, post-apocalyptic, or sci-fi related, and, as in life and in our dreams too, sometimes comical as well.

How bizarre?

Many of my fellow Dream Researchers have found that the bizarreness of what happens in our dreams usually far outweighs anything we could ever come up with in our waking state. Not only that, but Patrick McNamara at Boston University has theorised that this very bizarreness stems precisely from the Brain's attempts to represent, or to symbolise, the immensely complex feelings and emotions we often experience in life, in order to try and store them as memories. The more intense or complex the feelings then the more difficult they are to symbolise, henceforth, the more weird your dream gets!

Dreampunk

Dreampunk is a recently identified genre of fiction and art, partly influenced by Steampunk and Cyberpunk, which focuses on the strange qualities of dreams and the exploration of post-modern, often dystopian 'counter-culture'. Also featuring largely amongst Dreampunk's recurring themes are Jungian archetypes, and classical mythology, with protagonists using complex symbolic devices like 'dream logic' and fairy tales within their narratives, intentionally created to be interpreted in several different ways. Dreampunk artists and authors range from people as diverse as world famous movie maker David Lynch, and author Lewis Caroll, through to lesser known artists such as EC Steiner and writer Yelena Calavera.

Morpheus

Morpheus, the 'God of dreams', was originally a principal character featured in the long Latin 'poem' spanning a series of 15 books, called Metamorphoses. A partly mythological, part historical work, it was written by Roman poet Ovid in the year 8AD, and it tells the story of the creation of the World up to that point, and is still considered to be highly influential, even to this day. Morpheus has the power to appear to people in their dreams, and although he can change into human form, normally appears as a winged demon. As the God of Dreaming or Sleep, it's perhaps not surprising that he inspired the name of the powerful pain-killing drug, or 'opiate', called Morphine.

Olfactory Oddness

Have you ever dreamt of a particular smell? It's perhaps surprisingly uncommon to find yourself dreaming of smelling something. There have been many studies on the subject, and the likelihood of smells featuring in our dreams at any point is really low - around 1% of the time in fact. It's interesting to note that we CAN dream of smells though, despite its lack of popularity. Smells are so important to us in our daily lives, I really can't help but wonder why they don't appear more often and more prominently in dreams than they do.

Twin Peaks 'Zen, Or The Skill To Catch A Killer'

In the episode of TV series Twin Peaks 'Zen, Or The Skill To Catch A Killer' from 1990 one of the most infamous and downright strange 'dream sequences' in television history occurs. Twin Peaks had an odd, almost dream-like atmosphere anyway, so David Lynch really needed to make this dream sequence stand out. Agent Cooper experiences visions during REM sleep, leading him to Laura Palmer's killer. Very strange dialogue ensues between the people he encounters in his dream, with people's speech appearing to have been written and recorded backwards then played forwards, whilst one of the character's arms keep bending the wrong way, and all kinds of other odd elements combine to create a nightmarish, otherworldly quality to proceedings.

4, 7, 8

The 4-7-8 Breathing exercise, based on an ancient Indian practice 'pranayama', is a modern day take on an old method that's ideal for relaxation, and even helps in getting insomniacs to sleep. Put simply: stick your tongue behind your front teeth; exhale loudly from your mouth; inhale through your nose for a count of 4; hold your breath for a count of 7; exhale via your mouth again for a count of 8. Now repeat the whole thing three times and feel your troubles and the day melt away...

Innocent When You Dream

This is a rather lovely song written by world-renowned musician and actor, Tom Waits. His song reflects upon lost love, and how when he sleeps, his subconscious mind innocently conjures up beautiful memories of the happy times he and his long-lost love spent together, despite the fact that he was responsible for ruining the special relationship that they had. One of his most loved and popular songs, it has has been covered by a number of other artists, including Elvis Costello.

Dream Cheating

According to research by dream expert and author Lauri Quinn Loewenberg, the most commonly reported dream people have is one where their partner is cheating on them. She conducted a survey of 5000 people and found that infidelity based nightmares trouble us in our sleep the most, often recurrently. It's not usually anything to do with this happening in real life, though; it's more symbolic of the very natural fear of being left alone somehow, or of being 'wronged' in some way.

Night Terrors

Night Terrors are rather different to Nightmares, although often get confused for each other. A nightmare is a dream featuring fear, horror and anxieties and occur during REM sleep. Night Terrors, on the other hand, are frequently far worse... Often involving the physiological 'waking-horror' of sleep paralysis and suffocation, these occur during non-REM sleep when we are deepest in the realm of our slumber. Night Terrors make our heart rates and breathing escalate wildly. Around 6% of people experience Night Terrors, whereas most of us have nightmares from time to time at the very least

Waking Life - Movie

In the 2001 film Waking Life, the lead character - a nameless young man - lives in a constant state of lucid dreaming. Featuring much discussion and philosophising about the meaning of life and the appearance of reality, he ends up coming to the conclusion that the reason he never wakes up is that he might be dead. To make the film, and give it its dream-like visual effects, real life film was overlaid with clever technical animations, using Rotoscope, leading to it being nominated for several film-industry awards.

SLEEP

Composer Max Richter, consulting with American neuro-scientist David Eagleman, has created SLEEP; one of the long-est pieces of music ever recorded, designed specifically to be listened to... whilst you're asleep! His 'lullaby for a frenetic world' was made as an experiment to find out what effect hearing music has on our subconscious mind, and was broad-cast live on BBC3 as part of the 'Why Music?' series of broad-casts from the Wellcome Collection. Max says of the project: *"I think of SLEEP as an experiment into how music and the mind can interact in this other state of consciousness, one we all spend decades of our lives completely immersed in, but which is so far rather poorly understood. I consulted with the neuroscientist David Eagleman on how music can relate to the sleep state and have incorporated our conversations in the compositional process of the work."*

Book Of Dreams - Jack Kerouac

Famed for writing the classic book On The Road, Jack Kerouac (1922–1969) was a central figure of the Beat Generation, and a noted companion of Allen Ginsberg at the time. He also wrote an experimental novel composed entirely of his own dreams, based on his private dream diaries which he kept from 1952 to 1960. It's entitled, perhaps somewhat unimaginatively, The Book Of Dreams! He once said "All human beings are also dream beings" and "Dreaming ties all mankind together". In his book he manages to tie the narrative together in all manner of unusual, wild ways, featuring imagery, scenes and characters ranging from lost love, madness, and castration to cats that speak, cats in danger of their lives, and people giving birth to cats, to school classrooms, Mel Torme, Zsa Zsa Gabor, Tolstoy and Genet.

Tweeting Practice

Birds practice singing their songs in their sleep! In a study for Science journal in the US, Amish Dave of the University of Illinois and Daniel Margoliash, a biologist at the University of Chicago, discovered that brain cells of Zebra Finches fire in the same patterns as they do when they're singing as when they're asleep, although these patterns are absent when they're awake and not singing. The reason for all this? They're practising, in order to help them remember their unique songs, critical for marking territory and attracting mates. Recent experiments in humans and rats have demonstrated a strong correlation between learning and sleeping, and it seems birds need their sleep to help themselves learn too.

Frankenstein by Mary Shelley

After journeying through Germany and Switzerland with her husband-to-be Percy, John Polidori [author of The Vampyre, the first published vampire story] and Lord Byron, Mary Shelley and her companions decided to have a story writing competition with each other, to see who could write the best horror story. Days passed as she racked her brains for an idea; and then one fateful night, she had a dream, a dream which spurred her on to write one of the most famous gothic horror stories of all time, and one of the first ever science-fiction stories ever written. Her novel 'Frankenstein' was first published, anonymously, in 1818 and has gone on to become the world-wide classic it is today.

Alien abduction or Sleep Paralysis?

An increasing number of dream researchers believe that Sleep Paralysis, a very common plight to many people, might well be behind stories of supposed Alien Abduction reported the world over. Kazuhiko Fukuda, a psychologist at Fukushima University in Japan and leading expert on dreams, thinks that 'kanashibari' as it's known there, is currently more likely to be responsible for claims of such Alien activity. The reason for this he says, is that people will opt for the most plausible explanation for the mysterious and vivid experiences that accompany sleep paralysis, and Aliens seem to fit the bill for many people rather better than the more traditional witches and ghouls of folklore these days.

Bill Nelson

Dreams seem to be rather significant to award-winning legendary British musician, writer and artist Bill Nelson. He's featured dreams in the names of many of his releases since he began in the 1970s, right through his career. These include albums such as Northern Dream, Music From Dreamland, Quit Dreaming And Get On The Beam, Chamber Of Dreams, and The Dream Transmission Pavilion, as well as And We Fell Into A Dream, the song Do You Dream In Colour?, and even a collection of his diaries entitled Diary Of A Hyperdreamer. I wonder if all his titles come to him in his dreams too?

Google it.

So many creative, clever and inventive people have been inspired directly by their dreams. A recent notable example is Larry Page, the American computer scientist and CEO of Google no less, who actually came up with the idea for Google whilst he was asleep! With the help of Sergey Brin, Page created Google in order to "organize the world's information and make it universally accessible and useful". Google is currently the world's number one most visited website. And almost inescapable it seems...

The Cabinet of Dr. Caligari

Directed by Robert Wiene, Carl Mayer and Hans Janowitz's The Cabinet of Dr. Caligari from 1920 is a renowned classic, the most famous of all German Expressionist films ever made, and widely held as the first ever horror film. It tells the tale of a crazed evil hypnotist who exploits a poor young man who spends almost his whole life asleep, alone in his private world of dreams, in order to kill people. He manipulates the unsuspecting somnambulist's dreams and forces him to commit several murders whilst he is asleep, and the film raises many questions about our perception of reality and responsibility for what we do whilst we're unconscious.

The Sewing Machine

Our humble sewing machines are the product of a fortuitous dream. Elias Howe was trying to find a way of speeding up and automating the laborious sewing process with a machine he'd invented, but he couldn't get the thread and needle combination right. But in 1845, one fateful night, he had a dream which gave him the answer he was looking for; he found himself in a foreign country, surrounded by natives with spears, all thrusting their pointy sticks at him. He thought he was going to die - but then he noticed the ends of their spears all had holes in the ends. When he woke up, he applied this strange idea of a hole in the end of his experimental needle, to thread the thread through... and the rest is history.

Feeling anxious?

Dream researcher and psychologist Calvin Springer Hall [1909-1985] collected over 50,000 dreams from people, including many college students. What his research showed was, perhaps unsurprisingly, that the most frequently experienced emotion people have in their dreams was, basically, anxiety. We can experience all sorts of positive feelings and emotions as we snooze, like pleasure, happiness, pure joy, amazement, erotic arousal, and so on, but the more negative, unpleasurable emotions far outweigh these. Oh dear!

Free Association

Father of Dream analysis Sigmund Freud invented an amazing way of tapping into our subconscious thoughts with a technique called 'free association' - and it's been used ever since by artists, writers and musicians as a means of finding inspiration. Try it for yourself, it's fun and can be surprisingly revealing! Get someone to write down five random things or objects on a piece of paper, then read them out to you: for example

1. Hand 2. Motorbike 3. Apple 4. Chair 5. Love.

As you answer, say or write down the first thing that pops into your mind the instant they say each one. You can do this with almost anything really, and the things that come up can really take you in all kinds of interesting directions creatively... as well as perhaps discover a few things about yourself too, of course!

The House Of Fame - poem by Geoffrey Chaucer

An early poem by Geoffrey Chaucer named The House Of Fame, was a 'dream vision'. Written in 1379, and clocking in at a whopping 2,000 lines long, Chaucer's epic poem uses the concept of a dream to wax lyrical over the notion of fame. Once the protagonist of his poem falls asleep, Chaucer goes on, somewhat cynically perhaps, to examine the supposed truth and reliability [or lack thereof] of poetic 'accounts', tales and stories of famous lives throughout history.

All those songs are bad for your sleep

In a study of pop-song lyrics regarding the subject of insomnia, researchers found that typically a great proportion of them contained all kinds of unhealthy, very often in fact useless, supposed 'coping strategies' for dealing with sleeplessness. More often than not, song lyrics frequently recommend such courses of action as alcohol abuse, or the taking of drugs, reading or even watching TV in bed. And out of all these remedies for sleep disturbances, NONE of them ever really help anyone at all, and in fact prolong the very condition people are attempting to escape. Oi, songwriters - sort it out!

Saintless

Did you know there's no Saint of sleep? There's a few who come close though, such as good old St Vitus, the christian martyr, who amongst other things is also the patron saint of oversleeping, and St Dymphna who is the saint of sleepwalking and mental illness. I read that the old testament prophet named Elijah has apparently been proposed by some as a possible patron saint of sleep, due to his having allegedly slept for an exceptional amount of time in a 'divine slumber' once, but hasn't been granted Saintly status as yet. Well, what do you have to do to get someone Sainted these days eh? I dunno...

To See My Dreams

Spanish artist Jaume Plensa (born 1955 in Barcelona) created a huge sculpture of the head of a 14-year-old girl with her eyes closed, on Botafogo beach, in the Brazilian city of Rio de Janeiro. The white 12m (39-foot) tall head was made out of resin and marble dust, and called Olhar nos meus sonhos (To see my dreams). Juame said that the purpose of it was to inspire people to dream more. He made two other notable female head sculptures too; Echo, on display in New York's Madison Square Park, is the head of a nine-year girl 'lost in thought', and another, called Dream, can be seen in St Helens in England.

EEG

By far the most commonly used method of studying dreams by scientists is EEG or electroencephalography, which originated in the 1950s. The way it works is that because the cells of the brain communicate by electrical impulse, the EEG method is designed to measure all this exciting and mysterious electrical stuff going on. In turn, this helps them see what specific areas of our brains are talking to each other, firing off left, right and centre, as we dream.

Cheap Trick "Dream Police" song

The song "Dream Police" was a single in 1979 for the US rock group Cheap Trick. The songwriter Rick Nielsen claims it was inspired by something he had dreamt about when in deep REM sleep. It also appears on their album of the same name, and funnily enough - and this may well be utterly unique in the world of music - the song on the B-side "Heaven Tonight" was *also* a song about dreaming.

Nightmares are good for you

Recent research into Nightmares has led to two important discoveries which challenge conventional understandings about them to date. Firstly, that those who have these horrifying, disturbing experiences regularly are actually more likely to have significantly higher levels of empathy towards other people. And secondly, that nightmare sufferers experience enhanced levels of creativity in their daily lives too. This has seriously given our scientific perspective on nightmares a shake up, and shows us that we still have much to learn about dreams, the subconscious, and the human mind.

Persistence of Memory - Dali

"One day it will have to be officially admitted that what we have christened reality is an even greater illusion than the world of dreams." - Salvador Dali.

One of the great surrealist artists who ever lived, Salvador Dali dedicated much of his life's work to the subject of dreams, saying that when he did so, he was producing 'hand-painted dream photographs' rather than mere 'art'. Persistence of Memory, sometimes mistakenly called 'The Soft Watches' by people, is one of his most recognisable and famous of such paintings, completed in 1931, and has been on display in the Museum Of Modern Art in New York ever since an anonymous donor sent it to them in 1934. With its striking images of melting clocks and pocket watches, Dali wanted to illustrate to us how arbitrary and irrelevant normal concepts of time are in the world of our dreams.

Trees sleep too, you know

They may not require a bed, and do it standing up, but recently scientists have discovered that Birch trees actually 'go to sleep' at night. During their experiments, András Zlinszky and his colleagues of the Centre for Ecological Research in Tihany, Hungary claim that these trees go through physical changes akin to sleeping. The main thing they found was that a Birch tree's entire collection of branches droop as much as an extra 10 centimetres at night. No one had ever measured this kind of phenomenon before on such a scale, but they scanned trees in Austria and Finland with laser beams between sunset and sunrise, recording the time it took for the lasers to bounce back from the leaves and branches, determining their movement with incredible accuracy. It might even mean that other, or even ALL trees go to sleep! So please be quiet if you walk past a tree in the dark in case you wake it up.

Paranomia

Paranoimia was a Top 40 hit single in the UK in 1986, by British experimental synth pop group Art Of Noise, reaching number 12 in the charts. It uniquely featured a virtual guest vocalist, a computer and video generated TV presenter of the time known as Max Headroom, played by the American actor Matt Frewer. The lyrics of the song are based upon Max feeling scared and anxious, and totally unable to sleep at all, suffering a mixture of both insomnia and paranoia, so, hence the title! The song also features on the Art Of Noise album called In Visible Silence in a different form.

Ionizers

In a recent study by a group of French scientists, they made a surprising discovery about the effects of Ionizers on the quality of our sleep. Large or small, domestic ionizers are available from pretty much any hardware or electrical store, and designed to emit a steady stream of lovely negative ions into our home environment. Amongst the various usual physical health benefits of negative ions, they can also have an extremely beneficial effect on serotonin production in our brains, helping to healthily regulate not only our moods but our sleep patterns too.

The Changeling by Henry Fuseli

As a kind of precursor to his most famous painting, The Nightmare, painted in 1782, Henry Fuseli also produced another, earlier and notable artwork based on a scary old folklore tale. This equally somewhat unnerving nightmare scene is entitled The Changeling, drawn and painted in the year 1780, using chalks and watercolour paints. It depicts a witch stealing a baby from its crib, and escaping through a window into the night, leaving in its place a horrible replacement in the shape of a grotesque changeling. The mother is shown discovering her baby to be missing and the changeling sitting there in its place, to her obvious horror, whilst her nursemaid lies slumped to her side, possibly having fainted at the discovery I suppose.

Are all Religions just a Dream?

Lots of the most popular Religions actually began due to a dream or vision experienced by the early founders. En route to Damascus, Saul of Tarsus had a dreamlike vision starring Jesus, which lead him to become St Paul and spend the rest of his life helping to form Christianity. Muhammad, founder of Islam, got his religious revelations from a series of dreams involving the Angel Gabriel who told him to read what would become the start of the Quran. Even Buddha, on the very night before his enlightenment, had his 'five great dreams' and Joseph Smith, founder of the Mormons, was 'visited' whilst he slept in bed by a vision of the Angel Moroni.

A Dream poem

'A Dream' is a nice wee poem written way back in the 1780's by William Blake, the English poet. It portrays a dream of a nocturnal exchange between four main characters; the narrator, an 'emmet' or ant as they're known these days, a beetle and a glow-worm! Together, they all help the little lost ant find her way home to her children. Critics claim that this poem was Blake's comment on the usual idealised notion of maternity or motherhood, the notion of which being little more than a fantasy or dream rather than truly reflecting reality for most people. It was published in 1789, and appeared as part of Songs Of Innocence, a collection of 19 decoratively illustrated poems by Blake, accompanied 5 years later by Songs Of Experience. Both works were intended to reflect Blake's view of these two opposite states of the human heart and soul.

Our Subconscious Alarm clock

Have you ever woken up just before your alarm went off and wondered how or why? Just a coincidence? Or is there more to it than that? In a study conducted by the University of Lubeck, Germany in 1999, they discovered that our subconscious minds can rather mysteriously keep a pretty accurate track of time passing as we sleep. Not only that, but believe it or not, by just telling ourselves before sleeping what time we need to awaken by, we can 'set' our own internal biological alarm-clock, which uses stress hormone adrenocorticotropin to stimulate the waking process in us, rousing us from our slumber naturally.

The Dream inspired City of Germany: Karlsruhe

So legend has it, the lovely German city of Karlsruhe, which translates as 'Charles' Repose', had its origins and name bestowed upon it directly because of a dream!

The dreamer in question was one Mr Charles III William, the Margrave of Baden-Durlach from 1709 until 1738, who founded the new city after a dream he had of doing precisely that very thing, in 1715. Some say he only built the new city, replete with a brand spanking new Palace for him to swan around in, in order to escape from his nagging wife! I suspect that would be rather an over-elaborate undertaking to instigate just to get a bit of peace and quiet from his moany old Missus, don't you think?

Biphasic or Polyphasic Sleep

Like an afternoon nap, but feel a little bit guilty for having one? Well don't worry, you might just be tuning into your natural sleep patterns. A term first coined by early 20th century psychologist J. S. Szymanski, Biphasic or Polyphasic sleep is the practice of sleeping two or more periods within 24 hours, and said to be the natural ancestral sleep pattern for lots of animals, especially mammals. Essentially, sleeping like this all points towards you making more of your time when you're awake. As I mentioned earlier in the book, polyphasic sleep has often been employed by highly intelligent polymaths and prominent historical figures, including Eistein, Napoleon, Leonardo da Vinci, and so I hear, bringing things up to the modern day, Nikola Tesla.

#9 Dream by John Lennon

The song #9 Dream by John Lennon, from his 1974 solo album Walls And Bridges, was written because of a specific dream he had. It included the immortal phrase *"Ah! böwakawa poussé, poussé"* which came to him directly during the dream, although he had no idea what the words meant, but he 'just thought it sounded beautiful' so he used it. It has a dream-like quality and ended up being one of the most heavily produced tracks he ever did. Spookily enough, the song ended up reaching number 9 in the Billboard Hot 100 charts when it came out as a single.

Your Brain: Is it On or Off?

You might think you're awake when you're awake and asleep when you're asleep; but parts of your brain go to sleep and wake up all day long. Researchers at Stanford University found that many neurons in the brain cycle between being in an 'ON' state or an 'OFF' state, depending on what we're doing. Our brains use lots of energy, so in order for our brains to conserve energy, they switch off neurons that aren't required at a particular time, and keep the ones we want to use on.

Un Chien Andalou

Un Chien Andalou, or An Andalusian Dog, is an astonishingly strange 16 minute long film based on dreams, made in 1929 by Spanish director Luis Buñuel and the infamous surrealist artist Salvador Dali. It has no plot to speak of, neither the name nor the peculiar scenes in the film seem to make any sense at all, no one really understands what it's all about, and it's utterly nonsensical and very disturbing - exactly like our dreams can be sometimes. They got the idea to make the film after a conversation about how weird and disjointed dreams were, so they turned the bits they could remember of dreams they'd had into the scenes that make up this legendary short film, which has inspired the on-screen 'dream sequences' of movie makers ever since, and countless musical video projects from the likes of David Bowie to The Pixies.

Get more Sleep to get Sexy

Did you know that if anything is preventing you getting a decent night's sleep, it can seriously affect your sex-life? Well it can. Being tired all the time from things messing about with your sleep is a sure-fire way of zapping your libido and interfering with your sex drive. Stop going to bed too late, or getting up too early for a start! But if you have trouble getting to sleep, or have problems with sleep apnea, maybe you should relax more before going to bed, or try some natural sleep-promoting remedies. If those still don't help, talk to a homeopath, or perhaps your doctor, to try and improve the situation before your sex-life goes out of the window.

A Swinging Dream

After having experienced a stretch of relatively poor performances at numerous tournaments he played during 1964, world famous Golfer Jack Nicklaus stunned fans with an abrupt turnabout of events, and all because of a dream he had about how he was holding his club! And he still maintains what he learned from his dream to this day. Here's the man himself on what actually happened: "... *I had a dream and it was about my golf swing. I was hitting them pretty good in the dream and all at once I realized I wasn't holding the club the way I've actually been holding it lately. I've been having trouble collapsing my right arm taking the club head away from the ball, but I was doing it perfectly in my sleep. So when I came to the course yesterday morning I tried it the way I did in my dream and it worked. I shot a sixty-eight yesterday and a sixty-five today."*

PTSD Dreams change with the healing process

Some hopefully comforting news for sufferers of PTSD: the usually awful, very graphic and repetitive nightmares based on the experiences they have had often change, with their healing process, and become less specific to their trauma and less harrowing as a result. According to Deirdre Barrett in her 1996 book Trauma And Dreams, as PTSD sufferers conditions improve, their dreams become more symbolic in nature, and incorporate more and more elements of the dreamer's normal daily life.

Dreamcatcher by Stephen King

The story behind horror-writer Stephen King's world-famous 2001 novel 'Dreamcatcher' came to him in not just one, but a veritable series of dreams he experienced. After a serious accident he had where he was knocked down by a van in Maine, he luckily escaped with just a shattered leg and collapsed lung, but it was whilst recovering from his injuries that the dreams that became this novel began to flood into his subconscious as he slept. It was subsequently turned into a film, released in 2003.

Light Sleeper

Sufferers of sleep disorders and even jet-lag may soon benefit from new NASA research happening currently, called the Lighting Effects Study. The frequently varying light frequencies astronauts experience living on the International Space Station - up to 16 sunrises and sunsets a day - have a great effect on circadian rhythms, which in turn severely disrupts their sleep patterns. They've found that using variably controllable LED instead of plain fluorescent lights, therefore being able to precisely tailor the intensity of the light they experience, is helping them be more alert or sleep more soundly exactly when they want to.

Einstein's Dream

One of the most famous scientists ever, Albert Einstein, came up with one of the most famous scientific formulas of all time, as the result of a dream. E=MC2, known as the Theory of Relativity, came to him after waking from his sleep from a dream where he was on a sleigh, speeding down a mountainside. As his speed increased in the dream, he noticed that the stars in the sky changed their appearance as he approached the speed of light. When he awoke, he set to working out the now legendary mathematical formula, which proves that in theory time-travel is actually possible, and changed the way the world looked at physics and many other things in our collective culture forever!

Heal yourself from inside your dreams

To help patients overcome their crippling anxieties or fears, and do away with their terrible, persistent nightmares, psychologists have been discovering new and better ways of using lucid dreams as a way of helping people overcome them. Believe it or not, right now it's becoming possible for them to more easily induce such dream states, and then to contact and share two-way communication with a sleeping subject, enabling them to actually record what's happening in their dreams. They hope that this could pave the way in the future to fully treating such psychological issues in sufferers whilst they're still asleep.

Twilight

The idea for the now World-famous romantic vampire series Twilight came to author Stephenie Meyer in a dream. She says she had a dream on June 2nd 2003 about a vampire who was in love with a human girl, but despite his love for her, and true to form for all vampires I'm sure, he also had a strong urge to drink her blood. After writing her first draft of what ended up being chapter 13 of her first book, within three months she'd expanded her initial dream inspired idea, and completed a whole novel. Although rejected by many publishers, later that year she found herself signing a very lucrative publishing deal and has gone on to sell over 100 million books to date - and of course, it's even been turned into a string of blockbuster Hollywood movies. All that wonderful creativity, from just one small dream.

Precognitive Death Dreams

Precognitive or premonition-like dreams about death, of ourselves or others, in advance of the event itself, really do happen. No one can explain them, but such dreams are a fact of life and have happened many times to people all over the world throughout history. Some notable examples are Mark Twain dreaming of his young brother Henry's death, Abraham Lincoln dreaming of his very own death in great detail, a lot of the victims of 9/11 dreamt of the impending terrorist attack that was to kill them, and researchers claim there were 19 verified precognitive dreams about the Titanic disaster.

Dreaming by Blondie

One of the most popular singles by legendary new wave band Blondie, was the song Dreaming from their 1979 album Eat To The Beat, and got to number 2 in the UK pop charts. In this number, their rather exceedingly gorgeous lead singer, Debbie Harry, took fellow band member Chris Stein's original idea of using the phrase 'dreaming is free' and wrote the rest of the lyrics around the idea herself. If dreaming wasn't free, though, and we all had to pay to have them, I wonder how many people would do so? It might be a good idea... maybe you could pay for just nice dreams and make sure you never buy any nightmares, so you can just have lovely, happy night's dreams for the rest of your life.

Why some night owls can't help staying up late

Staying up way past everyone else's bedtime? Can't ever seem get to sleep before the cock crows? Well don't worry, you might well have no choice in the matter, because one of your genes is just hardwired that way. You may have a case of delayed sleep phase disorder, created by a mutation in the CRY1 gene which helps regulate your inner circadian 'clock' and sleep patterns. This common mutation, present in around 1 in 75 people, makes your circadian cycle longer than usual, so you tend to go to bed later than others.

Terminator

James Cameron is the creator of one of the most successful movie franchises the world has ever seen, 'The Terminator', and it all started with a dream. Or rather, a nightmare. He was ill in bed with a fever and had a vision in his troubled sleep, of the now iconic, skeletal metal figure, with its menacing red eyes, emerging from fire. That striking, terrifying image from James' dream helped to launch his career in Hollywood. His first movie, 1984's The Terminator starring Arnold Schwarzenegger as the cyborg-based lead character, and co-starring Linda Hamilton as Sarah Connor, went on to take over $70 Million at the box office.

Penelope's Dream from the Odyssey

Homer's immensely epic Greek 'poem' from the 8th Century B.C. is about the life of the Greek hero known as Odysseus, the King of Ithaca, and his wife Penelope, detailing his 10 year long journey home after the fall of Troy. Penelope was subsequently plagued by many undesirable 'suitors' during Odysseus's absence, and had a dream about an Eagle killing a gaggle of 20 Geese. She took her dream as a sign that her husband would someday return from his long voyage away and roundly thwart, foil, kill, deal with, and generally see them all off! There's even a wonderful illustration by John Flaxman (1755-1826) depicting Penelope dreaming, called 'Penelope's Dream' perhaps unsurprisingly enough.

Do we Sleep to Dream?

Some experts claim that the true purpose of sleeping is actually to allow us to dream. Dreaming plays a very important role, helping maintain our emotional stability and mental health. When we're asleep, our brains get busy sorting through the events of the day and the stimuli we've been subjected to, which correlates, somehow, with how much and how long we actually dream for. They've discovered the less stimuli our brains receive whilst we're awake, the less sleep we need, and the less likely it is we'll sleep, or dream, for long.

Edison's Naps

Mr Thomas Edison, inventor extraordinaire from America (1847-1931) had an unusual approach to unlocking his creative genius. When he wanted to generate new ideas, he would take a nap. But it wasn't quite how you might expect; he would nap in his chair, surrounded by steel pans, with his hands full of little balls or marbles. When he dropped off enough that his hands would relax, the balls would fall and hit the metal pans, waking him up instantly, and he'd be immediately struck with a new idea or two for what he was working on! He successfully filed over 1,000 patents whilst he was alive, so it would appear that it must have worked a treat.

Men Vs Women

Some dream researchers claim that Men and Women actually dream slightly differently! Apparently, they say that men's dreams tend to feature other men more than twice as much as they do women, but women are more likely to dream of either sex in a more balanced, fairly shared out way, with both sexes featuring equally. Also, unsurprisingly I guess, men are far more likely to dream of scenarios involving anger and aggression, whereas women tend more towards dreaming of caring, and romantic themes.

The Sandman and The Batman

The Sandman has appeared in many different guises over the years in popular culture, but did you know he was also one of the villains in the bonkers and somewhat psychedelic 1960s TV series of Batman? Played by actor Michael Rennie, Sandman was a classic Batman baddie of international repute, whose alias was 'sleep therapist' Dr. Somnambular, and used a special hypnotic sand on people to turn them into sleepwalking, somnambulistic minions. Once under his sandy spell, he could command them to serve his every whim, along with his henchmen named Nap and Snooze. He appeared alongside Julie Newmar as Catwoman in a very memorable episode, but Batman and Robin got the better of him, and Catwoman, in the end of course.

Dreaming Blind

Do people who are visually impaired or blind dream? The answer is a resounding yes! If someone lost their sight before the age of five, then their dreams are unlikely to include visual information. However, research has shown without a doubt that the Blind do indeed still have dreams, dreams which are just as complex and stimulating as the ones those of us with Sight can have. Their dreams comprise of sensory experiences from the other senses they possess, such as sound, smell, emotions, touch and so on, which are greatly enhanced in them, with way higher sensitivity than the rest of us, due to their lack of actual vision.

Lack of Sleep the cause of Alzheimer's?

There's been a significant increase in the number of people with Alzheimer's disease as people's life spans have become longer, but because of this, more crucially, because people's total time spent asleep has dropped. You see, the things is we don't get as much NREM stage (Non Rapid Eye Movement) deep sleep as we age, which is the time when our brains cement in place the requisite connections for storing memories, and basically stops us from forgetting things. It's this very sleep deprivation that plays a big part in exacerbating the condition and effects of Alzheimer's. Over 44 million people are living with Alzheimer's currently, but it seems that if we can each try our best to get as much decent sleep as we can, we might, hopefully, be able to stave off the possibility of ending up joining those poor 44 million sufferers... at least perhaps just a little bit.

The Discreet Charm of the Bourgeoisie

The 1972 surrealist film 'The Discreet Charm of the Bourgeoisie', by Louis Buñuel, is a cleverly made expose of the true nature of the bourgeois, middle-class people of France. As a cinematic device, he uses the dreams of six individuals who are attempting to hold a dinner party together, but keep getting interrupted, in order to give him license to create outlandish scenes to illustrate his ideas. In one 'dream' the French army invade the dining room, in another it turns out that the dinner party find themselves sitting on a stage with an audience watching them eat... suffice to say, it's a rather odd film, but even odder is the surreal ending: the whole thing turns out to be based on the dreams of just one of the dinner guests, who happens to have fallen asleep whilst hungry.

Colour vs Black And White

Did you know that on average 80% of dreams are in colour, just like real life - but some of us can experience dreams in black and white? And some people claim to only EVER dream in monochrome! Also, in a recent study, dreamers were asked to point at a chart to illustrate the kinds of colours most prevalent in their dreams, and the most commonly selected colour pallets consisted of soft pastel colours.

Disturbed sleep AND Brains

According to research published in 2010 in a journal called Neurology, sleep disorders which cause people to 'act out' their dreams, often including violent moves, screaming and thrashing about with their limbs, might be an early warning sign of potential brain disorders developing later in life. Parkinson's disease and Dementia are two of the most common neurodegenerative conditions, and such night-time disturbances as this could point to these illnesses eventually happening to someone, decades before anyone realises there's anything wrong.

A Benzene Dream

After many years spent studying the nature of Carbon to Carbon chemical bonds, in 1865 famed German Organic chemist Friedrich August Kekulé came up with a now world-famous theory about the, until then, mysterious structure of aromatic Benzene molecules... all from a dream he had. His dream inspired him to think of the structure of this elusive molecule as a ring shape, like an Ouroboros, the ancient symbol of a snake devouring its own tail. His theory turned into a ground-breaking, provable discovery, one thing led to another, and he literally changed the way the world of Chemistry looked at molecule structure forever.

The Night

Night time has always been a very special, magical time for Humans of every culture across the whole World. As our tiny planet revolves beneath our shining star, the hours of darkness have always held a deep fascination for us, it's just so different from daylight times, full of mystery, strangeness, fear and much more. The main thing I'm most struck by about the night, is that it really feels like a truly magical time where we can lose our inhibitions, connect with our more intuitive selves, and feel far more free from the social norms and expectations of behaviour. We analyse the dreams we experience as we sleep at night, have all kinds of varying customs attached to our traditional time of slumber, and even behave completely differently at night too. At night, it feels like anything could happen... and so often does, too.

I Can't Get No Satisfaction - Rolling Stones

Did you know that Keith Richards originally came up with the idea for this song in a dream? He dreamt of the lyrics and the iconic riff, woke up and recorded a little bit of it onto his handy little tape machine which he kept in his bedroom, just in case of times like this, then fell back to sleep again. Allegedly the rest of the band were a bit concerned that it was musically too similar to 'Dancing In The Street', but they went ahead with recording it in the end, as we of course all at least know, and a great many people love. It's become practically their anthem really hasn't it?

Critical Dreaming

One of the theories about why we dream in the first place, is that it gives our brains a chance to solve the various puzzles facing us in our daily lives. Without our pesky conscious minds getting in the way with all that worrying, reasoning and logic, whilst we dream our subconscious minds are given the green light to go ahead and explore whatever might be troubling or concerning us, in anyway it fancies. This unfettered critical thinking is very helpful, and so good for us in many ways, as it often sends us new ideas and perspectives on things through our dreams. Also dreaming gives our brains chance to 'reboot' too, which is essential to our psychological health.

Dreams Less Sweet

The second album released by British avant-garde experimentalists Psychic TV was called Dreams Less Sweet, and came out in 1983. Led by the splendidly notorious artist Genesis P. Orridge, previously of nation-shocking 'Industrial' music/art collective Throbbing Gristle, the band were one of the first to explore the areas of dream imagery and induced REM states for inspiration in their music and lyrics, and to great effect too. The band also featured members Peter Christopherson and John Balance, who went on to create the musical project Coil, who were arguably even more influenced by such dream research, and other such altered states, than Psychic TV were.

Enhance your REM Dream-sleep

Here's a really simple way to increase the amount of dreams you have... just hit the snooze button on your alarm clock, take more naps, or have a lie-in. The sleep we get in these extended or extra-time style snoozes is perfect for activating the all-important for dreaming REM sleep patterns. Basically, if you sleep more, and if you can, allow yourself to awake in sync with your body's natural rhythm, you'll soon find yourself dreaming ten to the dozen, and accessing your deep subconscious, along with all the valuable messages, information and lessons in there, usually hidden from your conscious mind.

Dreamlanders

The term 'Dreamlanders' is the collective name given to anybody who's regularly worked as a member of the cast, or crew, on the films of the notorious 'King of Filth' John Waters. Known for his fantastical, often bizarrely imaginative, independent movies portraying the rather more unseemly side of life and people, the term comes from the name of Waters' own production company, Dreamland Productions. He's most well known for his work with Divine, the sadly now deceased cult status icon, drag queen and singer, on films such as Pink Flamingos and Hairspray. Since starting his career in the late 1960s John has produced, directed and written many movies, and worked with some of Hollywood's A-list actors too such as Johnny Depp, Ricki Lake and Kathleen Turner.

Food and Dreaming

It doesn't have to be cheese! Or spicy food, or booze... eating anything at ALL before bed can interfere with your sleep and give you more vivid dreams. Basically, if you give your body things to keep your digestive and metabolic systems busy before bedtime, you'll have lots of REM sleep stages, and stay in them longer too, which means more dreams of course, and they'll far more intense too. However, this occurs very much at the expense of you experiencing any proper deep sleep, so you won't feel as refreshed when you wake up as a result.

Dream On

Another song with 'Dream' in the title, 'Dream On' is a Depeche Mode track which was released as a single in 2001. Coming from their album 'Exiter', it was sung by DM main-man Dave Gahan and written by their main songwriter Martin Gore, who penned so many of their huge hits like 'Enjoy The Silence', 'Master And Servant' and 'Personal Jesus'. The lyrics deal with a person who seems intent on self-destruct, who parties hard and seems to have lost their way in life, and gently suggests that they might do better to dream and love a bit more. I think we could all do with a bit more of that really, don't you?

Nocturnal penile tumescence

Unless they have a medical, physical problem, all men experience the phenomenon known as nocturnal penile tumescence - ie. getting spontaneous erections in the night! Normally this occurs between three and five times as a chap sleeps, usually during REM phase sleep when we're most likely to be dreaming, and is the cause of 'morning wood' in most cases too. But don't worry ladies, there also occurs a little known phenomenon in women called 'nocturnal clitoral tumescence', too! That's right; it happens to girls as well, albeit with perhaps somewhat less obvious results.

All aboard for Dreamland

Another kind of 'dreamland' is this. In the lovely old seaside town of Margate in England is a beautifully restored and refurbished 1920's Funfair, which goes by the name of Dreamland. I'm sure it wowed many a child, and plenty of grown-ups too in its heyday, when Funfairs truly were like a dream come true. Although I'm not sure how many of the rides and facilities are really the stuff of anyone's wildest dreams these days, it's a wonderfully quaint place to go, and is certainly lots of fun with its mixture of many old fashioned and super-modern rides, plus it even has a Roller-Disco, live music stage, loads of Arcade machines, and a pub too, to keep everyone suitably amused all day long.

Face it

Believe it or not, some studies claim that the faces of characters and people that appear in our dreams are in fact REAL faces, which we've seen at some point or other in our waking lives. We may not know or even remember them, but these studies suggest that we've certainly seen them, and our clever old brains have stored their faces for us. Imagine how many faces we might see in our whole lifetimes... hundreds of thousands or even, for some, more like millions! Now that's a hell of a lot of different faces for our subconscious to choose from to show us when we dream isn't it?

A Dream Play (*Ett Drömspel*)

Written in 1901 by Swedish playwright August Strindberg, A Dream play, or *Ett Drömspel* in Swedish, is a highly influential drama seen as the immediate precursor to surrealism and expressionism in theatre, which of course drew heavily on the subject and imagery of dreams themselves. In the play, Agnes, daughter of the God Indra, visits Earth to examine the kinds of problems we Humans have to endure. After meeting all kinds of heavily symbolic characters, and witnessing suffering from such things as poverty, the crushing routine of family life, cruelty and such like, she realises that people deserved the pity of the Gods. Then she returns to Heaven and awakens from the dream-like story of the play. It was first performed in Stockholm in 1907 and continues to be performed around the World to this day.

The Artist's Dream - George H. Comegys

This stunning painting from 1840 was painted by the artist George Comegys, the son of Benjamin Comegys and Ellen Hinsey from Maryland in the USA. It depicts an artist, with his head laid down on the table in front of him, searching for inspiration and dreaming of famous and prolific artists of the past like Da Vinci, Michelangelo, Rubens and Rembrandt. Immensely talented, Comegys studied under the artist John Neagle, but tragically died very young aged 28, of Phthisis, in the Blockley Almshouse of Philadelphia Hospital after suffering from mental illness for much of his short adult life.

Lucid Dreamers have higher levels of brain activity

Did you know that people who are capable of having lucid dreams, have incredibly enhanced levels of frontal lobe brain activity? Lucid dreaming is where the dreamer is aware of the fact they're dreaming, and can actually manipulate and control what happens in their dreams, and the frontal lobe is the area of the brain responsible for our sense of self, conscious awareness, as well as our language and memory skill levels. Essentially, what they're finding now is that lucid dreamers are way more developed in all these capacities than others, so if you want to improve your lot in life, you could do worse than try to learn lucid dreaming for yourself... it might just have a few other rather beneficial effects on you.

It's Who You Know

The people we meet in daily life have quite an effect on the content of our dreams. In a recent study, over 48% of the people who appear in our dreams were found to be known to the person having the dream. 35% of the people in our dreams were known by the dreamer due to the social or professional relationship they had with them, but less than 16% were totally unknown to them!

Srinivasa Ramanujan

The famous indian Mathematician Srinivasa Ramanujan (1887 to 1920) was a very unconventional man when it came to developing his 3,000+ successful, and sometimes groundbreaking, theorems. He claimed that the Hindu Goddess Namagiri regularly came to visit him in his dreams, giving him inspiration for new, wild and wonderful ways of solving difficult mathematical problems, some of which had been considered 'unsolvable' by the rest of the world.

Highly Illogical!

The reason events that happen in our dreams appear to be so convincingly real to our sleeping selves, is that during REM sleep our normally ever-vigilant logic and impulse-control centers are chemically 'shut off'. Norepinephrine and serotonin production are both temporarily suspended, which are essential neurotransmitters responsible for communication between brain cells; without which, our brains basically just 'accept' whatever our subconscious mind shows or tells us during a dream.

Lucrecia de León

Her prophecies about the coming loss of the Spanish Armada all came true, and was branded an 'evil dreamer' by the Spanish Inquisition - born in 1568 Lucretia de Leon had hundreds of documented prophetic, precognitive dreams in her lifetime regarding Spain's political future as a nation. She was fiercely critical of King Philip II's reign and she was both feared and revered by the government and the people of Spain due to the accuracy of her predictions. Eventually she was tortured and imprisoned by the Inquisition for her dangerously political powers of foresight, but ultimately only given a very light sentence, for the time at least, of 100 lightly delivered lashes of the whip - something she also predicted herself in a dream she had!

The Decline of Monochrome Dreams

In recent studies on the subject, findings indicate that around 12% of people without ocular problems dream almost entirely in black and white, whilst the rest of us tend to dream mainly in full colour. Researchers used to think we all dreamt in black and white, generally speaking, however, possibly due to the switch in the 1960's from black and white to colour TV broadcasts, such findings began changing to colour dominance! Less than 5% of people beneath the age of 25 these days dream in black and white; well, so long as we don't all start getting adverts popping up in our dreams like on the telly or Youtube, I'm sure it's all quite fine and dandy whether our dreams are multi-coloured or in monochrome.

The birth of dream analysis

It's been more than 50,000 years since early Mankind began painting depictions of their dreams on the walls of their caves. But can you believe, it's only in the last 100 years or so that the men and women of 'Science' started taking dreams seriously and started studying what they might mean. The first to delve into the world of dream analysis were the famous psychoanalysts Sigmund Freud and his disciple, Carl Jung, but it was a woman named Mary Calkins who in fact developed a more methodical, statistical and practical approach to dream examination.

Jimi Hendrix song, Purple Haze

The revolutionary, legendary guitarist, Jimi Hendrix, claimed in interviews that his arguably most famous song 'Purple Haze' was in fact inspired by a dream he had. In it, he dreamt he walked beneath the surface of the ocean, and quite literally, became enveloped by a purple-coloured cloud or haze as he did so. He also later added that he had been reading a sci-fi book, called Night of Light by Philip Jose Farmer, shortly before going to sleep that night...

Dream Dictionary

Here are a few suggestions of mine to help you analyse dreams yourself. As I mentioned before at the start of the book though, please don't take these things too literally! Merely food for thought is all I'm offering here, to help prompt you, or give you a few ideas about what might possibly be going on in your dreams, or anyone else's dreams for that matter, too.

A ctor

Ever dream you were a famous actor or actress? Have your dreams led you into the arms of one of your favourite stars of the stage, screen, or TV? Well here's a few thoughts as to what your acting-or-actor-infused dream could really be telling about your life...

Dreaming of an actor or actress symbolises your desire for something more in your life, such as more adventures, romance or interesting experiences.

Is a particular acting celebrity inhabiting your dream world? You might want to be more like them, physically, psychologically, or maybe feel you'd like to incorporate something about how they are in a certain role they're known for, which you identify with or feel you lack.

Were you an actor in your dream? Are you pretending to be something you aren't in your waking life? Perhaps you'd like to take on another life 'role' instead of the one you are currently 'playing' at because you just aren't happy. Is the role you play in your life really 'you'? Dreaming of being an actor represents aspects of the self yet unrealised, wishing to play a significant or different part or role in life or in a given situation, pretending to be something you are not.

If you dream of just being an extra in a film or tv show, you really aren't getting enough appreciation or recognition from people, you want more return for the hard work you've been doing, or to be approved of by others more widely.

Adult

Realising your potential, strong desire to attain your goals, seeking success or recognition

Aeroplane Finding you have an increased sense of freedom, or enhanced levels of mental or psychic energy. Things are becoming so much easier for you to handle, feeling on top of everything

Afternoon

Time to pause for reflection, gathering energies together, tasks yet to be completed

Air

Air is invisible to our naked eyes and, unless it's moving, we could be forgiven for not even noticing its existence - but we'd certainly notice if it suddenly disappeared. An essential life force, the element of Air is all around us, sometimes making its presence known to us with considerable force...

Dreaming of the air you're breathing relates to your creative spirit and energies. If you dream you're breathing faster than normal, but you feel ok with it, then this means you've got lots of extra creative energy to be able to put into something, like a project or task; if it feels uncomfortable though, then you're putting too much creative energy into a situation and need to do some-

thing about it to restore the balance. Dreaming of holding your breath for some reason shows that you're feeling particularly un-movable, stubborn and single minded about something, and may need to 'loosen up' a bit for your own good!

Moving air such as the wind represents your energy, your vitality, your 'life force', particularly at times when significant changes are occurring inside and around you.

If air is coming from somewhere mechanical or non-natural source such as for example an air vent, a propeller, a fan or a wind machine, it's likely that you're feeling as though certain changes are things you wouldn't have chosen to happen.

Airport

Freedom, ambition, hopes and dreams, new ideas about to 'take off' or come to fruition, and new career directions

Alligator/Crocodile

Hidden agendas, deceitfulness, unwelcome secrecy, treacherous behaviour towards you

Aliens

New and unusual people coming into your life in some way. Ideas and behaviour, which seem strange to you, not knowing what to do about someone who has come into your life, that you've never had to deal with before.

Alien worlds

New adventures or experiences, uncharted territories in your life, unfamiliar circumstances

Alice in Wonderland

Dreams can seem to be nothing but nonsense sometimes can't they? The most famous examples of dream-like nonsense in popular culture, which we all know and love, are the stories Alice in Wonderland and Alice Through The Looking Glass by Lewis Carroll - but when one of the characters from Alice enter our dream worlds, you can be sure there's more than just nonsense going on in our lives...

Alice herself represents distraction from reality, a thirst for adventure, and curiosity, especially about the mysterious aspects of life

Cheshire Cat grinning its way through your dream means deceit, mistrust, mockery or mischief. Carefully does it!

Dormouse from the tea party symbolises exhaustion with things, tiredness with life, or not getting enough rest in general

The *Jabberwock* looming into your dreams can represent ugly, horrendous, troublesome elements around you. Something is making you afraid

Mad Hatter is symbolic of strange, peculiar or odd influences and circumstances. You might be feeling as mad as him!

Mock Turtle symbolises a feeling of general sadness regarding nonspecific things, irrational worries, and misplaced concerns

The *Queen of Hearts* represents pompous, arrogant and unpleasant energies. Someone may be proving difficult to please or to deal with

White Rabbit can mean running out of time for something, that you're up against the clock in some way. Also, you might well have a difficult or confusing journey to embark on.

Alphabet

There are many differing associations in the world of dream analysis for the letters of the English alphabet. For example, some relate to historical context, previous or existing meanings in current society, others to folklore or mystical beliefs, and some are just very plainly related to how the letter in question appears.

A - Beginnings, new starts, ultimate achievement, the highest of quality, the best

B - Second choices, slightly lesser status, back-up plans, alternatives, something very good but not the best

C - Average or acceptable in quality or performance, third option or choice, to be able to 'see'

D - Below average in quality, lacking mental agility

E - Excellence, ecstasy, poor achievement level, east (direction), the East (geographical)

F - Failure, very poor standards, lacking satisfaction

G - Great or good things, graceful qualities

H - Happiness, achievement of a goal, help is needed, high energy level

I - A single thing of particular importance, the individual, something to do with yourself, observations

J - Jealousy, joyous situations

K - Unusual things in your life, hard or uncomfortable experiences, things being just 'ok' rather than good or better

L - Luxury, love, length, laziness

M - Masculinity, a motherly feeling or presence, liking something a lot, magical experiences

N - Negativity, not wanting to do something, refusal, denial

O - Resolving or repeating a situation, wholeness, completion, satisfaction

P - Possibilities, staying put/not moving, seeking relief

Q - Questions, needing answers, waiting for things

R - Right decision, correct choice, rudeness, competitiveness

S - Secrets, sneakiness, softness, unpleasant influences around you

T - Time is important or relevant, often not enough or too much of it, reaching the top, needing sustenance

U - Somebody else is significant or important right now, blaming others, unfortunate events, unhappiness

V - Strong emphasis on something, especially impressive, volatility, violent action or intent

W - Wondering, thoughtfulness, wishing for something

X - Seeing through things, deep perception regarding a situation or person, looking for or finding something, an extra level or degree

Y - Lacking understanding, agreeable circumstances, positivity, saying yes to something

Z - Reaching the end, the last option, no more choices to be made, tiredness

Amber

Old wounds need healing, feelings of entrapment need attention, realisation that a previous idea is no longer relevant

Amethyst

Peace of mind, spiritual contentment, success in personal life, professional achievements, psychic perceptiveness

Amusement Park

High interest in new experiences, willing to take risks to increase your enjoyment of life, physical gratification

Anal Sex

Other people's desires seem overwhelming to you, feeling lacking in personal empowerment or control – or strong feelings of lust and desire for something or someone, willingly submitting to a situation

Android

Feeling that things have lost their warmth or humanity, something seems lacking in spirit, desiring more or better abilities to be able to make the most of things in your life

Anger

Disappointment, unconscious frustrations, stress, restrictions, unexpressed opinions or feelings, repressive tendencies regarding negative emotions, aggressive impulses need your attention

Ankh

Especially fertile situations, life affirming events taking place, feeling more alive

Ants

You're working very hard at something important. Life appears to be constraining you - you've been going along with what others want instead of doing what you would really like to do.

Aquamarine

Increased sense of hope, communications improving, youthful spirits influencing a situation or relationship

Apple

Wisdom, knowledge, fertile and creative imagination, and the existence of harmonious aspects to a situation

Armageddon/Apocalypse

Utter and total destruction of something in your life, old ways becoming redundant, new beginnings

Arms

You need to protect yourself from something. An injured arm means you're feeling restricted in life

Armpits

Represent the way you like others to see you, and that you're looking for their acceptance

Artistic tools

Painting and drawing pictures is such a large part of our way of life, and of course it's been that way for thousands of years. Whilst pictures and paintings often include much in the way of symbolism, as dictated by the mind of the artist who made it, the paraphernalia which is used for the making of pictures also has a wealth of symbolism behind it too...

Bodypaint - *Self acceptance, experimenting with your identity, unusual perspectives*

Brushes - *Creative urges need satisfying, searching for the finer details in life, desire to create harmonious situations*

Canvas - *Personal potential, great possibilities around you, a chance to make a lasting difference in life*

Crayons - *A significant childhood experience, freedom of expression, unconstrained by the expectations of others*

Easel - *Feeling supported, other people's confidence in your abilities, feeling firmly grounded*

Marker pen - *Definite and clear ideas, having a significant point to make, important things to say*

Paint - *Emotions you want to express, innermost feelings or desires becoming stronger, wanting to express something very personal*

Pen - *Specific intentions, deliberate action, self-assurance*

Pencil - *Temporary situations, new beginnings, noncommittal tendencies*

Portraits - *Unique perspectives, singular ideals or ideas, admiration for another*

Self-Portrait - *Introspective thoughts, desire for self-improvement, reflection on one's present situation in life*

Sketchbook - *Being open to ideas, working out the best way forward, needing to make a decision*

Watercolours - *Idealistic views, having one's head in the clouds, vagueness, uncertainty*

Asteroid

Seeing an Asteroid looming into view can mean an important or life-altering change is coming

Art Gallery

Significant moments, things, and events in your life, desire to remember something especially, preservation of a memory, feeling or experience

Atmosphere

Freedom to act as you wish, liberation from a restrictive situation, invigoration, extremely positive feelings

Atomic energy

Huge efforts are required to make something happen, someone or a situation needs very careful handling, highly detailed and methodical approach to doing something, immense potential

Attic

Forgotten things, old memories, hidden secrets, repressive tendencies

Autumn *See **Seasons**

Baby

Dreaming of Babies can symbolise innocence, vulnerability, or new elements coming into your life, such as new beginnings, or making fresh plans. Life is blossoming with possibilities. Also they can represent your creative potential, or conversely, your weaknesses.

Back

Represents the strength of your own position in the world, an exposed back means you should be protective of a secret. To see someone else's back means you shouldn't lend them something, a hurt back represents feelings of weakness or inadequacy about your life in some way

Back Door

Covert methods, illicit behaviour, alternative solutions, finding a different pathway in life

Ballerina

Moving through life easily, graceful progress, ideals of beauty

Banana

Sexual urges and desires, especially male and typically masculine energies, as it's a significantly phallic symbol, quite understandably and obviously!

Barbeque

Deliberate action with expectations of valuable results, methodical processes, patience bringing great rewards

Barnacle

Possessing resilience, sticking to your decisions, firmly held beliefs, deliberately staying put

Basement

Fundamental driving forces, deep passions, subconscious desires and states of mind

Basketball

Passing on useful information, sharing a workload with others which alters rapidly, constantly shifting perspective on something

Bat

Acting covertly, acute perception of a situation, heightened awareness of how others see you

Battery

Independence of spirit, freedom, ability to move and act freely, temporarily enhanced stamina

Beach

Calm, lack of stress in general, easy to achieve what you want, two differing aspects of your life or state of mind are converging and meeting, anticipation of spiritual or emotional changes happening soon, seeking more stability in your life

Bear

Independence, awareness of beginnings and endings, life/death cycles, renewal of energies, fiercely single minded approaches and thoughts, protective behaviour

Bed

Feeling at peace with something, sense of safety, security, or perception of your own sexuality, desire

Bee

Life is harmonious and productive. Or, if they're stinging you, an unexpected problem needs dealing with

Beetle

Possible jealousy or hostility from someone at work, you need to be thicker skinned against the actions of others

Bell

Warnings, a need for preparation, important events, anxiety, sense of timeliness, time for action

Belly dancing

Getting in touch your femininity, Goddess/Mothering instincts, appreciation of feminine qualities

Bicycle

This represents the desire for harmony and an even-handed

approach to things. You want to establish more of a balanced situation somehow, feel more self-reliance, that you're working hard to achieve something, or that steady progress is being made towards a goal on your life path

Billboard Advert

Important lesson learned, clarity of understanding, a desire for everyone to notice something about you

Birds

Birds are magical creatures. Throughout the ages people have attributed a lot of mystical symbolism to birds, and many legends have been built up around them too. Specific Birds carry with them all kinds of unique dream symbolism; there are so many different kinds in this world, I could write an entire chapter of a book on them all - perhaps even a whole book! But dreaming of birds in a more general sense, has plenty of symbolism in itself. Birds in our dreams often represent our aspirations, our hopes and our aims in life, and usually in a very positive way. They tend to symbolise happiness, absolute joy, liberation, freedom, and our sometimes wild fantasies regarding our own potential, especially when seen flying, and soaring off into the skies. The more elaborate and colourful the birds in your dreams, then you can equate this directly with your perspective, on the condition of your life, and your progress toward your goals. For example, in relation to how attractive these prospects seem, or how happy or successful you subconsciously feel they are to you at the time you have the dream. Here are some of the most common birds that appear to us in our dreams and examples of what they can represent.

Blackbird – *Blackbirds represent temptation, lust, and dark desires regarding a love interest. You might well be looking for a serious partner to play with and keep you entertained in the bedroom department.*

Canaries – *Dreaming of a yellow Canary is a sign of happiness regarding relationships, especially if you dream of two of them together.*

Chickens – *Be careful of unpleasant gossip or the things that someone around you is saying to others about you.*

Cockerel – *A man in your life is being very forthright and stubborn about something, maybe even aggressive.*

Crow – *Often heralded as 'messengers from the other side' they carry with them important messages from the subconscious.*

Cuckoo – *Something in your life is undergoing a big change. You need to change the way you're looking at it, and maybe even try a completely different approach that you wouldn't normally feel comfortable or 'you' doing.*

Dove – *Tranquillity and peace are shortly to be yours regarding a previously troublesome situation*

Eagle – *You need to exercise courage and determination to achieve success in an area of life where your pride is at stake.*

Flamingo – *The way you're seen by others is very important to you right now, especially if you've just made a dramatic new change to your image.*

Hummingbird – *There's a lot more potential than you previously thought regarding a new idea or project of yours.*

Kingfisher – *Self-reliance and dignified behaviour is required from you to maintain your true position and power.*

Nightingale – *Beauty and harmony are abundant and all around you at the moment.*

Owl – *Insight and great wisdom are yours for the taking.*

Parrot – *Someone near you is speaking out of turn and will keep saying the same things unless you do something about it.*

Peacock – *Success is yours right now and you want everyone to acknowledge it, but be careful you don't become too proud.*

Raven – *One of the most mystically regarded birds in western culture, keep a sharp eye out for potential trouble, betrayal or bad* *behaviour from those close to you.*

Vulture – *Your previous experience of a particular type of situation will come in very handy soon, equipping you well to deal with something that could be potentially testing.*

Woodpecker – *Work hard at what you're doing because there'll be some great reward that comes your way as a result*

Birthday

Your wisdom is increasing, a sense of having learnt something, awareness of time passing, personal progression

Biscuits

Optimistic feelings, small pleasures, unhealthy urges, guilt over finding pleasure in something

Bisexuality

Looking at life in a more balanced way, acceptance of the pros and cons of a situation, wanting more from life

Blackboard

Seeing or using a Blackboard is symbolic of having something you wish to teach, and make clearly understandable for others, or that there is a lesson you yourself need to learn

Black cat

Spiritual independence, dark yet attractive sexuality, abundant psychic abilities, supposed connections with 'the other side', intuition, psychic tendencies, uncanny perceptiveness

Black Hole

Black Holes ominously symbolise seemingly impossible situations that you cannot escape whatever you try to do. They also might mean there's something unknowable that's troubling you, or something too difficult to comprehend happening. Your time and energy might be completely taken up by something beyond your control.

Black Widow

Black Widow Spiders signify perceptively dangerous situations, especially where relationships are concerned. And especially if it involves a domineering female!

Black Magic

Negatively deceptive methods, treacherous activities, unfaithfulness, disloyalty

Blackmail

Dreaming of Blackmail is a warning that you should be careful of your, perhaps normally hidden, competitive streak, or indeed someone else's manipulative tendencies.

Blackout

A Blackout in your dream means you're having difficulty seeing a situation for what it really is, or that you feel ignorant about something which is worrying you.

Blood

Women often dream of blood before their period, and when pregnant. If you're bleeding in your dream it means you're feeling drained of energy and emotion. Drinking blood shows that something's giving you new energy and strength

Blueberries

Healthy optimism, a certain youthfulness, or enthusiasm in general

Blue Sky

Calm, comfortable, gentle acceptance, freedom from past troubles

Bodypaint

Self acceptance, experimenting with your identity, unusual perspectives

Bonfires

Changing old ways, new directions in life, new ways of thinking

Bonfire Night (November 5th)

Sacrificing something for the good of others, the end of an old and undesirable situation, triumphing despite difficult circumstances

On this fateful day in History, November 5th 1605, Guy Fawkes, Robert Catesby and their cronies' dreams were (some say unfortunately) foiled, in their attempt to blow up the Houses of Parliament and King James 1st. British culture has joyfully celebrated his shenanigans, subsequent atrocious torture and death ever since, carting effigies of Mr Fawkes around town in pushchairs whilst begging for money, chucking them on massive bonfires, setting off loads of fireworks, and standing around in the cold eating badly burnt baked potatoes. Have you ever dreamt of any of the following Bonfire night or Guy Fawkes related things?

Baked Potato - *Grounding influences, earthly pursuits and interests are desired, seeking stability and comfort, especially during troubled times*

Throwing things on a Bonfire - *Old and outdated ways no longer of any use, wanting to get rid of specific unwanted aspects of your life or behaviour, finally letting go of certain worries or anxieties*

Burning - *Intense feelings, passionate instincts rising within, highly emotional states, an issue should not be ignored, enlightenment, transformation, destruction*

Effigy (Guy) - *Wishes and intentions need fulfilling, unable to express yourself sufficiently, substitution, actions that are only representative of true intent*

Explosions - *Sudden release, especially after harbouring pent up feelings or emotions, forceful and powerful energies coming to the fore, a much needed clearing of your path forwards, great outpouring of anger*

Fireworks Display - *Beautiful transformations, positive self expression, freedom of creativity, wishing to attract attention*

Gunpowder - *Dangerous situations, care needed regarding handling something, on the brink of losing control of a situation or temper*

Parliament - *Desire to help or control others, speaking out for what you believe in, improving something for other people's benefit*

King - *Strength, masculinity, powerful leadership, mastering of a skill, winning in a situation involving adversity*

Plotting - *Deceptive tendencies, employing underhand techniques, lying to yourself about something, wishing to mislead someone*

Rocket - *Greatly increased awareness, successful results, things going to plan extremely well, potent male sexuality*

Being a Traitor - *Feelings of guilt, lacking in pride, ashamed of previous actions*

Book

Reading a book in your dreams can mean you're working towards achieving something, steadily, with particular attention or focus. Books also symbolise wisdom, knowledge, and intellectual qualities. A closed book can mean you're feeling lacking in such qualities about something, and an open one generally means you have an open mind towards things, and are willing to learn about and accept new things into your life.

Born (Being)

New beginnings, starting to see the fruits of your endeavours, making a difficult big decision or move, challenging times

Bottle

Contained emotions, feelings or memories. Opening a bottle represents the accessing of such repressed aspects. If it's a bottle of alcohol you're opening, then you've been waiting a long time to develop or mature your feelings, and you sense you will be much happier as a result of you now accessing them.

Bowl

Collecting your thoughts, deliberately containing your emotions

Bracelet

Awareness of a need for protection, believing in someone, identifying with something

Brain

Dreaming of a brain means there's a problem you really need to think about how to solve. If it's there's something wrong with it in some way then your ideas and knowledge aren't getting enough of the attention you think they deserve.

Breakfast

A particular matter needs attention before any subsequent others, first steps of a new venture, easing an introduction to a situation

Breastfeeding - Feeling nurturing, love or tenderness towards something or someone. A desire to see something grow and blossom, to help in the success of an endeavour, idea or scheme.

Breasts

A need to be cared for, or to nurture others, high sexual energy

Brooch

Self-expression, telling others something personally significant, having unique ideas

Buffalo

Stubborn attitudes, conventional tendencies, fear of change

Builder

Personal ambition, self development, trying to improve things

Building

Buildings symbolise you and the way you see yourself internally too. If you find yourself in a very small one then you're feeling like you have something to learn in life. The bigger or taller it is shows you're becoming more aware and confident of yourself in the world. If your building is falling down or damaged in some way this is a sign that you've had a difficult time of it lately, especially regarding your relationships with other people. If it involves a particular kind of building, think about what it means to you and your feelings in general about it. For example does it make you feel safe or afraid, excited or unhappy? This will help you see a bit more clearly what your dream is trying to show you about yourself.

Bunny

Abundance, increased fertility, heightened sexual activities, hidden surprises

Burlesque

Attention seeking, strong sexual attraction, the need for approval, unsatisfied desires

Butterfly

You're transforming the way you think, romantic, happy and joyful times are in store, people seem very attracted to you at the moment

Bus

If you're waiting for a bus, this indicates that things haven't been going the way you want them to, you're hoping for something specific to happen. Riding along on a bus means you're avoiding making a decision for yourself, and instead, just doing what everyone else normally does, content to go with the crowd, doing what everyone else is doing, complying with popular opinions or choices.

Calf

Potential for growth, future plans, lacking much experience

Canal Barge

Canal Barges symbolise cool, calm, collected and ever so stable times for you. Almost nothing can ruffle your seagull feathers or overturn your vessel!

Candle

Gently dawning awareness, hope for the future, intellectual enlightenment

Canvas (Artists)

Personal potential, great possibilities around you, a chance to make a lasting difference in life

Car

Dreaming of driving a Car symbolises the progress of your life, especially related to your ambitions and determination generally. You feel that you are steering yourself in the right direction in life, that you have mastery over the relevant conditions, events or other factors. What's the car like, and the quality of the experience/drive?? Impressive? Comfortable? Fast? Or is it otherwise? These sorts of thing will have further bearing on things, and tell you how you truly feel your life is going...

If you're a passenger, you don't feel in control of your life journey. Maybe you enjoy being taken for a ride, or taken somewhere you wouldn't normally go.

If the Car won't start, do you feel powerless or lack sufficient self-esteem in some way?

Car parked? Time to stop what you've been doing and do something else perhaps.

Flat tyre? Something may be getting in the way and preventing you from progressing as you wish.

Driving an old Banger? Maybe your tried and tested methods or ways are now past their use-by-date' or are generally less useful than they once were.

Behind the wheel of a posh and pricey motor? Things could well be starting to work out for you, helping you to realise your ambitions.

Flooring it in a flash sports car? Things are progressing rather speedily indeed! Or are they moving too slowly for you, and you'd like them to get a move on?

Carnival

Desire to escape an ordinary situation, hiding certain aspects of the self, abandoning restraint and letting yourself go, hedonism

Carpet

Making your life easier, taking practical steps in order to achieve something, preparation of the psyche or physical self for the task in hand

Cartoon Characters

Most of us have grown up with a whole world of cartoon characters in our lives, from all the TV, films, comics and books of our childhoods, many of which still exist by way of new media, repeat showings, and the sheer longevity of the most popular ones, and so on. What could it mean if we find ourselves dreaming of one of them though? Here's a small selection for your perusal...

Bugs Bunny symbolises smart thinking, quick-wittedness, and an agile mind, definitely with a cheeky edge though

Daffy Duck represents unbridled enthusiasm, being overwrought emotionally and even feeling prone to bouts of jealousy

Donald Duck is a very different duck, meaning you could be feeling irritated, mischievous, or are having trouble getting others to understand you in some way

Homer Simpson might mean you're aware of being more lazy than usual, or feeling a bit daft or ignorant regarding something, or perhaps that you're feeling a fierce sense of devotion to your family

Mickey Mouse symbolises positivity, being a good person, and heroic actions generally

Roadrunner can interpreted as you attempting to avoid a nasty predicament, or that you want to run away fast from something or someone

Sylvester & Tweety Pie - Sylvester is symbolic of wanting something but not getting it, or being determined to do something

against the odds. Tweety Pie could mean you're seen as a potential victim by others but really you're too smart to let that happen.

Tasmanian Devil *represents your animal instincts, your wild side, and bad tempered or angry tendencies*

Cashmere

Possessing a gentle strength, extremes of comfort, pure luxury

Castle

Seeking security and protection, defensiveness, isolation

Catastrophe

What happens when all seems lost, hopeless or gone forever in your dreams? When things fall apart, collapse, get destroyed, become ruined, or even worse? Don't worry if it feels like it's the end of the world, it's not normally quite so dramatic. Dreaming of cataclysmic catastrophes signifies events happening and feelings we're experiencing which are much more subtle - even though at the time of having the dream, it doesn't half feel like it COULD be the end of it all!

Caterpillar

Personal transformation, humble beginnings leading to greater things, the discovery of beauty in something

Cauldron

Fertility, nurturing someone or something, deliberate actions, methodical processes

Ceiling

Upper limits, reaching a point you cannot pass, needing a break through, spiritual matters on your mind

Celebration

Celebrations in general, represent recognition of important personal changes or goals achieved, and significant growth developments occurring.

Cemetery

Sadness, re-visiting painful memories, burying or hiding something about yourself

Centre of the Earth

Feeling ungrounded, interests in unknowable aspects of a situation, getting to the real heart of a matter, investigating something extremely thoroughly

Chainsaw

Big changes happening, severe alterations to plans, cutting through obstacles

Chastity Belt

Feelings of being prevented from doing something, blocked emotional pathways, not being able to express yourself as you wish to, especially sexually

Cheetah

Healthy sense of purpose, the active pursuit of an important goal, an 'anything is possible' approach, willingness to strike quickly in order to gain

Chest

Abundance self confidence, pride, painful chest means someone's being aggressive and confrontational toward you

Chick

Not yet able to do something, searching for an answer, unveiling results of previous endeavours

Chiffon

Delicate situations, the lightening of an emotional load or responsibility, careful handling is needed

Child

Natural curiosity, a desire to begin nurturing something within yourself, old childhood worries or behaviour patterns need dealing with or resolving

Childbirth

If you dream of the birth of a child, this is one of the nicest things to dream of, as it shows that there's so much promise for your immediate future. Even if it's a painful or difficult process in your dream then this signifies that even though it could be difficult in some way to actually achieve what you want, you're going to have some truly major positive changes in your life, and pretty imminently too. If the birth is easy on you in your dream, then you're shortly about to be released from a situation that has been worrying you a lot, without too much happening that will unsettle you at all.

Chimney

Finding a way to remove something unwanted in life, sexual prowess, familial warmth, or a lack thereof of either

Chimney Sweep

Strangely attractive, unusual qualities, innate cleverness, psychological skills

Chisel

An important point needs to be made, making small improvements, steady progress

Chocolate

Indulgence in excesses, heightened sensuality, self-reward, needing more pleasure in life

Christmas

Dreams of Christmas time have various meanings, depending on which particular aspect of the festive period you dream of. To dream of Christmas during any other month in the year than December is a great sign of how productive and happy your life is soon going to be, in the short term at the very least. If you dream of it during December itself, then that suggests that this upturn in events is more specifically money orientated – maybe you'll get a lovely Christmas present from someone who's feeling a bit flash with their cash!

Christmas Dinner

If you find yourself dreaming of enjoying a huge Christmas lunch with all the trimmings, this is generally symbolic of the strength of feeling and fulfilment you're receiving from your loved ones, be that family, your partner or friends. If the yuletide banquet in your dream involves lots of family members, especially if it includes those you haven't seen for a long time or even family members that are no longer with us, this is a strong indication that you're developing spiritually to quite some degree, and in a really positive way!

Christmas Party

Dreaming about being at a Christmas party means that, although in your dream you may well be enjoying yourself and having a grand old time of it, you're are a bit over cautious in your relationships with people, especially with new friends. Try to loosen up a bit with them, and you'll find life becomes a lot more enjoyable, and that you feel more comfortable around them too!

Christmas Present

Presents are obviously a big part of the whole Christmas experience for most people, and dreaming of receiving them actually means that rather than getting some interesting looking, beautifully wrapped gifts, you should rather be experiencing some kind of wonderful reunion with an old friend or acquaintance. Be careful if in your dreams you receive lots and lots of presents from someone, though - this is a sign you should be wary of the motives of the person giving them to you!

Cinema

Feeling distanced from events happening around you in life, or perhaps wanting to distance yourself from those events - what's happening on screen? This will reflect your state of mind in some way - seeking adventure, a break from the norm, yearning for ways to experience more fun or excitement. Whatever is happening in the movie you're watching reflects what's happening - or not - in your world. If you're standing in a queue at the cinema though, this highlights even more the 'waiting around for something to happen' aspect to your life.

Circle

Perfection, wholeness, completion, life-cycles, open-minded-ness, also monotonous activities, routines

Circus

Enjoyment of present circumstances, or alternatively, feeling a lack of stimulation, looking for entertainment

City

A busy City symbolises a hectic time of it, a busy schedule, or an active social life, but don't forget to look at the context too - is it a happy or unpleasant experience? It might all be fine and dandy and represent there being lots of positive things around you, yet could also mean you want to connect more with people, but are finding it hard to do so, so it can also reflect feelings of loneliness, things seeming overwhelming, feeling lost in the crowd in some way

Classroom

Learning new things, new lessons in life, understanding some-thing more clearly than before

Cleaning

Getting rid of outdated attitudes and undesirable influences, organising, sorting out your priorities

Cleopatra

Exotic desires, powerful feminine qualities, feeling worshipped, living in luxury

Cliff

Large, imposing and often scary decisions looming, major turning points in life, 'jumping off into the unknown' emotionally

Climbing

Climbing on or over things is fun and something we do lots when we're children. As we get older, climbing is something we do in many different, frequently non-physical ways too...

Generally, climbing is symbolic of steady progression towards a goal, or specific point, like reaching a significant milestone in your life. The qualities of what and how you're climbing in your dream give you further context to reflect on regarding your experience of doing so.

Hills and Mountains are harder to climb than most things. The steeper or higher they come, the harder to surmount or transverse you feel the task or journey ahead of you is.

Struggling uphill means you're facing very tricky circumstances or a really difficult situation to cope with indeed.

Climbing Ladders can symbolise your career or business progression, or your perceived social status, and for some, your views on your own sexual prowess - especially if you're a bloke! Very phallic, those ladders.

Climbing stairs represents a slower, more calculated or deliberate progression forwards towards where you wish to be. 'One step at a time' and all that.

Reaching the top of climbing something signifies the pinnacle of achievement, a goal is reached, something has been conquered at last.

Clocks

Dreaming of Clocks represents the significance of time in our lives, also our sense of progress, or lack thereof. A clock is symbolic of time being a very important factor. Consider the nature of how the clock appears, as this provides additional context and perspective to what the dream may mean...

Is the clock running fast? Perhaps time is running short for you. If it's running slowly, maybe you have too much time on your hands, or something is taking too long.

Winding up a clock means there's something we need to put more energy or effort into, to achieve the results we desire.

A clock showing the wrong time represents our frustration with something we want to occur not happening yet, or an inability to find the right time to do something.

A stopped clock could mean the end of a situation, something having reached a conclusion, or perhaps even an end of a life, although not usually the dreamer's.

Clockwork

Rewards for previous efforts, work needs to be done before you can move forward, many things need to be organised for something to work properly

Clone (of yourself) - Reluctance to take responsibility for own actions, feeling overworked or that there's not enough time in the day or energy to do what you want to, strong self-regard and self-belief, narcissism

Clothing

Dreaming of your clothing tends to symbolise something

about how you feel you're perceived by others, and how you wish to be seen, indicating your current state of being. The clothes we put on and wear everyday, are made of all kinds of familiar material and fabrics, which protect us, comfort us and help us live our lives in so many different ways. In the world of our dreams, consider what unique strengths, weaknesses and qualities an item of clothing might possess, then apply this to what's happening in your waking life, to try and help you find out what's *really* going on underneath it all...

Dreaming of wearing clothes that don't suit you means you're putting on a fake 'front' to others, that you're pretending to be something you are clearly not, and possibly being hypocritical in some way.

Dirty clothing shows that there's something you need to change about yourself, in order to benefit more greatly or avoid doing yourself a disservice.

Wearing old clothes means you have an old way of doing things which needs to change, or a previous mode of thinking or behaving of yours is no longer relevant, or has stopped being of use or interest to you.

Wearing new clothes symbolises new attitudes to life, new ways and new approaches to self-expression generally are on the cards, you're either thinking about improving some aspect of yourself or have recently done so.

Wearing clothes that are too small for you means you're feeling restricted by a situation, or that it's totally wrong for you.

Clothes not fitting because they're too big symbolises a sense of inadequacy or that you're unsuitable to fulfill a specific role.

The materials the clothes are made of can have further meanings too...

Cashmere - *Possessing a gentle strength, extremes of comfort, pure luxury*

Chiffon - *Delicate situations, the lightening of an emotional load or responsibility, careful handling is needed*

Cotton - *Purity of thought, simplicity, seeing the many differing benefits of one thing, simple pleasures yielding great reward*

Denim - *Hard working qualities, intrinsic resilience, labour intensive activities*

Fleece - *Feeling left out or ignored, desiring affection, longing for family support*

Leather - *Self-reliance, self-protection, animalistic or sexual desires, connections with nature*

Lycra/Spandex - *Flexibility, needing to alter an approach to suit circumstances, willingness to maneuver a position or viewpoint*

Nylon - *Resistance to change, tenaciousness, maintaining integrity under difficult circumstances*

Polyester/Viscose etc - *Convenient solutions, unnatural experiences, synthetic and unrealistic results*

Rubber - *Strange and unusual tendencies, extremes of experience, exploring your sensuality, perversion of the norm*

Silk - *Unbreakable bonds, very strong connections, feelings of everlasting love, ultimate pleasure*

Velvet - *Smooth transitions, self-indulgent behaviour or circumstances, satisfaction with a situation, lofty ideals, noble achievements*

Wool - *Traditional values, practical approaches, reliability, natural feelings or interests*

Clouds

Lack of clarity, missing information, searching for something intangible, something is proving hard for you to fully understand, fear of impending failure, a sense of something in the air about you

Cloudy (Overcast sky)

Negativity, tendency towards self-pity, depression

Clowns

Clowns appear in people's dreams much more often than you might think! The clown, 'joker' or 'fool' is an archetype deeply ingrained into nearly all the differing human societies, from images of the court jester and circus clowns, film and comic book characters, through to the heavily symbolic depiction as the basis of 'The Fool' card in Tarot card decks the world over. The presence of clowns in a dream can have a lot of significance for us, dependent on the context within our dream world that it appears, and our own notions or fears associated with them too.

Dreaming of yourself as a happy clown shows the playful, child-like, even silly side of your personality being brought out, and you're feeling much less inhibited than usual. It could be that a relationship is making you feel this way, or that someone is appreciating you for who you really are and loves your company.

If you have cheery clowns around you, then you're very happy and excited to be involved in something going on around you, a family situation, social events or even perhaps a project at work.

If you're an unhappy dream-clown, you're feeling as though something is no longer as enjoyable in life for you, as though what you liked about something has been 'spoiled' or taken away.

Are scary clowns frightening you as you sleep? You suspect that someone around you is not being their true self with you, and are hiding their thoughts from you or behaving in a 'disguised' fashion, literally as though behind a mask or a clown's makeup.

Clubbing

Wanting to have more fun with, and to be more involved with the people around you. A need to feel more socially active, to really enjoy yourself for a change

Coal

Slow but eventual progress being made, a beneficial situation needs regular attention to be maintained

Cockroach

Your psychological and spiritual side needs a 'spring clean', you'll benefit from changing an old habit that doesn't serve you so well anymore, unpleasant memories are troubling you often

Coconut

Rewards await those who persevere with hard work, hidden treasures are to be found within unappealing or difficult situations/tasks

Coffee Table

Concerns about your immediate social circle, time out needed from a situation

Coins

Valuing something, positive opportunities around you, being given something relatively small which is helpful or that you need

Comets

Escape, fleeing old unpleasant situations, rare occurrences

Concert

Harmonious influences around you, exciting events occurring, feeling connected to others

Condoms

Wanting to feel protected, or to offer protection, knowing you are safe to live in the particular way that is chosen, having confidence in a decision, sexual interest or anticipation in or around you

Confusion

Finding a decision difficult to make, inability to settle on a viewpoint with any sense of certainty, lacking clarity

Contortionist

Difficulty working out what to do, literally tying yourself up in knots about something which is bothering you, being able to stretch your abilities or tolerance beyond that of the norm

Cooker

Loyalty, devotion, harmonious company or situations, nurturing a true desire or passion

Cooking

Food plays a really HUGE part in our lives doesn't it? If we're not shopping for, eating or thinking about our next meal, then it's pretty often that we're in the kitchen, cooking or preparing something to eat. Here's a few cooking based dream symbols I've rustled up...

Baking something means you have a special plan or idea in your mind at the moment, and that you're perfectly, patiently, happy to carry on as normal whilst waiting for it to come to fruition and take effect.

Boiling something in a pot, saucepan or cauldron? You want something dealt with, efficiently, cleanly, and soon. All for your own benefit and satisfaction!

Chopping things up for a meal symbolises a desire to meticulously ensure you have everything you might possibly need for a particular task or job you want to do, and need to make things as manageable as you can too.

Frying tonight? There's a situation that seems pretty hot to handle right now, and you need to be careful you don't burn yourself by getting to close to it, or spending too long in it either. Get it sorted and get out!

Seasoning food in preparation for a meal represents a literal need for more flavour, spice and enjoyment in your life. Try some new ingredients and allow a few brand new, more exotic influences into your world!

Stirring things about shows that you're considering all the elements of your life at the moment, people, things, situations, and hoping you can make it all work out not just in your favour, but for the benefit of all, too.

Coral

Hidden depths, concealed beauty, discovering life or at-
tractiveness, especially in things previously thought the opposite

Cotton

Purity of thought, simplicity, seeing the many differing benefits of one thing, simple pleasures yielding great reward

Country - *See Different Country

Countryside

Being in the Countryside means you desire a stronger connection with nature and calm, a need to escape from normal life.
You might want the very opposite to a City based dream, but
look at what's happening in the dream too for more insight.
Do you desire a simpler time, with less stress? You might crave
more freedom than you are getting

Crab

Strength beyond expectation, clingy and possessive tendencies, unusual directions of movement, strange decisions

Crayons

A significant childhood experience, freedom of expression,
unconstrained by the expectations of others

Crescent

Versatility, emerging femininity, change is coming, new life in
old situations, renewal

Crescent and Star (symbol) Sense of wonderment, universal mysteries, heightened emotional states, thinking of higher things

Crisps

Temporary situations, unfulfilled goals, lack of satisfaction regarding a significant issue

Cross

Choice to make, indecision, new directions, possible religious or moral connotations, rejection, sacrifice

Crossed Fingers

Hoping for something, a desire for success, optimistic points of view, difficulty achieving something

Crown

Ultimate goals achieved, success in life, being in a position of power, elevated sense of status

Cruise

Going on a Cruise? You're on an emotional adventure right now. Who knows what exotic delights await? Or it could be that you really WANT to experience such an adventure, and that such things are missing from your life currently.

Cub

Playful approaches, immature behaviour, innocence

Cup

To dream of a cup can mean several things, depending of course on the conditions and circumstances in which it appears. Cups are generally seen to represent emotional states and feelings, especially related to love and healing.

If the cup is full and in your hands, this symbolizes satisfaction, or fullness of feeling, that you have the thing you desire in your grasp. It could be that you are feeling loved and are happy with this, or particularly valued by someone you care about.

If it is empty, well then I'm pretty sure it's not going to be too

much trouble to your imagination to think of what this may signify. But did it used to be full? Have you lost something you once had? Are you looking for something specific in life with which to fill your cup, to heal your heart, mind or soul somehow?

Is your cup half empty, or is it half full? Depending on which, you may be feeling somewhat negative about something or, conversely, positive instead.

If your cup is overflowing, you have more than you need or want emotionally, and could even feel that an emotional situation is out of control.

If the cup has a broken handle, something in life is proving hard to cope with, you quite literally cannot 'handle' it.

Is your dream cup broken entirely? This indicates feelings of loss, emotional desperation and sadness. It may be that you feel powerless, leaving you feeling helpless to prevent a problem gaining momentum, power and control, especially over you.

Curtains

Repressed thoughts, secretive actions, wanting to hide or prevent something being noticed, concealment of an aspect of yourself

Cushion

Protecting yourself from an unpleasant reality, denial of home-truths, fear of pain, seeking comfort

Cutlass

Hostile feelings, destructive emotions, frustration with life

Cycling

Feeling self-reliant, self-motivated, balanced, steady progress

Cyclops

Intently focused on something you see, maybe even too much focus, concentration, a broader view is needed

Cylinder

Lack of expression, limited options, controlled feelings, contained emotions

Dancing

Happiness, joyful situations, having a positive outlook, celebration, freedom, liberation, self expression, sensuality, sexual energies, living life, and behaving how you truly feel you want to...

Dancing in any way, shape, or form in your dreams is usually a wonderful sign, symbolic of so many perfectly positive, and marvellously kinetic, energetic things happening in our lives. Finding yourself dancing in your dreams signifies nothing less than your own happiness, finding yourself in joyful situations, and feeling in possession of a generally positive outlook.

Dancing alone denotes a sense of real freedom, and joyous liberation, especially if you've been experiencing restrictive situations or energies around you. It symbolises self expression, and a renewed lust or love for life, and a sense that you feel you can now behave however you truly wish to.

Dancing with a partner represents a joining or unifying of the yin and yang energies, sometimes literally regarding the masculine and feminine. It symbolises harmony with sexual energies, and your sensual side, frequently symbolising new, positive connections with others.

Darkness

Lack of understanding or information, negative perspectives, depression, unhappiness

Dawn

Enlightenment, awakenings of the spirit or soul, realisation

Dead (deceased loved ones)

Dreaming of loved ones who've died isn't a portent of impending doom, and it's not meant to scare you witless either. Many believe that people who've died and passed over to some sort of 'other side' sometimes make contact with us via our dreams, to speak with us, give us an important message or to help us in some way. Also, as a natural part of the grieving process, it can be a way that the subconscious mind is trying to help us come to terms and cope with the loss we've experienced, even years after the person has died. We can dream of reliving experiences we used to have with them, and sometimes we want so much to be able to say our 'last goodbyes' as it were, that the subconscious actually arranges for this to happen in the world of dreams, to help us live our lives a little more peacefully in the 'real' world. Much research has gone into this tenuous area with no real conclusions, and an enormous number of theories abound. The myriad personal and religious belief systems of the human race continue to attempt to explain such phenomena and possibilities to this day...

Death- *See also **Dying**

It's going to happen to us all in the end of course: but what the devil does it mean if we dream of death and dying? Apart from often ending with waking up in a cold sweat, sometimes terrified, but usually thankful we're still here of course...

Dreaming of yourself dying isn't actually as bad as you might imagine. It signifies serious change in your life, such as positive transformations and enlightenment! Out with the old and in with the new and such like. Leaving the past you behind, and time to embrace new energies and things coming to you to light up your existence. So in a way, it's actually potentially fantastic news if you have a dream about popping your clogs!

Dreaming of someone else dying symbolises the end of an era regarding your relationship with them in some way. It might be that the way you used to be with them is no longer relevant, or that you've moved on.

To dream of faking your own death, or others thinking you're dead but you know in the dream that you aren't, represents a desire to stop living a certain way, or being how you are, and to be able to rid yourself of unpleasant or negative influences around you.

Demon

Deliberately hidden aspects of the self, worrying about undesirable character traits, feelings of persecution

Denim

Hard work, something has an intrinsic resilience, labour intensive activities or requirements

Desert

Finding yourself in a boiling hot Desert can signify loneliness, isolation, or feelings of being 'deserted' (excuse the pun) by others. It can also mean you need somewhere to be alone, away from people

Devil

Afraid of negative consequences, negative aspects, fear of something 'evil', temptation, forbidden desires

Diamond

Purity and wholeness of the self, extreme resilience and strength, personal vanity

Diamond (shape)

Determination, self-perfection, absolute clarity, extraordinary self-belief

Dice

Willing to take a risk, gambling with especially significant things in your life, unknown results, indecision

Different Country

Dreaming about being in another country means that you're feeling there's something lacking in your life, and you need to change something fundamental about your general situation. Things could be getting on top of you a bit or maybe it's that you aren't finding the satisfaction or happiness you need, and that a change of scenery is required. This could be something as simple as changing your routine a little, or perhaps a lot too! It doesn't literally mean you want to go or even move to somewhere else - although I must say, you can't beat having a nice holiday to blow your cobwebs away can you.

Different Planet

This represents your desire for totally new experiences in your life. It's a strong sign that you're willing to push yourself as far as you can in order to see what's 'out there' for you to explore. Also, if it's one of the planets in our solar system, then have a look at its astrological meaning as that could help you understand further just what area of your life your subconscious might be telling you something about .

Dim light

Uncertainty, vague ideas, unclear motives, ill-informed about something

Dining Table

Seeking encouragement from family, emotional nourishment needed, there is a big family issue to tackle

Dinner/Evening Meal

Main subject or task, awareness of a significant source of information or energy, an important issue needs to be dealt with

Directions

Left - Hidden meanings, seeking alternatives, wanting challenge, unusual ways or methods, emotional difficulties

Right - Direct action, progress or movement, obvious or logical decisions, rationale, doing what seems 'right'

Up - Awakenings, emergence from restrictive situations, positive perspectives and actions, or possible sadness in waking life

Down - Uncertainty, unhappy about something, negative feelings about something, dis-ease regarding current happiness or positivity

Backwards - Being counter-productive, failure, undoing a good deed, spoiling something, under-achievement, ruining things

Forwards - Moving onwards, progressing positively, success, building on achievements, change

Sideways - Avoiding something, tactical maneuvers, maintaining similar circumstances despite change

East - Feeling hopeful for the future, spirituality, spiritually based decisions or actions, wisdom, enlightenment, deep thought, beginnings

West - Fulfilment, potential, opportunities, growth, a sense of finite awareness, something ending, or the realisation a thing will end, growing older

North - The reality of things, coldness of thought or deed, progress/moving forwards, on a journey to completion, seeking *guidance*

South - *Life-path questions or expectations, enduring something difficult, looking to a brighter future, longing for warmth or comfort*

Circular - *Repetitive actions or thoughts, cycles of behaviour, repeating same mistakes, caught in a negative pattern of activity, going round in circles*

No Direction - *Stagnation, depression, lack of progress, detrimental inaction, not knowing what to do next*

Disease

Something is wrong in your life, slow and unpleasant disintegration of a situation, a small but destructive process in underway

Dishwasher

Feeling a need to lighten your workload, or that you've had a lot of nurturing experiences or life lessons lately and want to feel ready for more

Diving

Decisively dealing with something, confidence in your decision, exploring new areas of life

Doctor

You want to examine your life more closely, to find out what's wrong with it, in order to 'make it better'. When you dream of someone else in a doctor's uniform, you feel that someone else holds the real answers to your life questions, that only they can truly help you.

Dolphin

Highly intellectual activities, intelligence, spirituality, emotional intelligence and connectivity

Dominatrix

Wishing to be shown a better way of doing something, lacking physical self-confidence, admiration or trust in a particularly strong feminine presence

Door

It's pretty much damn near impossible to avoid encountering a door, one way or another, during any given day isn't it? Well, they're everywhere aren't they? Just as well really, or how would we get into places; or for that matter, leave them… but when doors appear in our dreams in some way, there's a whole load of interesting things they can symbolise.

Going through a doorway into a house represents passing from one state of self, or perspective on yourself, to another. Also, new opportunities are possibly presenting themselves

A door opening outwards is symbolic of opening up to other people, especially to their views or opinions on you

Doors opening inwards suggest a time for reflection upon yourself, or that you're feeling introspective. It's likely that a time for self-examination is overdue

Letting someone in particular in through a door symbolises an interest or willingness to interact and cooperate with them, or perhaps to learn from them

If there are lots of different doors, and you don't know which to go through, you might be having difficulty in making a choice or decision, and are feeling overwhelmed by this

Locked or closed doors represent opportunities you've had that appear to be impossible to take, you've missed out on, or that you've been prevented from taking for some reason

Not being able to find a door to get out of a room or building could mean you're finding it hard to express your thoughts or feelings in life, about a specific thing

Doughnut

Seeking growth, desire for development, looking for completion

Dragonfly

Be careful - something in your life is not what it seems to be, life is teaching you a lesson that'll be helpful for you to learn, magical protection, mystical warning, look beyond first impressions, a change in circumstance will happen

Drawing/Sketching

The desire to express yourself in your own way without any interference from others, to deliberately live life in your own way. Also idealistic views, feeling unsure how to express your thoughts adequately, creative urges need satisfying

Dried Fruit

Concern about old age, feeling drained or spent, something may be past its best

Drinking

Our lives would be pretty dry if we didn't drink things, and so would our dreams, if the things we drink regularly didn't feature in them on occasion. And in the world of dreams, other than their usual properties, they all possess additional, rather interesting attributes too...

Alcohol - *Drinking booze in your dreams, as in waking life, often suggests pleasurable and fun times, but not always, as although it sometimes signifies a strong desire for pleasure and indulgence, it can mean a much needed escape from 'too much normality' and humdrum routine is the order of the day*

Tea - *Feeling serene, calm, a sense of contentment, mild satisfaction*

Coffee - *Sudden awareness, sharpening of the senses, feeling alert, impetuous desire*

Water - *Seeking clarity, clear intentions, emotionally revitalised, sense of refreshment of the mind and body*

Red Wine - *Sensual pleasures, indulgent tendencies, strong desire for companionship*

White Wine - *Searching for inner peace, relaxed situation/approach, the need for reflection*

Champagne - *Complete success, joyous celebration, achievement of an ultimate goal, triumph over adversity*

Beer - *Tranquility, sociable inclinations, wanting a little distance from normal life, new perspectives*

Spirits - *Self-reward, a significant point has been reached, desire for personal change*

Hot Chocolate - *Throwing caution to the wind, enjoying being decadent, looking for comfort in the external, emotional satisfaction*

Fruit Juice - *Feeling 'alive', connected to the life-force, positivity*

Fizzy Drinks - *Momentary happiness, a 'quick fix' of fun, light-heartedness, empty but enjoyable activities*

Energy Drinks - *Physical intensity, enduring current conditions, drive, intent on action*

Herbal Tea - *Spiritual cleansing, a sense of purity, revitalisation of the soul*

Driving

Sense of control, direction, purpose, moving forwards

Drill

New discoveries, searching for something hidden, getting to the bottom of a situation

Drunk

Abandonment of responsibilities or concern, carefree actions, wishing to escape, trying to hide from or block out painful truths, feelings, or situations, recent personal breakthrough or event

Duckling

Starting to be more flexible in your views, discovering new abilities

Dungeon

Feeling like you're being prevented from living or being how you want, limiting circumstances, repression

Dusk

Unhappiness, sadness, experiencing a temporary gloomy disposition, negative outlook

Dying

Don't worry if you dream of yourself coming to the ultimate end - that is to say of course, dreaming of actually dying. This is in fact a positive thing, as it reflects the fact that not only do you recognize the fact that something in your life is in need of a change, but you are trying to change that something as you feel that it has outlived its useful purpose for you.

This is a very common and important occurrence in most people's dreams at one time or another, and mainly shows that you are experiencing a particularly transitional phase which you're willing to go through, whatever it takes, to make your life more how you'd like it to be. You're becoming more enlightened, and perhaps even spiritual in your approach to your existence, and are about to enter into a new, and likely far more productive time.

*See **Death** and **Common Dream Themes** for more

Ears

If ears are dreamt about this means we need to pay more attention to the things others are telling us. If they're bigger than normal or there are lot of them, it's because you really want to learn or know something. If you don't have any and can't hear in your dream, then you're feeling that there's something you'd rather not know or don't want to hear someone say.

Earring

Someone could be telling you what they only *think* you want to hear, you have a desire to hear something pleasurable or personally complimentary

Earth

The Earth is a beautiful thing. Viewed from above, far away past the upper stratosphere in Space, video imagery from the International Space Station gives us an astonishing perspective on our planet and all it's visible characteristics, allowing us to observe and discover things about it previously beyond our wildest dreams or capabilities. And when we dream of the kinds of things which go to make up our planet, hidden meanings are also waiting to be discovered...

Atmosphere - Freedom to act as you wish, liberation from a restrictive situation, invigoration, extremely positive feelings

Beach - Two differing aspects of your life or state of mind are converging and meeting, anticipation of spiritual or emotional changes happening soon, seeking more stability and calm in your life

Clouds - Lack of clarity, something is proving hard for you to fully understand, fear of impending failure, a sense of negativity in the air

Country - Identifying with a particularly strong characteristic, an overriding impression about something, desiring or needing a change of circumstances

Desert - Lacking the particular stimulation you want, undesirable circumstances, feeling lonely, abandonment

Forest - Searching for deeper personal insight, awareness of transitory elements passing through your life, trying to understand

things better

Island - *Individuality, single-mindedness, unique qualities*

Landscape - *Dreaming of a landscape symbolises how you see your own body. The more beautiful it seems, the better opinion you have of your body and self-image, but the more unpleasant the landscape appears, well, that means you are having more than just a bit of trouble with how you view your physicality in some way.*

Mountain - *Important task to undertake, a significant issue in your life, having an impossible goal to achieve*

Ocean - *How you see your emotional life, something is affecting you emotionally in a really big way - consider the state the ocean is in as an indication of the emotional effect it's having on you*

North Pole - *Positive energy, feeling elated as in 'on top of the world', clarity of thought, feeling 'cool' and calm*

South Pole - *Seemingly insurmountable tasks, difficult conditions surrounding you, a long journey lies ahead, wanting more adventure in life but on your own, isolation*

Both Poles - *A situation involving opposing issues needs dealing with, you're torn between two choices, two points of view*

The World - *Ability to 'see the bigger picture', appreciation of many aspects contributing to one overall thing, wholeness, unity. Seeing the planet Earth in your dream indicates that you're comfortable with your perspective or view of life, that you feel very realistic and 'down to earth' about life in general.*

Earth (Physical Element) - Dreams involving the element 'Earth' in some way symbolise your perspective or view on anything from the physical forms it can take, to the effects it can have on us, to the very soil we rely on, not just for giving our feet something to stand upon, but of course to enable us to grow and nurture things other than ourselves, too.

Dreaming of being covered in earth and all muddy means you're having to cope with a very messy problem which you'd prefer your life to be cleansed of, rather than have to deal with, as if it could all be just 'washed away', like mud. If you're struggling to walk through thick, sticky mud in your dream, you're feeling restricted in your movement and actions in some way, that something or someone is impeding your progress.

When earth, in the sense of soil, features strongly in your dreams, this can signify that a new endeavour or project or relationship is founded on 'stable ground' and bodes very well for the future. Also, it represents a real sense of growth in life, and that there's plenty of opportunity around you.

Earthquake

Fundamental instability, feeling ungrounded, things being shaken-up, a change is needed: an Earthquake occurring in your dream means that there's a real lack of comfort or stability in some area of your life right now, and that you feel powerless to help the situation. You may even feel overwhelmed by it, although if you 'survive' it unscathed this is a sign that you'll get through it all somehow, whereas, if you find yourself becoming trapped or buried in your dream 'quake' this may mean that you'll find whatever situation it is much harder to deal with.

Easel

Feeling supported, other people's confidence in your abilities, feeling creatively grounded

Easter

New projects are underway, old ideas being given new relevance, something or someone coming back into your life

Eating Out

Lack of substance or inspiration in normal life, the search for psychological or emotional nourishment elsewhere than in your normal circumstances, looking for spiritual joy, emotional fulfilment through sharing with another, pleasure and gratification

Electricity

Personal power is increasing quickly, positive self-awareness and discovery, exciting times and projects are underway at last, an increase of psychosexual stimulation is occurring

Electric Fire

Emotional contentedness, strong family ties, feelings of warmth towards someone

Electric Light bulb

Artificial impressions dispelled, new ideas, inventive solutions

Electrician

Life force, wanting/needing more energy, revitalisation

Elephant

Faithfulness, patience, intellectual wisdom, holding on to old ways, dwelling on past memories

Elvis Presley

Strong masculine presence, irresistible charisma and attraction in someone, powerful energies around you

Embarrassment

Self-conscious awareness of something, discomfort with self-expression, wanting to hide something from others

Emerald

Commitment to something or to another, longevity of life, immortality of creations, emotional healing

Emotionless

Weakness of will, lack of self-confidence, unwilling to accept something, unable to comprehend a situation

Endings

Dreaming of things ending in some way does often indicate that you have reached a point in your life where you are or about to achieve something important to you, such as a goal you've been hoping to reach or an event occurring that you've wanted to happen for some time. It can also indicate that you're embarking upon a new venture or phase of your life, or that a problem that's been present in your life is being resolved

Endless Knot

Equality, awareness of normally hidden connections, continuity, harmonious situations

Erection

Strong sense of own masculinity, high levels of self-reliance and confidence, prominent and potent creative forces coming from within, sexual excitement or lack thereof

Evening

Endings, something closing down or stopping for good, or potential in the air, a sense of excitement and anticipation

Evil Eye/Eye of God (Equilateral triangle with a solitary eye inside)

Observation, watchful or investigative activities, feeling under the scrutiny of others

Exercising

Wanting to improve something in your life somehow, the desire to build upon what you already have, to expand your world

Exhibition

Needing to examine something, observing your own life and the life of others, a different approach may prove beneficial

Eyes

Seeing your own eyes means you've started to understand something more clearly. If there's something in your eye, this represents something being in your way or something that you don't understand. Dreaming of having a third eye means you should look within yourself to gain clearer insight into a situation. If your eyes are shut (in your dream that is – I think we can assume that your actual eyes are shut as you're asleep!) this means you don't want to believe the truth about something.

Eye Liner

Extra attention needs to be seen to be given or received, enhanced perceptions, wanting more clarity or understanding from others

Eyepatch

Unable to see things the way others do, one-sided viewpoint, lacking a sense of perspective about something

Eye-shadow

Alluring or mysterious qualities, deliberately emotionally deceptive, wishing to create dramatic situations

F ace

We all have one, it's our front door in many ways, and each one is entirely individual and unique to us. Our faces matter to us greatly. And when we dream of our face there's a wealth of meaning hidden behind it...

Dreaming of seeing your face symbolises the way you'd like to be perceived by the world around you, rather than how you feel you truly are. Does it please you or do you feel something else about it?

Two faces? You're feeling conflicted about something, behaved in one way when you may have preferred another, or expressed something other than your true thoughts.

Damaged? Something has happened to make you feel you've been emotionally attacked or wounded, that you or your reputation have been sullied in the eyes of others

Spotty? Things are going on in your thoughts about yourself which you're not happy about, and finding tricky to conceal from the world.

Washing your face is symbolic of wanting to cleanse yourself of things that are troubling you, or to actively save your public reputation with others

Fairground

Wanting to enjoy things more, a need for fun and adventure, not wishing to take something so seriously

Fairy

Magical qualities in the people around you, mischief, naughtiness, especially children's, needing help in little ways, wanting something greatly

Falling - * Also see Common Dream Themes

Falling generally symbolises some kind of lack of control in your life, which is making you feel especially ungrounded and uneasy. It might even be that your position is seemingly downright precarious in some way and you don't know, right now, anyway, what to do to stop it or change things.

Famine

Needing encouragement, wanting stimulation, lack of love, need for emotional sustenance

Fast

Lacking information, requirement of resources, avoidance of that which you may want or need

Father Christmas

Being provided for, receiving things from others, unexpected surprises

Fawn

Nervousness, over-sensitivity, afraid of something, tendency to overreact

Fear

Resistance to change, distrusting someone, lack of faith, unhappiness with life, insecurity, needing reassurance, lack of support or guidance around you. Feeling afraid, or experiencing anxiety, are two of the most common emotions we feel when we dream. In fact, along with anger and sadness, in the world of dreams these more negatively perceived emotions tend to be more likely to surface than the happier, more positive ones! Fear not though... when we have feelings like this in our dreams, these experiences actually help us come to terms with, and handle much better, such trying emotional situations as these in our daily lives.

Feast

Physical needs, sexual desires need satiating, wanting to increase personal power or influence, an abundance of things, having more than you may need or want, excess, indulgence

Feet

Where would we be without our trusty feet? Apart from lying down that is. They take us everywhere we go, support us all day long, provide balance throughout our lives, and take a huge amount of physical punishment. We should say thank you to them sometimes really, don't you think? Here's a few foot-ish dream symbols for you...

Your Feet - *Feelings of stability, practical matters being important right now, the need to be more sensible, and to feel grounded*

Beautiful feet - *Contentedness, happiness, being very satisfied with life*

Ugly feet - *Embarrassment, dissatisfaction, helplessness*

Walking - *Independence, movement, being yourself*

Running - *Complete liberation, a strong need to leave something behind for good*

Injured feet - *Something has gone wrong, or you've made a mistake*

No feet - *Inability to change something or escape from the truth, feeling well and truly stuck*

Field

Healthy influences, comfort, space to exist happily, harmonious aspects or events

Fingers

Skilful manipulation of a situation, a finger pointing at you means you're blaming yourself

Fire

To see fire in our dreams represents all kinds of powerful passions and energies, and especially the transformation of aspects of our lives that are extremely important to us.

When something is burning it generally means that something is disappearing from your life to be replaced by something new instead.

Dreaming of being burned by fire yourself suggests that something is literally 'burning you up' and that your temper is becoming increasingly bad with it too. If it's your house that's on fire, this means that you're feeling a strong passion inside you, and that you have a lot of love that you really want the chance to show.

Putting out a fire means you've come to terms with something lately through your determination to do so, and that you've 'vanquished' a problem once and for all.

Wildfire means that a swift breakdown of a situation is occurring, seriously detrimental influences sweeping across many people's lives, the effect of someone's carelessness

Fire-Breather

Harmful words being said, control of anger or destructive tendencies, wanting to impress others with your voice or words

Fired - *See **Job**

Fire Engine

If a shiny red fire engine is the subject of your dream, this means you're urgently concerned with looking after other people's needs and desires, more than your own - perhaps you need to try putting yourself before others a bit more.

Firefighter/Fireman

Someone near you needs to be saved from a potentially dangerous situation they aren't aware of. You know you have to be brave and fearless to make something happen the way you want it to. If you're being saved from a fire by Fire-Fighters, you feel that life is finally helping you to get what you truly want. Also, being a hero figure, calming a heated situation down, action is required, dangerous situations

Fire light

Intense sexual desires, strong passions, transformation, death of old ways, new beginnings, anger

Fireplace

A lovely cosy lit Fireplace symbolises home comforts, peace, contentment and emotional warmth. Stoking that fire means you're feeling strong desires for something, possibly for romance or love.

Fireworks

Release of pent up energy or emotions, feeling overjoyed about something, completion, success

Fish

Generally, Fish symbolise being emotionally adept, able to deal or cope with strong feelings and their effects, having a talent for evading difficult emotional circumstances, also conception, pregnancy, and swift directional changes in your emotional life.

Dreaming of Fish swimming around symbolises important emotional insights and messages coming straight from your subcon-

scious, although it's likely not quite clear what they might be yet - so very much a time to pay attention to what else is happening in your dreams, as whatever it is will be highly significant to you, and may even help you in your current situation.

Going Fishing in your dreams is symbolic of wanting answers, wisdom or assistance with something troubling you. Catching a fish means that you've understood messages from your sub-conscious, which have now literally 'surfaced' in your conscious mind.

Shopping for fish in a fish market often represents nothing less than the potential for all kinds of wondrous, joyous times around you, and a strong likelihood of pleasurable experiences occurring in your life.

Cooking or eating fish means you are starting to incorporate lessons you've learned, or beginning to apply and understand the benefits of whatever insightful things about life you've discovered or been shown recently.

Seeing flying fish is a lovely symbol of your own emotional liberty and freedom, that you've broken free of a situation which was holding you down or limiting your enjoyment.

Dead fish represents the end of a run of positivity in some area of your life, maybe a loss of personal power in some way, or realising that you aren't quite as knowledgeable about something as you used to be

Fist
Being forceful, defensive or definitive moves, threatening actions

Flamenco
Fiery passions, dramatic events in your love-life, direct and positive happenings, fierce drive to perform flamboyantly

Flaming Torch
The pursuit of a cause, important discoveries, self confidence,

realisation of love

Fleece

Feeling left out or ignored, desiring affection, longing for family support

Floating in mid-air

Contentedness, acceptance, letting go of worries, freedom to move as you wish, achievement of desires

Flood

Being overcome by emotion, too much to deal with, extremely emotional times

Floor

Solid foundations, good grounding, feeling supported

Flying

We all fly so frequently these days, that many say it's almost become like taking a bus - well, apart from all that long-winded bag check nonsense and the enduring of such huge long queues at passport control. What does it mean if we dream of things related to flying though?

Aeroplanes can mean you're rising above problems, overcoming obstacles, or gaining a higher perspective on things, perhaps an increased sense of freedom, too

Airports signify a desire for new projects or endeavours to succeed, such as new relationships, new jobs or new ways of living, and generally that you have ambitions to get something underway. They can also symbolise births or deaths in your life, as in the arrivals or departures areas of an airport.

Checking your bags in at Bag-check? You want to get rid of old baggage weighing you down in order to get on with something more important to you. Do you want to lighten your life's load so you feel less hindered by other things?

Using a Parachute symbolises a need to escape from a dangerous or impossible to cope with situation. Perhaps it's time to give up on an old ideal or troublesome issue.

If you're a Pilot in your dream that means you feel really in charge of your destiny in some way, that you know where you are heading and feel supremely confident that you are in control of your life.

Being talked through the onboard Safety Procedure represents your subconscious need for reassurance before you make your next move or decision.

Going through Airport Security? If an Air Stewardess or Steward is helping you in your dream, you want some help along the way with what you're currently busying yourself with, in order to really feel you can make a go of it. If you're taking on such a role yourself, then it means you feel that you want to help others in a similar capacity who're involved in what you're doing.

Foal

Uncertainty, lack of confidence in taking action, feeling unsteady or unsupported

Foetus

New ideas forming , feeling like taking a fresh approach, inspirational events in life

Fog/Mist

Vagueness, indistinctness, uncertainty, complete lack of clarity, confusion

Food

People often dream of food. Food is such an integral part of all our lives, it's no surprise that, at one time or another, we all have dreams featuring it in some way. However, food appearing in our dreams doesn't simply mean that maybe we're a bit peckish, or that we missed out eating a meal during the day! To dream of food represents the fact that there's something we're hungry for in our lives; something we really need, or something we want, that we aren't getting or experiencing in real life.

Of course, Food is literally what we need to survive. It gives us the energy and fuel we need to exist. Sometimes people do have very literal dreams involving foods that contain nutrients their body is missing, like when they have a deficiency in their diet. It's important to take note of dreams where you are eating things like fruit and vegetables, like oranges or spinach etc, because your body probably needs the vitamins and minerals at that time.

We wouldn't ignore pangs of hunger for too long before we made sure we ate something, and so, in a way, it's useful to acknowledge when our subconscious mind is telling us something about our emotional needs - our 'life-pangs', if you like! If we try to understand the things that our dreams are telling us, it can be really helpful to our lives both in the short-term, and in the long run too.

So, what does dreaming of different types of food represent symbolically? Here's a few thoughts on some of the most common ways that food appears to us in our dreams...

Forbidden food - *Chocolate, cakes and sweets etc - with the pressure to be stick thin and size 'O' disturbingly all around us these days, it's understandable that many people, especially women, dream of rich, indulgent foods like this. It's usually a signal that you need to be nourished emotionally, and can certainly mean you feel that food is a problem in some way for you.*

Strange food, scary food - *If you find yourself confronted with awful, inedible things to eat, things you absolutely cannot stand to eat in real life or even frightening things before you at the dinner table, this is a sign of real emotional upset. Something has truly upset your apple-cart in life, and your subconscious is trying to show you this in your dreams.*

Parties and Feasts - *Including everything from tea parties 'mad hatter' style with fictional characters come to life, to huge banquets with every kind of food under the sun! Parties, feasts and banquets in your dreams are a bit like what it was like when you were five and made an imaginary tea party with your teddy bears, it's the imagination running riot and giving you some fun! It can also be a sign that you aren't indulging yourself in what you would like to be doing in life enough.*

Sexy food - *Aphrodisiac foods like Oysters, Chocolate etc. appearing in your dreams reflects the fact that you could do with more sensual pleasures in your life. It could be that you aren't experiencing enough of these earthly delights currently, or that your desires aren't being fulfilled, and that you are feeling dissatisfied with this area of your life.*

Football

Belonging to a social or work group, working together with others in a collective effort to achieve something, personal responsibility within a team

Footwear

We spend huge amounts of money on protecting our feet - we dress them up in all manner of fancy coverings such as shoes, boots, trainers, high heels and flip-flops. Here's a few examples of footwear-based dream symbolism!

Baby booties - *Innocence, purity and vulnerability are keenly felt, and you feel a strong desire for nurturing, loving or being loved.*

New Shoes - *New directions, unfamiliar situations, improved conditions in life*

Old shoes - *Character traits, habits, the way things usually appear to be in your life*

The Wrong Shoes - *Doing something in a way other than your*

own, doing something you feel you shouldn't do

Can't find your shoes - *Understanding who you are, why you do the things you do, looking for a truer sense of yourself, and your own identity*

No shoes! - *(Feet comfortable) Breaking away from normality, non-conforming, a significant change in attitude.*

No shoes! - *(Feet Uncomfortable) Lack of confidence, low self-esteem, unhappy with something*

Trainers - *Finding life easy going, success, dealing with things effortlessly*

Baby shoes - *Vulnerability, innocence, naivety, purity, the need to be loved and to be cared for*

Boots - *Strength, powerful situations, feelings of personal superiority and confidence*

Flip flops - *Unsure about what to do at the moment, thinking of changing something but don't know how to*

High Heels - *Powerfully feminine, attractive, the sexual side to a situation or person*

Platforms - *Platform shoes symbolise a sense of elevated status, or a high opinion of yourself. Perhaps you want such things, as you don't possess them, or regard yourself as superior in some way. Or maybe you simply want more clarity or information about something, by gaining more perspective.*

Wellies - *A sense of being safe and protected, or of being prepared for something*

Forest

Searching for deeper personal insight, awareness of transitory elements passing through your life, trying to understand things better

Fork

Helpful situations or people around you, easily reaching goals, effectively dealing with things

Four Leaf Clover

Extraordinary events taking place, highly unlikely discoveries, bizarre or unusually rare situations

Frankenstein's Monster

Feeling you've done something wrong, ashamed of something you've done, unnatural and horrible situations, scared of events surrounding you, negative effects of being overly ambitious, discovery of unpleasant truths

Freezing

Hard attitudes, lack of emotion, bitterness, inhibited self-expression, rejection

Front Door

New chances to take, new opportunities, moving on from how you were, time to move forwards

Fruit

Fruit is not only very good for you, but comes with a whole world of ancient symbolism surrounding it too... and sometimes, when you peel back the usual outer layers, it can be quite surprising what hidden meanings you might find inside...

Apples represent wisdom, knowledge, fertile and creative imaginations, and the existence of harmonious aspects to a situation.

Bananas symbolise sexual urges and desires, especially male and typically masculine energies, as its a powerful phallic symbol, quite understandably!

Blueberries indicate a healthy optimism, a certain youthfulness, or enthusiasm in general.

Coconuts (yes, ok, technically not a fruit, but I included it here anyway... cos I can!) mean rewards await those who persevere with hard work, hidden treasures are to be found within unappealing or difficult situations/tasks.

Oranges symbolise a re-energizing of something, positive ener-

gies, a lust for life, and plenty of joi de vivre!

Pears *represent feminine fertility, nurturing and growth, caring feminine qualities, although sometimes can literally be taken as 'two of something'.*

Pineapples *mean exuberant self-confidence, 'showy' tendencies, a desire to stand out in some way, healthy qualities, awkward beginnings becoming positive situations.*

Raspberries *are symbolic of bittersweet energies, situations that can be taken either way, something that isn't to everyone's taste but that some may like very strongly.*

Strawberries *mean fabulously sensual seductions, especially regarding highly feminine sexual qualities, indulgence par excellence, lots of pleasures to be found.*

Frying Pan

Acceptance of a situation, inescapable truths, going from one bad thing to another

Full Moon

Emotional fulfillment, over-emotional situations, feeling well connected with nature and earthly things

Funfair

Funfairs symbolise an increased interest in new experiences, that you're willing to take risks to increase your enjoyment of life, or need more physical gratification than you're getting

Future

Idealistic hopes, impatience, ambitions, improvements, dissatisfaction with current conditions as they are

Games

Sometimes we find ourselves playing games in our Dreams - but that doesn't mean our subconscious just feels like mucking about and having a bit of fun! Consider things such as what kind of game you've dreamt about, what the aim of the game is, how you felt whilst you were playing, and how it might relate to the situation in which the game in your dream occurs...

Roulette - *Taking chances, risky behaviour, uncertain conditions, untrustworthy people*

Bowling - *Masculine energies, sexual desires, work ambitions, performance issues in both - are you bowling strikes or missing the pins?*

Pool - *Many decisions to be made, small details need sorting out, swift reconciliation of several minor factors, direct action required*

Cards - *Protectiveness, secretive actions, collecting information, avoiding detection, private information*

Chess - *Strategic approaches, tactical decisions, removal of opposition*

Scrabble - *Power of your own words, trying to make people understand you, winning arguments, persuasive speech, intellectual superiority*

Jenga - *Difficulties, unpredictable and unstable situations, fear of someone spoiling things somehow*

Monopoly - *Family issues need sorting out, home and property worries, complicated financial situations*

Draughts - *Taking evasive action, changing your direction, having limited options.*

Galaxy

Creativity, artistic accomplishments and the effects you have on the immediate environment surrounding you.

Garden

Development, natural growth, nurturing experiences, inner

growth, self-reliance, expecting results for your endeavours, abundance of potential.

Gardening

Ever dreamt of doing the garden? A spot of nocturnal lawn-mowing perhaps, or weeding your flower-beds in your sleep? Let's take a look at what it could mean...

Harvesting your very own crop of vegetables or picking fruit symbolises the pay-off for all your hard work, literally the fruits of your labours are ready to be enjoyed. You've been cultivating new aspects to your life or self and are beginning to see the results.

Planting flower bulbs represents a desire for beauty, tranquility, sweetness and happiness in your world. You have nurturing instincts which you want to exercise and use.

Pruning a bush is symbolic of you wishing to organise your life better, to be more rational or sensible and not waste your time on things that no longer work or benefit you.

Pulling up flowers from their beds can mean you're seriously upset with certain things you used to find made you happy or fulfilled, and you strongly want to destroy or put a timely end to them.

Sowing seeds represent new plans, projects or energies coming into your life, which you hope will grow into positive things for you.

Uprooting a tree means you've really undone something that was good in your life, or acted very unwisely. Also it could suggest that you now distrust some old knowledge, or suddenly realise something you once respected to be false or useless.

Weeding is symbolic of spiritual messiness, unwanted aspects of the self which you've let infiltrate or take over your thoughts and daily life, causing you problems. Are you dealing with them suc-

cessfully? Maybe you need to try a new approach.

Genitals

They can represent your feelings and attitudes towards a situation, sex, and the sexes themselves. In what context do they appear – positive, negative, or something else?!

Male Genitals - *Overtly sexualised power trips, potential potency, direct actions or intentions, yang energy*

Female Genitals - *Attraction, effortless persuasion of a masculine presence, seeking comfort, love, fertility, fruitful endeavours, yin energy*

Ghost

Anxiety about unpleasant experiences, fear of death, feeling disconnected with society

Giant

A daunting task looms ahead, someone is behaving overbearingly, chaos surrounds around you, feeling inferior

Gifts

We love to give or receive gifts and presents don't we? Along with this of course goes the whole rigmarole of thinking about what someone might like as a present, writing lists, tramping off to town, looking for bargains in the shops, finding the perfect gift for so-and-so, arms full, bags bulging, buying lovely elaborate wrapping paper and bows and oh everything... good grief, there's so much to it. Here's a few thoughts about gifts in our dreams anyway...

Giving a gift - *Generosity towards other people, expressing your feelings carefully, consideration of others feelings or wishes*

Giving lots of gifts - *Emotional honesty, a strong desire to help someone, the possession of knowledge you think others would find useful*

Expensive gifts - *Emphasis of someone's importance to you, sacrificing your own happiness*

Searching/Shopping for gifts - *Your desires, searching for opportunities, wanting to impress, looking for some kind of attention, wanting a solution to something*

Receiving a gift - *Rewards, appreciation for your efforts, feeling valued*

Expecting but receiving none - *Things being unlike you imagined they would be, disappointment, being let down by someone, disillusioned*

You not liking a gift - *Unwanted praise, lack of value in something, inappropriate attentions coming your way*

Others not liking a gift - *Feeling undervalued, being excluded in some way, lack of interest in your contributions or ideas*

Wanting gifts - *Needing a particular kind of attention from someone, wanting something to happen to or for you*

Wrapping gifts - *Being careful about the way you are perceived, wanting to be understood in the right way*

Wrapping them badly - *Feelings of inadequate preparation, bad planning, fear of being caught lying about something*

Elaborately over-wrapping gifts - *Needing or wanting others approval far too much, unhealthy obsession with something or someone, duplicity, deception*

Unwrapping gifts - *Realising the truth, understanding a situation, seeing the facts as they really are*

Can't unwrap a gift - *Lack of understanding, the need for more information*

Gig

Seeing a gig by a live band can mean you want to express yourself more, and get more attention somehow. Or, maybe you want to feel that others are making more effort to please you.

Giraffe

The need to have a broader perspective on things and to take a wider overview in general, a pinnacle of achievement being reached or finally within your grasp, imminent success

Giving

It's better to give than to receive, as they say, but is that always true? In the world of dreams giving things to others can take on entirely different meanings. Let's have a look at some of the different types of things we can give to others, how they can feature in our dreams, and their meanings...

Advice - *Searching for answers, seeking wisdom, feeling unsure where to turn or what to do next, desire to feel respected or wise*

Care and Attention - *Your nurturing instincts are strong, you're possibly lacking the care or attention you require or want, wanting to contribute to the positive growth of a situation or person*

Love - *As with Care and Attention, you have a lot of love in you to give, and could also feel a distinct lack of such love in your life, harbouring the desire for a great love to enter your world, needing to feel adored, or to adore someone in particular*

Money - *Valuing someone's presence or influence around you, helping someone succeed or prosper, wanting to feel of worth and especially to others, exchanges of energy taking place*

Something Desirable - *Desiring someone, or wanting something else greatly yourself, expressing your gratitude, divesting yourself of worldly goods in order to benefit others, wishing to please*

Something Horrible - *Unexpressed negativity, possibly towards the particular person in the dream, someone has upset you and you want to tell them, resentment to others, unhappy duties need to be done*

Something Practical - *Helping, assisting, enabling others or a situation in a positive way, for the greater good, wanting to build something up, to improve things, needing to be of use*

Something Unwanted - *Feeling unappreciated, rejected, devalued, someone no longer wants you or what you do in the way they used to*

Time - *Fear of not having enough time yourself, acute awareness of time passing, wanting to be able to do all you want before it's too late*

Too Much - *Desperate actions, strong desire to have something you don't have, or get what you aren't getting, going too far, going above and beyond the call of duty*

Too Little - *Inadequacy, falling short of the mark, unable to have* *the effect you want, not enough of something in your life*

Giving birth – See *Childbirth

Giving Thanks

Giving thanks for what you have in your dreams can literally mean you actually do want to do that to someone in particular, but can also indicate a pleasing aspect of yourself you've become aware of that you wish to accept or acknowledge.

Glasses

Looking at life through a normal pair of Glasses means you're having trouble seeing a situation clearly enough, or that you need a little more clarity about a subject than you currently have. Seeing through dark Glasses means you're finding something hard to deal with directly, that something is too much for you to cope with on your own without some assistance or help.

Gorgon

Undesirable feminine presence or qualities, fear of consequences regarding a confrontation

Gorilla

Forceful presence, bullying, competitiveness, exaggerated masculine aspects, aggressive tendencies

Grasshopper

There's a spiritual question you'd like to be answered, you desire and value your freedom very strongly

Gryphon

Personal strength and resilience, feeling divinely protected, finding faith in something

Guide/ Manual

Unsure of which way to turn or what to do, wanting to know everything about a situation, the desire to know or understand someone intimately

Guilt

Remorse over decisions made, feeling responsible for something unpleasant happening, concern over doing something you know you aren't supposed to do, repressed desires, past or present failures

Gun

Aggression, arrogance, desire to exercise or establish your power over others, sex drive

Gymnastics

Agility of mind, strong self-control, flexible approach

Hair

H air

Our hair is more than just a trivial hirsute decoration of our body and personal dream factories - it says all sorts of things about us and our personality. When our hair becomes the focus of our dreams, the way it appears, and what we do to it, says a lot...

Brushing/Combing - *Organising your life, tidying your thoughts, making sense of your true feelings, wanting to feel confident in your opinions, to have courage in your convictions*

Cutting - *Getting rid of some now undesirable aspect of yourself, time to move on, self-improvement*

Dying - *Wishing to alter other people's views of you, change is needed, new modes of behaviour*

Falling out - *Fear of loss of power or control, diminishing sexual attraction, losing your strength, lacking self-esteem*

Hair Extensions - *Giving an impression of yourself which is different to usual, pretentiousness, taking credit for other's achievements or abilities*

Semi-permanent colouring - *Trying out new ideas, experimentation in your personal life, doing things you haven't done before*

Shaving - *Making a complete break with your past, severing close personal ties, fresh starts*

Styling - *Trying to be perceived in a different way to usual, desire to change something important to you in your life, concern over how you're judged by others, wanting more order in your life*

Tangled - *Difficult situations, confusion over something, uncertain feelings*

Turning white - *Acute awareness of something happening, surprising or shocking events occurring, acquiring new wisdom, in-*

sight or knowledge

Washing - *Getting rid of unwanted attitudes or feelings, changing old ways of thinking for new ones, new approaches to emotional situations*

Wig - *Giving a false impression to someone, attempting to disguise something, passing off someone else's ideas as your own*

Hallowe'en

Unconscious fears, distrust of others, false impressions, scared of doing something

Hammer

Forcefulness, great masculine power required, determination, strength

Hands

Your communication skills are excellent, a left hand means you're feeling very receptive, right hands symbolise being more active. Big hands represent great success in your endeavours

Harvest Festival

The fruits of your labours are finally apparent, end results, giving something of value away

Haunted house

Repressed memories, troublesome past events, old thought processes resurfacing

Heart

Love, affection, romance, emotional expression, truth, 'the heart of the matter'

Heat-wave

Creativity, abundance of energy, powerful energies around you, heightened desires

Heaven

Idealistic tendencies, lack of will to confront reality, hope, delusions, unrealistic expectations, perfection, ultimate joy, escape from unpleasant circumstances, optimism

Hell

Fear of suffering, deep unhappiness, depression, misery, very unpleasant circumstances or influences, guilty conscience, self-criticism, inescapable situations

Hero

We all need a hero from time to time! But what does it mean when heroes and heroines appear in our dreams?

The Romantic Hero

The hero dreamt about by most by women is the Indiana Jones type, representing the archetypal romantic adventure, flying off into the sunset to explore new exciting worlds together! Dreaming of a hero like Harrison Ford's famously handsome on-screen character symbolises a lack of fulfilment in these areas of your life. You crave new experiences somehow, maybe a different job is in order, your social life might be feeling dull and flat, or maybe your personal life is lacking in real romance.

The Superhero

If a Superhero like Superman, Batman, Catwoman, Spiderman or even Wonder Woman, flies, leaps, swings or explodes into in your dreams to accompany you, it represents difficulties present in your life. You're feeling as though the only way you can get out of it is if someone comes along who has some kind of 'superpower' and makes something happen, to change things for the better! If you're the one with the superpowers in the dream though, this is more of a sign that you're dealing with a really tricky situation way better than you'd ever thought possible before.

The Ordinary Hero

As indeed we all should realise, ordinary people are far from that, and are in fact the true heroes in life. You don't have to be able to leap tall buildings, or fight armies single handed, or travel to the other side of the world just to find adventure! If we dream of someone close to us who suddenly appears to assume the abilities or characteristics of fictional hero characters like Indy or Spider-man, this is an indication of the respect we have for them, or how amazed we might feel about them for example doing so much for us or those around them in real life, or a particular thing they've gone through or survived – we're seeing them as the real heroes that they truly are.

Hexagram/Six Pointed Star

Seeking insights, balance, the balancing of energies, unity

Highwayman

Someone taking something you value away from you, unwelcome strangers interfering in your life

Hippopotamus

Unforeseen show of strength, previously hidden powers, effortless progress in difficult times

Hitler

Restrictive situations, ignorance of something significant, fear of someone else's power or anger

Hitting

Unexpressed anger or frustration, keeping unsettling thoughts private, wanting something so change without knowing how to do it

Hoe (Garden)

Nurturing energies, harmonious conditions for growth, the evening-out of unbalanced situations

Hogmanay – See *New Years

Holiday

Feeling overworked, a temporary change in circumstances is

needed, something has changed in your life in a positive way

Homosexuality

Personal harmony, acceptance of your sexual self, sense of comfort in your dealings with someone of the same sex

Hook hand

Deceitfulness, inability to achieve intimacy, social awkwardness, dangerous connections

Hopping

Things impeding your journey or path, difficulties, unusual circumstances

Horseshoe

A possible wedding, an important union taking place, turned upward - energy flowing positively, downward - energy flowing negatively

Hospital

Desire to be healed by others, feeling uncared for, psychological concerns

Hot-air balloon

You're doing something that's very important to you, following your own instincts will be very beneficial to yourself and others

Hourglass

Time passing, time running out, endings and beginnings, balance, harmonious aspects

House

Your inner self, your soul or internal spirit, how you see yourself, and all the different aspects of you contained within

Hover Car

Considering yourself 'above' other people, high hopes for your personal life ambitions, your life path generally, or how your career might progress

Human body

Health worries, obsession with physical appearance, anxiety

about the human condition

Hunger

Lack of recognition, feeling spiritually unfulfilled, unacknow-ledged, reminded of old wishes

Hyena

Manipulative energies, tricky circumstances about you, find-ing yourself in humorous situations

Ice Cream

Heightened pleasures, satisfaction with life, your love-life could well be improving

Illusionist

Disillusionment, lying or being lied to, being fooled by some-one, people or things being other than they seemed

Indiana Jones

Hero figures, potential for adventure in the air, excited by a dangerous situation

Infant/Toddler

Unpredictable circumstances, uncertain situations, change-able prospects, finding something hard to handle

Infidelity

Feeling guilty about something, knowledge that you did something you feel was wrong, possible lack of excitement in your own sex-life

Invasion

Unwelcome occurrences, overpowering presence, changes being forced to happen

Island

Individuality, single-mindedness, unique qualities

Jade

Personal growth, the power to heal others, harmonious situations, important developments within the soul

Javelin

Sharp insights, pushing your ideas forward, making an important point

Jealousy

Desire to feel love from someone, dissatisfaction, vulnerability, fear of experiencing personal intimacy, something is lacking in your life, feeling disadvantaged, wanting more success

Jesus Christ

Wanting to help people, acting for the greater good, feeling 'divine', peace, strength in times of trouble

Jetpack

Independence, wishing for a quick exit or wanting to get out of a situation fast

Job

To start a new job in your dreams represents the fact that you're changing the way you approach life in some way, although you're feeling that it could well take you some time to settle into this new way of thinking, but ultimately you know that you're doing something you know is the best thing for you to do. Dreaming of being fired from a job shows that there is something in life that you desperately want to leave behind you or get rid of, and that you couldn't care less if that thing was magically removed from your life in an instant

Joey

Seeking refuge, a close maternal bond, feeling unprepared for something important

Jogging

Inspiration, the desire to improve something, acknowledgment of a goal to aim for

Journey

The journey of life is different for everyone. The subconscious mind loves to make literal and often very visual puns on things, to show us where we seem to be or to give us clues to help us. So, when we dream we're going on a journey somewhere, especially if it's by a particular mode of transport, this tells us things about how our 'life journey' is going! Consider the conditions you're travelling in, the nature of the journey, and how you are travelling, for further insights.

Juggler

Overwhelmed by life, many tasks to cope with, attempting to do too much

Juicer

Extracting the real essence from a situation, the purest and most essential qualities. It might also be that you want to really make the most of what you have in life and get as much from it as possible.

Jumping

Overcoming obstacles, major progress is happening, impulsive actions, risk taking, trying to avoid unpleasant tasks

Jungle

Chaotic situations, lack of clarity on things, confusion, fear of unknown dangers

Kaleidoscope

To view the World through a Kaleidoscope represents the beauty, magic and wonder, or perhaps the complex mysteries, you feel life is showing you, or maybe that you want life to be full of, instead of your current, rather less magical experiences.

Kicking

Aggressive action, forcing something to happen, or victimisation, being taken advantage of

Kid

Stubborn actions, starting to develop a fixed view on something, willing to try anything new

King

Dreaming of being King symbolises your more masculine ambitious traits coming to the fore. You want to take control or take charge of a situation, or even feel you need more respect from those around you.

Kissing

Acceptance of someone or something, desiring closeness, genuine love and affection

Kitchen

Search for spiritual warmth and nourishment, home comfort, desire for transformation of your life

Kitten

Seeking your own independence, transitional times, seeking affection, wanting to be loved by others

Knife

Cutting something out of your life, putting things under close scrutiny, sexual frustration or aggression

Kraaken

Worry about unimaginable horrors lurking within a situation, feeling overwhelmed by something immense and scary happening in your life, extreme emotional anxieties

L abour

Being in Labour can mean your aims and goals are proving difficult to achieve. There's a lot of hard work that needs to be done in order to see the results you want.

Labyrinth

Working out complicated problems, feelings of persecution, unsure where to go, lost

Ladybird

Traditionally a symbol of good luck, pleasant surprises, unusual gifts or pleasure, beauty, joy, attractive femininity, favourable conditions for creative pursuits

Lampshade

Concealment of your desires, protection from overpowering influences, wary of being too optimistic

Laser

Total clarity, acute or sudden perception or insight, extremely penetrating awareness and knowledge, highly detailed comprehension

Leather

Self-reliance, self-protection, animalistic or sexual desires, connections with nature

Leech

Something or someone is sapping your vital energy, avoid those who seem to be demanding a lot of your time and attention

Letter

Personal revelations, emotional honesty, direct communication

Letters - *See Alphabet

Lights

Each type of light source comes with its own set of hidden meanings in the world of our dreams...

Flaming Torches symbolise a strong desire to hunt something down and find something out, whatever may lie in your path. They can also symbolise self-determination, a wish to shine out amongst others in this world.

Fairy Lights represent mysteries and magic, you want something or someone to bring such things into your life. But perhaps your current situation is giving you these things, and life seems so much more interesting and pleasing now.

Lamp-posts indicate light being shed on a dark situation or event in your life, possibly from afar.

Lampshades mean you're trying to protect yourself, or even hide from some great power around you. Do you fear being noticed?

Oil Lamps symbolise a yearning for the kind of comfort and support you feel existed in days long past, or nostalgic feelings for someone you looked to for advice and reassurance.

Striplights suggest that you want to have absolute clarity and information about something, or that you need to examine a situation clinically and coldly with as little emotion involved as possible.

Sunlight symbolises joyful successes, reassurance about your decisions, and emotional happiness especially.

A Torch represents a need to illuminate a specific thing or aspect to something. You want to look deeper into things, to gain insight into a very personal, maybe even sexual situation.

Lightning

Sudden insights or revelations, acute awareness, alarming events, recklessness

Lion

Great physical strength, the desire for or perception of strong leadership, influential characters in your life, attaining a position of personal power

Lipstick

Enhanced sensuality or sexuality, saying what you want others to hear, not what you really feel, a sense of mistrust or pleasure from what another is saying to you

Living beneath the Ocean

Being overwhelmed by your emotional life, delving into 'the depths' of your inner psyche and desires, deep introspection

Living on the Moon

Sense of isolation, emotional loneliness, feeling helpless due to your own oversensitivity, misanthropic tendencies

Lock

Opening a lock means you have finally escaped a situation you have been unwillingly restricted or inhibited by. You have found an answer to a problem, or finally understood the true nature of something.

Lost

From socks, umbrellas, keys, cars, bags, cats and teeth, to friends, points, abilities, strengths, minds, selves and beliefs; on the whole, as a species, we seem to be very good at losing and finding things. In fact we lose or find things so regularly that it would seem extremely odd not to lose or find something at least once a day, wouldn't it? But have you ever had a dream where you've lost or found something? I've put together a list of things that people most often dream they've lost or found, together with what they can symbolise we're lacking, or have gained, in our waking lives...

Socks and shoes - Comfort, feeling grounded, life-path progress, *warmth and protection*

Umbrellas - *Protection from the unexpected, emotional security, avoiding problems*

Bags and suitcases - *Responsibility, life's burdens, worries*

Purses and wallets - *Secrets, private desires, personal value or power*

Teeth - *Confidence, success, concern over appearances, finances*

Keys - *Opportunities, hidden abilities, answers and solutions*

Home - *Basic needs, how you see yourself, perspective on life*

Car - *Motivation, direction, progress, control of your own destiny*

Weight - *Self esteem, self worth, self belief, indulgence*

Jewellery - *Significant achievements, important people in our lives, precious spiritual qualities*

Gloves - *Ability to handle things, issues regarding creative expression*

Mobile phone - *Communication, connections with others, privacy*

Passport - *Complete restriction of movement, strong desire for freedom, feeling a total lack of progress, urgent home issues need attention*

Glasses - *Lack of understanding, inability to perceive something, striving for knowledge or information*

Ticket - *Fear of incompletion, small obstacles to be dealt with, slight hindrances around you*

Love

Finding genuine contentment in something, pleasurable connections with others, positive understanding, joyful revelations

Love spells

New love, a strengthening of your feelings towards someone, letting your emotions lead you, possible lack of objectivity about things

Lucky Charm

Unwilling to take responsibility for your actions, wanting to connect with your spiritual side, looking for support from others

Lunch

Starting to get to grips with things, a manageable workload, a welcome influx of new energies or stimulus

Lycra/Spandex

Flexibility, needing to alter an approach to suit circumstances, willingness to maneuver a position or viewpoint

agazine

New perspectives, new ideas, useful insights, gossip

Magic

New approaches, radically different changes, creative thought, discovering amazing new qualities or abilities, using your imagination well

Magician

Situations more difficult to deal with than at first thought, seemingly impossible demands being made, wanting to master or successfully deal with a tricky situation, deception, creating an illusion regarding how something is seen by others rather than the reality, astounding revelations

Magic Carpet

Escapism, leaving a relationship, moving on from a situation, running away from responsibilities

Magic Wand

Sensing your own power over other people, or someone else's power over you, controlling events, dictating circumstances

Magnifying Glass

Viewing something through a Magnifying Glass symbolises your desire to examine something in your life very closely indeed, in order for the truth or information you seek to be found.

Map

Life-path, periods of transition, wanting to realise your ambitions, [reading it correctly] feeling you're going in the right direction, [reading incorrectly] things literally going in the wrong direction to how you would wish in your life

Marilyn Monroe

Femininity, attractive female energies, beauty, emotional ideals

Marker pen

Definite and clear ideas, having a significant point to make, important things to say

Mascara

Emotional expression, more subtle intents than eyeliner or eyeshadow, enhancing feminine qualities

Masturbation

Not doing enough to satisfy your own needs, not paying yourself enough attention in some way, displaying egoistic tendencies

Matchstick

Striking a Match means you now have a new idea, or tool, to help you solve a puzzle or that you've gained a little more clarity about something, and now you can see a bit better what the nature of a situation might be.

Maypole

Creative energies flowing, fertile time for new projects, relaxed sexual attitudes and approach to life

Mealtimes

Dreams are a psychological feast, often providing wonderful food for our soul and spirit, nourishing our lives in so many ways. Our actual mealtimes provide us with more practical sustenance of course, but what does it mean if we dream of them...

Breakfast - *A particular matter needs attention before any subsequent others, first steps of a new venture, easing an introduction to a situation*

Dinner/Evening Meal - *Main subject or task, awareness of a significant source of information or energy, an important issue needs to be dealt with*

Fast - *Lacking information, requirement of resources, avoidance of that which you may want or need*

Feast - *An abundance of things, having more than you may need or want, excess, indulgence*

Lunch - *Starting to get to grips with things, a manageable work-*

load, a welcome influx of new energies or stimulus

Outdoor Barbeque - *Deliberate action with expectations of valuable results, methodical processes, patience bringing great rewards*

Picnic - *Pleasure in doing something, giving your contributions to others, a change of circumstances regarding a usual habit or task*

Skipping a meal - *Not desiring anything further at present, enduring hardship to achieve the results you require, simplification of a situation*

Snack - *Small amount of assistance wanted, looking for a helping hand, seeking or offering encouragement*

Tea-break - *Temporary relief or respite from something, a fresh, new perspective on a situation is desired, pausing for thought*

Mermaid

Emotional deceit, beware of somebody's duplicity, charming lies

Meteor

Urgent, energetic action required, especially emotionally

Microwave

Searching for a faster way of doing something, quick results being needed, impatience

Midday/Noon

Important times or events, a significant point is reached, appointments to be kept

Middle Aged

Deeper understanding of things - perhaps one thing in particular, acceptance of yourself for who you are, true knowledge of your abilities and limitations

Midnight

Powerful spiritual situations, incredibly important decisions or actions, complete change is imminent

Mime Artist

Finding it hard to get your point across, failing to make your voice heard, difficulty communicating with others clearly

Minotaur

Earthly and practical concerns are troubling you, summoning up of your own determination, confused about where to turn next for the best

Mirror

Mirrors reflect an awful lot more than just your face in the world of dreams. Dreaming of a mirror is symbolic of your true subconscious views on yourself, and on the world about you, how you really see things...

Mirror - Own Reflection - *Seeing yourself in a mirror means you're examining the truth about yourself and your life, literally reflecting upon how you see yourself in your own eyes, rather than how others might see you.*

Mirror - No reflection - *You are having major issues with your sense of self-identity, as though you absolutely can't see or understand who or what you are, somehow. You may have lost your sense of self entirely for now.*

Fogged up/Misty Mirror - *Something is indistinct or difficult to see to you, but not totally. You almost have a grasp on whatever it is, but still something obscures your view.*

Weird/Fairground mirror - *Life feels distorted, something definitely feels not right at all, maybe even disturbingly so. Things are not how you expect them to be.*

Broken Mirror - *A situation or ideal has been shattered. What you thought was there is suddenly no longer there at all, instead its been destroyed, and is now unsalvageable.*

Black mirror - *Perhaps you're using your smartphone or iPad/ tablet device a lot more than you need to, or should be, for your own health or state of mind.*

Rearview Mirror - *You might be looking back at your past a lot, or dwelling on how things once were, immersing yourself in regrets instead of concerning yourself with the now or your future.*

The Moon

There's certainly no escaping the effects of the Moon on not just our planet, with all its tidal to-ing and fro-ing, but as Astrology shows us, on ourselves too. Symbolic of magic, unusual activity, and feminine aspects such as life cycles, intuition and emotions, when we dream of the Moon it reveals hidden information about what's happening in the more mysterious realms of our existence...

Dreaming of the Full Moon represents times of hope, and often long awaited illumination of our darker, normally less apparent desires. Emotional awakenings are in the air.

An eclipse of the Moon symbolises normal aspects of yourself being temporarily unclear or somehow obscured to you. Perhaps you are feeling overshadowed or even compromised by something or someone.

A new Moon, or crescent Moon, means renewal, and that new forms of energy are coming into your life. Brand new starts, new people, jobs, projects or ideas are gently forming, or beginning to make themselves known to you.

A waxing Moon can mean such new endeavours are now really underway, gaining momentum and taking shape.

Waning Moons symbolise old cycles ending, and no longer useful energies or things leaving our lives, to make way for new ones coming in later on.

Howling at the Moon? You need to release that emotional blockage and NOW! There's a strong desire to express yourself emotionally and you aren't getting the chance to do so. What's holding you back? You might also feel a desperate need to communicate with someone special to you.

Morning

Starting of a new venture, early stages of development, there is progress to be made somewhere

Moshing

Aggression, anger, desire to vent or let off steam

Mother's Day

Feeling a desire to nurture something or someone, needing to look after yourself better, showing your appreciation of the support you've had

Motorbike

You want more adventure and thrills in your life, especially in your sex life. You're also feeling quite rebellious and you'll do whatever it takes to make it happen

Mountain

There's an important task to undertake, a significant issue in your life to deal with, having a seemingly impossible goal to achieve. Mountains often symbolise those big issues and challenges we sometimes have, things we need to try to overcome or make a great effort to deal with.

Mountain Bike

Overcoming whatever obstacles lie in your path, feeling able and equipped to handle whatever difficulties come your way, deliberately taking the path less travelled

Mouth

Mouths in our dreams mean we feel that we really need to express ourselves in some way, and if the mouth can't open for some reason then we're finding our ability to do so very restricted somehow. If it's a really big mouth then this means we're feeling we've said something we shouldn't have, and if you have no mouth at all in your dream it's because you either don't know what to say about a situation or feel like whatever you did say you wouldn't be understood or heard.

Moving

We're almost constantly moving aren't we? Even if we think we're not - we're made of trillions of subatomic particles which are constantly on the go, vibrating this way and that and changing all the while. And when we're asleep and supposed to keep still, we can still get up to all sorts of physical things. With our dreams, the way we might be moving in them subconsciously tells us many different things about ourselves...

Walking - *Confidence, easy going attitude, steady progress being made*

Running - *Determination, motivation, success, or avoiding issues, not accepting responsibility for your actions, avoiding confronting fears*

Jumping - *Overcoming obstacles, major progress is happening, impulsive actions, risk taking*

Dancing - *Happiness, joyful situations, having a positive outlook, celebration, freedom, liberation, self expression, sensuality, sexual energies*

Skipping - *Frivolous disposition, needing to lighten up, childlike innocence*

Hopping - *Things impeding your journey or path, difficulties, unusual circumstances*

Kicking - *Aggressive action, forcing something to happen, or victimisation, being taken advantage of*

Hitting - *Unexpressed anger or frustration, keeping unsettling thoughts private, wanting something so change without knowing how to do it*

Spinning around - *Unsure of which direction to take, feeling overwhelmed, total confusion*

Swinging - *The natural cycle of life, balanced perspective, ability to see both sides of a situation*

Climbing - *Struggling, big ambitions, determination to succeed at all costs*

Sliding - *Something is out of control, inevitability, helpless to change circumstances*

Jogging - *Inspiration, the desire to improve something, acknowledgment of a goal to aim for*

Stretching - *Relaxed attitudes, growth, feeling overburdened, strained, exhaustion of energies, a need to slow down*

Mummy

Feeling trapped by others, being held back by a situation, unable to express yourself as you wish

Museum

Your own past, learning from previous mistakes and experiences, using your own wisdom for a current situation or challenge, things you value

Music

Whether it's blasting out of speakers in shops, on the radio or TV, at concerts, on home stereos, iPod earphones, or escaping from someones mobile phone at the back of the bus, there's no escaping the fact; music is literally all around us! Although everyone's taste in music varies, can 'hearing' music in a dream have any particular symbolic meaning? Yes indeed! Music can play a very significant part in our dream worlds, and the 'collective unconscious' we're all a part of. Here's some examples of what dreaming of a few differing popular styles of music could symbolise...

Rock - *Strong passions, single-minded desires, direct actions, over-the-top reactions*

Pop - *Shallow emotions, light hearted feelings, interest in surface details*

Classical - *Powerfully emotional times, many different kinds of feelings about something, overall views of life, dramatic situations*

Jazz - *Random events, disordered thinking, easy going attitudes*

Blues - *Simplicity, honesty, basic values, unhappiness with something*

Country - *Longing for something you once had, trappings of adulthood, compassion for other people*

Soul/R&B - *Sexual desires, an inner need to be found attractive*

by others, wanting to feel accepted and valued

Punk - *Dissatisfaction, tension, anger, disillusionment, disregard of established rules*

Dance - *Joyfulness, freedom of self-expression, letting go of inhibitions, going with the flow of life*

Electronic - *Unusual situations, interest in the finer details, heightened sensitivity, introspective tendencies*

Hip Hop - *Aggression, feelings of superiority, also feelings of insecurity, emotional immaturity, arrogance*

Indie - *Wanting to be seen as being different from others, finding your own way of doing something, trying to think more individually*

Musician

Aiming to create harmonious situations, wanting to control how people feel to your own end, seeking attention, working with others for a common goal

N ail Polish (Fingers)

Focusing more on important activities or tasks, a desire to accomplish something creative, enhanced self-expression

Nail Polish (Toes)

Meticulous concern over your progress towards a personal goal, sensitivity regarding other's opinions of your chosen life path, wanting things to progress beautifully

Nausea

Upsetting times, unpleasant duties, yearning for inner change

Neck

You need to control your feelings. An injured neck means your heart's desires are different from that of your mind

Necklace

Pride, intellectual superiority, recognition of personal achievements

Newspaper

Interesting developments in life are fascinating you, a drive to find out more information about the things affecting you, also judgemental tendencies, lack of trust, lies, extraneous information

New Year/Hogmanay

Dreaming specifically of New Year celebrations is a sign that your life is changing for the better, perhaps even right now – time to hold tight for some surprising and welcome changes. Should you dream of spending it with lots of friends, then this is a sign to be more careful of whom you're spending time with at the moment socially, as someone may not be quite as true in their intentions as they'd have you believe. If your New Year's dreaming includes you getting married on this day this is an indication for the future of your current relationship; it might be worth diverting your attention more strongly to what you both want out of it right now. However, if you dream of proposing on New Year's it's a good sign that your relationship is going strong, or that a new person is coming into your life bringing you a lot of happiness.

Night

Dark energies, obscured feelings, something has been lost, desperation, helplessness, not knowing what to do, cannot see the reality of a situation

Nose

Noses in dreams symbolise the fact that we're working really hard to succeed at something, and can also mean there's something that we're curious about going on in our life.

Nose Ring

Appearing very conspicuous to others, being *especially* curious, heightened personal powers of intuition

Nosebleed

If our nose is bleeding that's a sign for us to be very careful about looking too much further into an unusual situation.

Note

Trying to remember a small detail, poor communication, having little information about something

Novel

Escape from normality, idealistic thoughts and wishes, wanting to live a different life

Numbers

Numbers feature so frequently in our daily lives, that most of us probably don't realise just quite how important and significant they truly are. We just take them for granted really, and quite right too - they're very helpful little things, and their very existence means we can do things like tell the time, measure things, and keep track of how much cash we don't have compared to what we thought we had, and so on.

Interestingly, the more significant numbers amongst them all carry with them a host of other, hidden symbolic meaning, and have done since time immemorial - and when particular numbers feature prominently in our dreams, you can count on the fact that there's a lot happening...

Here's 1 to 10, and I've also selected a couple of the more 'peculiar' numbers that tend to pop up in life, too.

1 - Single mindedness, individuality, confidence, originality of thought, deliberate decisions, solitude, spiritual pursuits, loneliness

2 - Diversity, loving union, partnerships, cooperativeness, directly opposing forces or complementary energies, such as light versus dark

3 - Creativity, vitality, life force, imagination, broadening your horizons, new experiences

4 - Earth energies, grounding, stability, physical strengths or

limitations, materialism, practicality

5 - *Daring tendencies, dynamic situations, bold actions, spontaneous decisions, heightened awareness, over sensitivity*

6 - *Emotional states, psychic abilities, harmonious situations, positive family life developments*

7 - *Mental healing, highly intuitive behaviour, elevated spirituality, unusual self expression, Attainment of spiritual goals, positive individual growth, unique abilities*

8 - *Wealth, success, prosperity, valuable gains to be made, regenerative activities, instinctual actions and thoughts*

9 - *New inspirations, development of a situation, feeling 'reborn', reformation, improving old ideas*

10 - *Finality, completion, immense power, total control of something*

13 - *Superstition, births and deaths, transitions, changes, obstacles, challenges ahead*

18 - *Conflicts, extremes of opinion, search for truth, self centered thoughts, deceptiveness*

23 - *Mysterious circumstances, unexplained activities, paranormal phenomena, close connections to the spirit world*

Nurse

Compassion, caring, spiritual or mental healing, looking after someone else's needs

Nuts

Prosperous actions, looking for truth or genuine reason for something, attainment of something valuable to you

Nylon

Resistance to change, tenaciousness, maintaining integrity under difficult circumstances

Ocean - *Also see **Water**
How you see your emotional life, something is affecting you emotionally in a really big way, consider the state the ocean is in as an indication of the emotional effect it's having on you

Octopus

Able to grasp several ideas at once, doing several things all at the same time, feeling molested or troubled by someone or something

Old/Senior Citizen

Wisdom regarding an important decision to be made, reluctance to alter your view point on something, worried about the passing of time, needing to discard an old worn out attitude

Om

Saying or hearing something particularly significant, elevated consciousness or awareness of something, something is beginning or starting to happen

Opal

Positive energy boosting, raising of libido levels and vitality generally increasing, but beware of impulsive actions

Oral Sex

Finding what someone is saying pleasurable to hear, strong desires to tell someone how much you really feel for them

Orange

A re-energizing of something, positive energies, a lust for life, plenty of joi de vivre!

Orgasm

The need to release something energetically, getting rid of something in order to make yourself happier, enjoying life more, whether in actuality or just desiring to do so

Oval

Birth, female sexuality, feminine power, mothering instincts, creative potential

Oven

Ovens represent the presence of emotional warmth and deep care for others, especially where your family are concerned. They also mean that there's something important you want, but although you know it will be a long wait, you are happy to let it come in its own sweet time.

Oven Glove

Fear of being hurt in love, trying to protect yourself from getting too close to someone or something

Oyster

Hidden secrets, discovery of something you value greatly, concealed treasures or rewards

Packaging

Packaging
Wanting to see beyond the surface of a situation, fully comprehending all details, awareness of false impressions being given to you

Page (paper)
Summarising, reflecting on a situation, evaluating something

Pain
Self criticism, lack of control, physical or mental issues remain unresolved.

When we dream of aches and pains happening in a specific part of the body, they're potentially symbolic of underlying issues we may have, and the things that we would do well to focus our attention and energies on...

Arms - *Self protection, unable to care for others sufficiently, feeling restricted, limited*

Back - *Stress, pressure from others, your views or your beliefs are being challenged, lack of support*

Bottom - *Discomfort, unsettling influences, restlessness*

Chest - *Lack of confidence, diminished vitality*

Ears - *Unwelcome words have been said, hearing unpleasant things*

Eyes - *Unable to see a way of changing a situation, seeing disagreeable things occur, something seems amiss with your point of view*

Feet - *Difficulty following your chosen path, something feels less stable than you'd like*

Genitals - *Sexual dissatisfaction, unhappiness with previous sexual partner or encounter, wanting a positive sexual experience*

Hands - Guiltiness, ashamed of past actions, feeling incapable of action

Heart - Emotional problems, discomfort regarding a relationship, lacking enthusiasm

Head - Confusion, trying to understand something, psychological pressures, difficulty accepting something

Legs - Your progress is impeded, lack of balance, trouble regarding your desire to move

Mouth - Trouble expressing yourself adequately, not liking what you have said or have to say, feelings of distaste regarding a situation

Neck - An unwelcome presence or person in your life, wanting a situation to change, conflict between the hearts desires and those of the head

Tummy - Some news is proving hard to digest, dissatisfaction with things, a situation is making you upset

Painting

Emotions you want to express, innermost feelings or desires, wanting to express something personal

Paint brush (Artist's)

Creative urges need satisfying, searching for the finer details in life, desire to create harmonious situations

Paint brush (DIY)

Improving a situation, covering something up, hiding the facts, new starts

Pamphlet

Limited knowledge, discovering a basic fact or truth, needing to know a little about something

Panther

Hidden dangers around you, fear of enemies 'lurking' in your life, uneasy silences, gracefulness, a sense of elegance and beauty

Paper

A blank piece of paper symbolises new beginnings, fresh starts and that you sense lots of potential in the air around you. It's a really positive symbol, especially in relation to creative actions and situations...

Lots of little bits of paper means you have rather a lot of small but relevant things that need doing, that many small jobs or elements to a situation require your undivided attention.

A bundle or pile of paper represents some large task having to be done. It can mean things seem a bit overwhelming as well.

Paper bags are symbolic of secret things inside a person or situation, or that something has been concealed from you, and that you are curious to know the truth about something hidden.

Paper planes often represent fun, sometimes silly, ideas, that don't really go anywhere, and can indicate there being a lack of productivity regarding something work related.

Paper plates reflect unreliable and unsustainable gains and rewards, a lack of proper emotional or psychological 'nourishment'.

Paper towels are symbolic of temporary troubles needing to be dealt with, that something needs 'cleaning up' and sorting out in order for you to move onwards.

Scrumpled-up paper means you've finished with a project or job. You don't want anymore to do with it, and have no further interest in it at all.

Parade

Being distracted from the task in hand, awareness of the passage of time, attracted to ideas other than your own

Paranoid

Harbouring suspicions about other people's motives or actions, overly concerned over impending commitments or agreements which need to be made, imagining more problems than there are

Park

Resting from activities, renewal of energies, spiritual growth

Parrot

Much is being said, someone around you is gossiping, finding something or someone repetitious

Party

You need to let your hair down and have more fun, feeling unhappy with something in life

Past

Negative non-acceptance of the present, sense of regret, wanting to change previous events, feeling unsafe, disillusioned

Peace

New beginnings, inner conflict resolved, end of a cycle, stability

Pear

Feminine fertility, nurturing and growth, caring feminine qualities, although sometimes can literally be taken as 'two of something, also in a negative context can suggest an imbalance, disproportionate ratios, imperfections

Pen

Specific intentions, deliberate action, self-assurance, feeling equipped to do or say something

Pencil

Temporary situations, uncertain of new beginnings, non-committal tendencies, beginning to see a clearer view, an idea or situation is taking shape

Piercing: Lip/Tongue

Having something unusual or significant to say to others, or possible lack of confidence in your own opinions, inability to adequately express yourself, fear of telling people what you really think

Piercing: Nipple/Genital

Heightened physical awareness, ownership of your own sexuality and sexual power, being extremely comfortable with your own body

Pendant

Romantic ideals, giving or receiving love, acknowledgment of a deep emotional connection

Pentagram

Transformation, thoughts or ideas taking shape or form, behaviour patterns

Petrol

Volatile tendencies, perpetual hunger for sustenance, wanting frequent stimulation

Phoenix

Feeling reborn, new ideas/influences/situations, healing of old psychological wounds

Pickled Herring

Enjoying the results of past labours, appreciating the benefits of being prepared, saving or preserving an emotional response or feeling for another time

Picnic

Pleasure in doing something, giving your contributions to others, a change of circumstances regarding a usual habit or task

Pig

Acceptance of qualities some may find undesirable, awareness of and understanding/accepting such qualities in yourself or others

Pilot

You know where you're going and feel totally in control of where your life is headed. If someone else appears to you as a pilot, you may not be feeling as confident as you'd like about a recent decision you made or direction you've taken.

Pirates

Ahar Jim Lad etc! Pirates feature pretty regularly in the worlds of books, films, games, TV and a million other ways too - you practically can't move for all the swashbuckling, treasure chest hunting and general pirate-booty around us these days. What does it mean if you dream of such Piratey type things though? Let me just don my eye-patch and I shall take a look (through just one eye though, obviously)...

Wielding a Cutlass or Pistol represents aggressive, hostile feeling towards others or about a certain situation. You strongly want to exert your influence and personal power.

If a Pirate's Parrot is perched on your shoulder, be careful of gossip or seemingly important messages coming your way - all might not be what it claims to be, and could cause you problems.

To have a Pirate in your dream is symbolic of an element of potential trouble or chaos in your life, or could mean you desire more freedom, liberty, or excitement, or intend to start taking what you want from life

Donning a Pirate's Hat means that you want to temporarily behave more wildly, or in a more libertarian way than usual.

Pirate Ships symbolise a quest for adventure in your emotional life, possibly even dangerous adventuring! If it's flying in the sky you're really succeeding at indulging in your wildest fantasies, but still feel in control of things too.

If a Skull and Crossbones Pirate flag is flapping away on your mast, then you want to show the World that you mean business, and are not to be trifled with. Woe betide anyone who gets in your way!

Plague of insects - Many negative occurrences culminating in a larger overall effect, loss or damage of anything essential to your requirements

Planets

Exploring new territories and areas of your life, finding out new things about your own capabilities - if a specific planet is dreamt of, then these capabilities are in particular relation to the astrological qualities associated with the planet in question.

Plants

Whatever kind of plant life we might dream about, from the tallest trees down to the smallest flowers, each represent different aspects of our lives, and echo our emotional responses to the world we find around us...

Flowers - *Beauty, pleasure, love, harmony, kindness - also, the different colours of a flower carry with them further symbolism*

Trees - *Growth, hope for the future, knowledge, wisdom, strength, self-development, stability, longevity*

Grass - *Protection, comfort, safety, security, contentedness*

Bushes - *Concealment, disguise, privacy, hidden actions*

Cacti - *Resilience, endurance, self-protection, adaptable, individuality, defensiveness*

Ferns - *Self-reliance, determination, resourcefulness*

Vines - *Natural progression, organic processes, acceptance, gradual development*

Moss - *Long term developments, slow progress, gradual achievements, old ideas, old habits*

Weeds - *Unwelcome influences, unwanted thoughts, problems, nuisances, undesirable circumstances*

Crops - *Positive growth, feeding your desires, the learning process, planning for the future, cultivating ideas*

Herbs - *Improvements, actively changing things for the better, new perspectives, mysticism, significant factors or elements*

Venus Flytrap - *Restriction, being tricked, unexpected unpleas-*

antness, extreme desires, unhealthy appetites

Plastic Surgery

Having plastic surgery in your dream means you seriously want to change your life, or how people look at you, and what they see in you which is of any value or use to them. You literally want to improve your circumstances so much you are considering similarly drastic (plastic) measures regarding changing yourself or your life!

Plate

Giving or accepting of a task, a situation needs to be dealt with, challenges before you

Pliers (A Pair of)

Deliberate removal of something, extracting information, needing to get a better grip of a situation

Plus sign (+)

Adding additional aspects, more information, introducing another element to a situation; or dividing something into separate parts

Poles (Magnetic)

The North Pole - Positive energy, feeling elated as in 'on top of the world', clarity of thought, feeling 'cool' and calm

The South Pole - Seemingly insurmountable tasks, difficult conditions surrounding you, a long journey lies ahead, wanting more adventure in life but on your own, isolation

Both Poles - A situation involving opposing issues needs dealing with, you're torn between two choices, two points of view

Police

Concern for rules, regulations, or morals, personal power, controlling others, possible desire to guide or control the behaviour of those around you.

Seeing a Police uniform on someone you know who's behaving sternly to you? You possibly haven't been acting in a way that meets with their approval. If they're behaving kindly towards you, this means that you're feeling protected by their presence or their actions.

Seeing strangers dressed as Police around you; you need to think before you act, as you know others could get annoyed or upset by what you do, and may even try to stop you doing whatever it is. If they're being protective, this indicates you're feeling accepted by society or your local community.

Polyester/Viscose (synthetic fibres)

Convenient solutions, unnatural experiences, unrealistic results or goals

Portrait

Unique perspectives, singular ideals or ideas, admiration for another

Postman

Communication with others, significant messages or information, getting your own message across effectively

Post Office

Messages from your subconscious, important information, the need to communicate something to others

Potions and Spells

Powerful influences, experiencing manipulative tendencies, strong desire for something, transformation

Pregnancy

An aspect of yourself is developing and increasing in significance. Something in your personal life is growing bigger in size, or becoming more important to you, perhaps a new idea, direction or venture.

Pregnancy Test

Dreaming of taking a pregnancy test represents you entering new eras or phases of your life. Your subconscious is asking you 'Are you ready for this? Are you prepared for what you have to do?'

Prince/Princess

To dream of being a Prince or Princess suggests a need to feel appreciated or wanted by someone, especially romantically speaking. It may also symbolise a certain satisfaction with your achievements, or feelings of pleasure about your life right now.

Profession (ie. if you dream of doing a different job to one you normally do)

We all daydream sometimes of what life might have been like if we had made different choices, and ended up in a different job to what we do for a living. It's fun to imagine in this way isn't it, but 'the grass is always greener' of course, and dissatisfaction or boredom with how things are tend to be the chief reasons for us thinking this way from time to time.

Dreaming of being a Doctor, Nurse, or generally in the medical profession symbolises a desire to make people's lives better, to be supportive and helpful to them. But it could also be a desire to 'heal' your own problems or psychological 'wounds'.

It's a popular dream to be a famous Rock Star or Musician, and dreaming of being one suggests you want your life to be more harmonious, exciting or glamorous. Maybe you want to be seen as particularly entertaining or attractive, even sexy, to other people - or maybe one person especially. Perhaps that you don't have a suitable outlet for your own talents. Are you getting the recognition you would like or feel you deserve at work or at home?

Mechanic or Engineer? Something in your life needs fixing. You need to thoroughly understand the reasons something or someone is behaving a certain way, in order to know what to do next. Have you got the right tools you need, be it physically, emotionally or psychologically speaking, to get to grips with a particular situation?

To dream of being in the Fire or Police service can mean that you like to be seen as a 'hero' to others. There may be problems, or even real emergencies, that you need to deal with, either alone or part of a team. Or do YOU need a hero in YOUR life?

To dream of being an Artist, Painter or Sculptor means you wish to express yourself in your own unique way in life. Do you want to create a situation, or even literally make something, according to your own tastes and desires?

Prostitute

Enjoyment of personal gain, being rewarded for work you find pleasurable to some degree, or unhappiness with your job, feeling exploited or ill-used

Pub

Needing to get out of the house more, wanting to relax and socialise with people, life seems to be lacking in fun or stimulation

Puppy

Wanting to be taken care of, behaving childishly, having a carefree nature

Puzzles

Psychological and emotional challenges are around you and need your attention, something is troubling your peace of mind and you want to work it out

Q uarry

Searching for or discovering hidden aspects to something or someone, unearthing valuable secrets, something of value lies within a seemingly ordinary situation

Quartz

Balancing of male and female energies, amplification of an idea or thought, clarity of mind and intention, cleansing of the spirit taking place

Queen

If you find you're a Queen in your dreams, then this symbolises the feminine side of your subconscious, in a similar way where you feel you lack a certain status or respect from others. But also that you desire an increase or breakthrough in your own personal development, intuitive powers or growth generally.

R abbit

Fertile situations, sexual liberation and expression, faith in the power of nature

Radio

Dreaming of listening to the radio could indicate that you want to feel more connected to the outside world, or need more information or influence in your life from sources further afield or far removed from your usual circles of family or friends

Rain

Fertile conditions, renewal, cleansing, spiritual enlightenment, emotional liberation

Rainbow

Unusual or rare events happening in life, sexual liberation and acceptance, hoping for something amazing and magically life changing to occur

Rain showers

Moments of clarity, erratic progress, emotionally uncommitted

Rake

Gathering information together, examining all the details you can find, trying to make clear a way or path forwards

Raspberries

Symbolic of bittersweet energies, situations that can be taken either way, something that isn't to everyone's taste but that some may like very strongly

Rectangle

Material desires, grounded emotions, permanence, solid foundations

Refrigerator

Emotionally remote and cold, lack of response to others needs, inability to progress

Rejection

Inability to change, wishing to change a situation, forced acceptance, unhappiness with imposed circumstances, refusal to go with the flow, lack of self-worth, unassertiveness - giving too much of yourself to others, unwilling to accept part of yourself or life

Restaurant

Desire for spiritual nourishment or replenishment, needing

more energy

Reversed aging

Dissatisfaction with own ageing signs, feeling youthful and energetic perhaps despite your age, renewed enthusiasm for something

Rhino

Aggressive determination, unswerving dedication, being 'thick skinned' and impervious to the hurtful and negative words or ways of outside influences

Rickshaw

Letting someone else do the hard work, relying on others for your own profit, goals or end results

Riding a bicycle

Self-reliance, working hard to achieve something, steady progress being made

Ring

Emotional bonds are being established, commitment to a task or person, lifetime ambitions, promises made, firm beliefs

Ritual

A habit needs breaking or changing, vicious circles of behaviour, old routines are getting to you and need to change, attempting to make something happen, searching for spiritual or emotional clarity and control

Roads (And paths) - Roads and pathways are a feature of all our lives, and always will be - and when we dream of any of the differing kinds, there's a whole world of rich symbolism waiting for us...

Motorway - On your way somewhere, making headway, headed towards a goal. Possibly, life seems too predetermined, or even boring. You feel you're on the same 'journey' as many others in some way, and want more excitement or fun.

Narrow - *Feeling somewhat lacking in choices or options regarding your life path, or that there's no realistic option but the path you're taking right now.*

Unmarked or rough - *Unsure of your direction or way forwards. Treading new ground, or taking 'the path least travelled' is making you wary of the potential dangers and pitfalls of doing so, but also the rewards, ultimately.*

Long/endless - *Things have been feeling like a constant procession of things to be dealt with, always something for you to sort out or do, one thing after another, seemingly without end.*

Winding or hilly - *Struggle, 'an uphill battle', serious obstacles need all your strength and willpower to overcome them. Having to manoeuvre your way around or through difficult situations.*

Chicane - *A sense of being deliberately constricted or controlled by forces outside you and around you. Feeling compelled to make a decision or move that you feel is awkward or uncomfortable*

Rocket

Deliberate action to ensure future efforts are grounded in solid foundations, expectations of success and fruition of ideas or plans, male energy, phallic symbol, a real sense of achievement

Rocket Fuel

An extraordinary amount of effort or energy is necessary in order to achieve something, powerful emotions, a much needed boost

Rolling Pin

Control of creativity, positively decisive action, ability to shape things or events however you want

Rollercoaster

Everything's going up, down and all around you emotionally at the moment, and you're not really sure how things are going - apart from that it's getting quite confusing

Roof

Protection, shelter, security, being cared for or looked after

Rowing a boat

Emotionally difficult journeys, a lot of effort is needed to stay on course, working hard and sticking at something, determined to succeed on your own terms

Royalty

Have you ever had blue blood running through your veins in your dreams? Do you have dreams of being King or Queen, born into regal grandeur, and of being the head of state of your country, or did you even just dream you were wearing a crown once? Whether you disagree with the notion of a monarchy, or are a fervent supporter and admirer of our rulers on their appointed thrones, there's no denying the significance of Royalty in our society, or in the world of dreaming...

Dreaming of being King symbolises your more masculine ambitious traits coming to the fore. You want to take control or take charge of a situation, or even feel you need more respect from those around you.

If you find you're a Queen in your dreams, then this symbolises the feminine side of your subconscious, in a similar way where you feel you lack a certain status or respect from others. But also that you desire an increase or breakthrough in your own personal development, intuitive powers or growth generally.

To dream of being a Prince or Princess suggests a need to feel appreciated or wanted by someone, especially romantically speaking. It may also symbolise a certain satisfaction with your achievements, or feelings of pleasure about your life right now.

Rubber

Strange and unusual tendencies, extremes of experience, exploring your sensuality, perversion of the norm

Ruby

Vitality, sexual passion and desires, fleeting infatuations, headstrong affairs of the heart

Running

Determination to succeed, motivation, pursuit of something, urgent desires, or avoiding issues, not accepting responsibility for your actions, avoiding confronting fears

Sacrifice

Something needs to stop, desiring the removal of an unnecessary presence in your life, willing to give something up to gain something much better

Sadness

Imminent achievement or success, realisation of personal goals, happiness is within your grasp - or disillusionment, realisation of an unwelcome truth, introspective tendencies, reminded of past disappointments, missing something you cherished, unwelcome events occurring, sorrowful situations around you

Sailor

You as a sailor; you have a great interest in exploring life's possibilities, and you want to have more adventures than usual. If sailors are around you, you're feeling emotionally inexperienced in comparison to others, particularly regarding relationships

Sales Assistant

Helping others get what they want, wanting to be of use, trying to make people happy

Salsa Dancing

Feeling sexy in your own right, in a party mood, being social

Sapphire

Protection, divine influence and inspiration, truth and honesty, ultimate goals, heavenly or angelic ideals and actions

Satellites

Communication issues, in relation to the wider spectrum of your life. The need for getting your message or thoughts across clearly and effectively

Satyr

Subversive energies are around you, possibly dangerous situations, someone behaving like a rogue

Saucepan

Combining many things together to make one special thing happen, pooling resources, careful planning

Saw

Making deliberate decisions to change, dividing something up amongst many, breaking down a larger problem to ease coping with it

School Child

You as a school child; you feel like there's a lot you don't know in life yet, that you're lacking in knowledge in some way.

If school children are in your dream, but you aren't one, you either think you're wiser than certain people around you right now, or possibly that others seem to be having more fun and enjoying life more than you

School Lessons

Whether you liked it, loved it or hated School, we all had to go, and had to study the same old classes/subjects didn't we? Memories of our classroom studies inspire considerable emotions and deep rooted feelings in us all. Let's go back to school for a moment (not long, promise) and see what those school lessons can teach us about ourselves in the world of dreams...

Maths - *Making calculated decisions, evaluating situations, working something out, judging the true measurable value of something*

English - *Communicating, self expression, desire to be understood, clarity of purpose*

Geography - *Knowing where you are with things, comprehension of the situation you find yourself in, desire to travel, seeking a change of environment*

Biology - *Natural processes, unforced or organically occurring situations, appreciation of what you have, seeing the miracle and wonder in 'ordinary' life*

Chemistry - *Significant reactions; seeking certain reactions or avoiding them, experimentation with combining different aspects of your life together, then seeing what happens as a result*

Physics - *Material interests or pursuits, wishing to deeply understand something tangible, wanting to know how the universe works*

IT/Computers - *Helpful assistance in doing something, needing the right tools for a job, communicating your ideas socially, high intelligence, lacking knowledge, or a strong desire for knowledge, connections*

Art - *Idealistic interpretation of things, unique and individualistic visions or perspectives, imaginative solutions or creations, creative tendencies and technical skills*

Music - *Harmonious surroundings, moving emotional situations and discoveries, pleasurable influences, desiring harmony in life, getting into a particular rhythm of working or living, how you emotionally feel about life*

Drama - *Acting out your desires, wanting things to be different to how they seem*

Languages - *Wanting your wishes to be understood by everyone, intent on widely spread communication with others, getting your ideas across to as many people as you can, interest in a certain culture or country's ways and/or values*

History - *Concern over your past experiences, wanting to learn from your mistakes, dwelling on previous occurrences in life, hunger for information about what has gone before*

Scorpion

You've been experiencing an unpleasant situation lately because of someone else's words or actions, be careful of following a course of action that you know deep down is unwise... in case you get stung!

Screws/Screwdriver

Careful action, desire for security, fixing something in proper place in your life, working hard for the result you want

Sea - *See **Ocean** and **Water**

Seahorse

Faithfulness, a masculine presence is taking on a more feminine role in your life, peculiar perspectives

Seaside

Searching for emotional fulfilment, a more spiritual balance is needed

Seasons

From sprightly spring to sultry summer, autumnal days or winter wonderlands... what does it mean when we dream about the different seasons? Depending on the context each season appears to us in our dreams, they represent some very interesting aspects that could be going on in our lives...

Spring - If spring has sprung in your dream this is a good sign for new starts in general, especially business orientated matters and anything creative. New sexual encounters look set to be very happy ones if spring is in the air in your dream world. People often experience a strong sense of having been energetically 're-charged'. There could be a birth or even a re-birth happening for a close family member or friend. You could be changing an old habit or way of doing things.

Summer - Expect some lovely surprises in store if you dream of summer time, it's a sign of growth, knowledge and maturity in an important area of your life. You're feeling more compassionate and understanding towards someone close to you, and plans will start to come together, and bear the 'fruit' of your previous labours.

Autumn - Expect rewards, friendly advice or help from quite unexpected places. Represents a strong feeling of the passing of time and the differing stages of life, the end of a project or a stage in your life, giving way to a new perspective or challenge. A relationship could be changing in some way.

Winter - Finances often get a boost in some way, also a sign that you're entering into a period of fun and excitement. Or, you may be feeling less interested in a person emotionally speaking, and

behaving colder towards them. It can sometimes be a sign that you're feeling unhappy about a given situation you have to deal with.

Seeds

New ideas, preparation for the future, fertile situations around you

Self-Portrait

Introspective thoughts, desire for self-improvement, reflection on one's present situation in life

Sex

Wanting more sex in general, possibly repressed or unexpressed desires need satisfying, requiring deeper intimacy with someone else than you are currently experiencing

Sex (Abstaining from)

Fear of the consequences of over-indulgence, awareness that you're overdoing things lately

Sexual Fetishes

Complicated situations, an activity is lacking in some aspect and inhibiting fulfilment, questionable decisions made for the wrong reasons

Shapes

We see all kinds of shapes around us constantly, and many that are so familiar that we usually don't even notice them. Wherever we look, shapes are absolutely everywhere in life, and the more common ones have their own very particular symbolic significances. When they feature within our Dreams, they bring with them their subliminal messages, to inform our subconscious minds in all kinds of ways, depending of course on the context they appear to us within the dream we're having...

Bell - *Warnings, a need for preparation, important events, anxiety, sense of timeliness, time for action*

Circle - *Perfection, wholeness, completion, life-cycles, open-mindedness, also monotonous activities, routines*

Crescent - *Versatility, emerging femininity, change is coming, new life in old situations, renewal*

Cross - *Choice to make, indecision, new directions, possible religious or moral connotations*

Cylinder - *Lack of expression, limited options, controlled feelings, contained emotions*

Diamond - *Determination, self-perfection, absolute clarity, extraordinary self-belief*

Heart - *Love, affection, romance, emotional expression, truth, 'the heart of the matter'*

Hourglass - *Time passing, time running out, endings and beginnings, balance, harmonious aspects*

Oval - *Birth, female sexuality, feminine power, mothering instincts, creative potential*

Pear - *Imbalance, disproportionate, imperfections, natural situations*

Rectangle - *Material desires, grounded emotions, permanence, solid foundations*

Square *Stability, strength, conventionality, limited views, conservative tendencies, the desire to express yourself*

Shark

Feelings of hostility, anger, or aggression, an emotional threat around you, possible danger in your life

Shooting

Specifically targeting something, accuracy, aggressive tendencies

Ship

Emotional exploration is very important for you, your subconscious wants you to expand your horizons emotionally, trying to gain a better, deeper understanding of yourself

Shops

Shops are so intrinsic to all of our our daily lives, especially in the western world - we're always shopping for something aren't we? To the point of obsession, for some people. We shop to stay alive, to make life more comfortable, to make ourselves feel better, and to make others feel better too. Online shopping is all very well, but really, where would we be without actual shops and all their paraphernalia? Well, at home I suppose. Or living in internet cafes. So long live shops and shopping I say! And here's what dreaming of certain shop related things can mean...

Assistant - *Needing help, lacking support, or wanting to help, inclination to give of yourself to others*

Barcode - *Feeling unrecognised for who you truly are, automatic responses to situations, fast assimilation of information, quick to understand*

Changing Room - *Wishing your life was different, anxiety regarding the varying roles you have to play, trying to fit in with a new situation or circumstance*

Check-out Counter - *Acknowledging the results of past actions, a price needs to be paid for previous decisions, taking stock of things, working out where you are in your life*

Customer Services - *Dissatisfaction, wanting things to be different, feeling betrayed or let down*

Door Alarm - *Concern over recent actions, worried about the possible consequences of leaving, feeling caught out by a situation*

Mannequin - *Inaction, unable to move forwards, projecting idealistic views of how you'd like yourself or someone else to be*

Price Sticker - *Personal values, questioning how much something is worth to you or to others, awareness of the price you'll have to pay for your actions*

Products - *Things you want or need in your life, abundance (many things) or desperation (too few), wanting something specifically*

Sale/Reduced Section - *Feelings of lessened worth regarding something, looking for an easier way to achieve a goal, unexpected success*

Security Guard - *Wanting to feel more secure in life, worried about being caught out, feeling something private or personal is under threat of being discovered*

Shop - *Opportunities are all around you, potential choices to be made, many different options and paths to take in your life*

Trolley - *(Filling it/full) Seeing results for your efforts, gathering together proof of your endeavours, (empty) feeling that your life is missing these elements*

Window Display - *Idealistic dreaming of what you want, thinking of how you'd like life to be, being attracted to something special*

Shopping

Dissatisfaction or boredom with things as they are, opportunities in your life need considering, personal needs and desires, seeking solutions to problems, wanting new influence or direction, searching for satisfaction and seeking fulfillment

Shopping Centre

Decisions need to be made, many options, too much advice from others

Shoulders

You feel you have too much responsibility in your life. Having big, strong shoulders means you're a great support to others

Shovel

Coping with large issues quickly, clearing backlogs, feeling sufficiently equipped to deal with a heavy workload

Silk

Unbreakable bonds, very strong connections, feelings of everlasting love, ultimate pleasure

Singer

Possessing unique and individual opinions, wanting to or even succeeding in getting your voice heard by others, having something important to say

Singing

Communicating positively with others, feeling in tune with

those around you, harmonious situations, enjoying life

Sink

Getting rid of unwanted things in your life, experiencing an emotional purge, cleansing yourself of old feelings

Skateboarding

Wanting maximum results from as little effort as possible, seeking exciting or different ways of doing mundane things, showing off your abilities to others

Skeleton

Guilty secrets, hiding something from others, fear of being 'found out' somehow

Sketchbook

Being open to ideas, working out the best way forward, needing to make a decision

Skipping

Frivolous disposition, wanting to lighten up about things, childlike innocence

Skipping a meal

Not desiring anything further at present, enduring hardship to achieve the results you require, simplification of a situation

Skull & Crossbones

Be wary of others motives, intending to act in ways normally unexpected of you, wanting people to fear something about you

Sky

A clear Sky represents hope, freedom of self expression and all kinds of creative wonders that might be possible to you. A cloudy, darkened Sky above you means something else though - time to prepare for things coming to a head, there could well be trouble afoot, or even you might subconsciously sense something might be ending.

Sledge/ Sleigh

Zooming about on a sledge can symbolise having a childlike perspective about some aspect of life, which you still retain a sense of wonder and fun about. Also, unusual or fun ways of getting from one point to another, and smooth transitions

Sliding

Something is out of control, inevitability, helpless to change circumstances

Sofa

Rest or relaxation, being very comfortable with something, dissipation of stress, feeling supported

Soldier

You as a soldier; you're prepared to have to fight for your own opinion or viewpoint to be heard, because no one seems to be accepting how you think things are or should be. If lots of soldiers are around you, you're feeling unable escape a situation. Also they can represent discipline, structure, imposing your will, or defending your own beliefs

Snack

Small amount of assistance wanted, looking for a helping hand, seeking or offering encouragement

Snake

Did you know that one the most frequently dreamed of creatures on the planet is the Snake? They are positively overflowing with all kinds of symbolism attributed to them the World-over, and can represent complex aspects to our lives...

What is the snake in your dream doing? What is your reaction to it? The way it appears to you and the context in which it pops up says much about your current state of mind or what's happening in your life.

Seeing a snake appear in your dream suddenly can mean there's something, or even someone, around you that is unpredictable, out of your control, which you feel trepidation or fear towards.

If the snake is interacting and talking with you as a person would, then there IS a person around you who could very well be behaving in an underhand, slimey, and untrustworthy way.

Seeing a Snake hiding somewhere, indicates that you have suddenly become aware of a possible threat, possible betrayal or danger to you. If it's a tiny or baby snake, you don't see it as too much of a problem though. Also, it may mean that there is a hidden message from your subconscious that you need to pay heed to.

A snake shedding its skin is wonderfully symbolic of transform-

ation in your life, usually positive changes, growing, renewal of the self, and self-improvement in general.

A Snake biting you is your subconscious trying to alert you to something which you are not aware of yet, which has not entered your conscious mind for you to be actively wary of

To kill a snake symbolises your triumph over adversity! You have successfully dealt with a difficult task, or overcome the odds regarding something

A snake in your bed represents your sexuality, sexual power and sex drive. Freud considered the snake a potent phallic symbol. If you are not afraid of it at all, and feel happy about it being there, then you are feeling sexually active, powerful or strong - especially if it's poised to strike! If you feel scared or unhappy or afraid of it, then you have similarly unpleasant feelings towards sex, or your own sexuality.

Eating a snake is symbolic of a current lack of sensuality, passion or even a diminishing sex drive - You need to get some lust back in your life and NOW!

Snow

Fresh new perspective, sense of spiritual tranquillity, overwhelmed by something

Solar power

Positive energy, happy developments, inner joy radiating outwards, good omens for your endeavours

Spaceship

Unusual creative approaches, adopting a different perspective on things, independence from others, courageous endeavours, exploration, finding new ways to do things, originality, singular ways of life, i.e. existing and living in an uncommon way

Spade

Ease of progress, constructive endeavours, working hard to create something according to a plan

Speed Boat

Speed Boats represent your flighty side, you aren't interested in sticking around regarding a certain affair of the heart that you feel is holding you back, and would much rather have a fun, exciting time instead.

Spider

You feel like you're separate from those around you, but happy to be so, something you've been working towards will come to fruition soon, or something you fear is threatening you currently

Spider Web

Spider's webs symbolise the success of a creative project or endeavour, being stuck in a web reflects a relationship situation you aren't sure how to deal with

Spinning around

Unsure of which direction to take, feeling overwhelmed, total confusion

Sports

Dreaming of playing, or observing, sport can indicate a strong sense of competitivity, a burning desire to achieve certain goals, or to exert great influence over people around you, especially those with opposing views. Here's a few sports I've chosen to examine, and some of the things they can signify if you dream of them...

Cycling - *Feeling self-reliant, self-motivated, balanced, steady progress*

Diving - *Decisively dealing with something, confidence in your decision, exploring new areas of life*

Gymnastics - *Agility of mind, strong self-control, flexible approach*

Javelin - *Sharp insights, pushing your ideas forward, making an important point*

Jumping - *Taking large risks, trying to avoid unpleasant tasks, impulsiveness*

Rowing - *Difficult paths, a lot of effort is needed, staying on course*

Running - *Determination to succeed, pursuit of something, urgent desires, confronting fears*

Shooting - *Specifically targeting something, accuracy, aggressive tendencies*

Swimming - *Emotional needs, seeking emotional support, overcoming overwhelming feelings*

Trampolining - *Resilience, ability to cope with life's 'ups and downs', striving for higher and higher goals*

Weightlifting - *Hidden strengths, serious effort to make something happen, under/overestimating how much hard work might be required*

Wrestling - *Dealing with something hard to control, fighting to make a point, struggling with another person's ideas or personality*

Spring - *See **Seasons**

Square

Stability, strength, conventionality, limited views, conservative tendencies, the desire to express yourself *See Shapes

Stairs

Dreaming of ascending some stairs is often symbolic of progress being made, and the attaining of new levels of achievement in life, from the material plain, to the emotional, and even spiritual successes too. It can also reflect a deepening of your understanding and perceptions regarding something significant to you.

Being afraid to walk up stairs means you have a reticence to progress, or to achieve your dreams, for fear of losing what you are familiar with.

Walking downstairs, rather than simply meaning the opposite of walking upstairs, is more likely to represent difficulties or hindrances in life, or that progress is being lost in some way. If you dream you're too afraid to walk down some stairs, this often symbolises something in your past you're unhappy about confronting, or a fear of unconsciously repressed emotions or thoughts.

Falling or tripping on stairs indicates that you are lacking in con-

fidence or conviction about something. If it happens going upwards, you're trying too hard to do something, working too fast or unrealistically. Tripping going downstairs can mean you're not feeling ready to access or confront feelings or thoughts that you've previously hidden.

Sitting on stairs is symbolic of being unsure which way to go next, or quite what move to make, or what decision to take.

Star

Hopes for the future, aspirations, wishes, desires and pursuits, creativity, high ideals, imagination, fortunate aspects around you, 'fame' or attention, fate

Starfish

Fascination with the unusual, someone or something having healing or even regenerative qualities

Star light

Guiding influences, mystical directives or direction, angelic inspiration, self-fulfilment, luck, chance, fate

Stately Home

Admiration or respect for the finer things in life, being concerned about your material wealth, wanting to improve your own social status

Stomach

There's something happening in your life that you really can't stand, and want to change, a bare tummy means you need to express your natural, basic instincts

Strawberry

Fabulously sensual seduction, especially regarding highly feminine sexual qualities, indulgence par excellence, lots of pleasures are to be found

Stretching

Relaxed attitudes, growth, feeling overburdened, strained, exhaustion of energies, a need to slow down

Strip light

Harsh facts coming to light, unwelcome realisations, experiencing a 'reality overdose'

Stripper

Sexual exploration, physical especially sexual self-expression, repression of desire

Strobe light

Confusion, disorientation, unrealistic expectations

Summer - *See **Seasons**

Sun

The Sun is one of the most potent and powerful symbols in our entire existence. When our huge fireball in the sky is shining its light in our dreams, there's all kinds of different meaning that could be attributed to it, dependent on the context, conditions and ways in which it appears to us...

The Sun - *Generally speaking, this symbolises such things as positive energy and power, peace, success, strength of purpose, clarity of mind, fertility, life, joy, happiness, enlightenment, good omens, and a very strong sign you're on the right path.*

Sun Rising - *New beginnings, renewal, new endeavours, new energies entering your life*

Two Suns - *A choice between two differing paths to potential happiness, indecision regarding an important issue because you stand to gain either way*

Many Suns - *Overwhelming choices to be made, seemingly endless possibilities, a multitude of positive influences around you*

Huge Sun - *Immensely positive events taking place, abundance, great happiness*

No Sun - *Lack of productivity or inspiration, feelings of unhappiness, despair, hopelessness, sadness*

Exploding Sun - *Sudden realisations, life-changing events, astonishment*

Pale Sun - *Uncertainty of direction or purpose, wary of new developments or energies in your life, lacking confidence in your own abilities*

Red Sun - *Definite decisions being made, moving forwards aggressively, positive but tough action being taken*

Black Sun - *Strange or unusual spiritual activities, becoming aware of new unfathomable depths to what was once familiar to you, discovery of intense personal power, arcane secrets, magick*

Solar Eclipse - *Views are temporarily obscured, inability to see your own path or abilities, difficult times*

Sun Setting - *Phases of life changing, awareness of something coming to an end, a cycle of your life is nearing completion, introspection, time to rest*

Surfboard

You're quite happy just going along with things for the time being, you're enjoying your current emotional state and how things are at the moment

Swastika

Desiring peace and harmony, potential misunderstanding or confusion regarding someone's intentions; alternatively, extreme decisions, actions or circumstances

Sweets

Wanting something forbidden, something that makes you happy is within reach, perhaps a little indulgence is needed

Swimming

Immersing yourself in an emotional situation, handling an emotional problem effectively, emotional needs, seeking emotional support, overcoming overwhelming feelings

Swinging

The natural cycle of life, balanced perspective, ability to see both sides of a situation

T adpole

Yet to achieve your potential, wishing for pregnancy/ fertility, large changes are coming

Talisman

Needing protection, fears of the known or the unknown, desperate thoughts, helplessness

Tango

Seduction, love, being strongly sexually focused exclusively on one partner

Tap Dance

Attempting to appear impressive toward others, 'showy' tendencies, being highly skilled at something

Tattoo

Although Tattoos have become way more popular and common in the last 20 years, they still represent something of a sense of rebellion and are a significant method of self expression to most of us. They often come with a lot of meaning attached to them for many of us, but if they appear to us in the world of our dreams, whatever a tattoo is of, and even where, can contribute even further meaning to the dream - but I'll just deal with some of the basics of dream tattoos here...

Having a tattoo done represents your desire to be seen as unique and individual regarding a particular endeavor, or that you wish to express something about yourself to others in your own special way.

Owning a tattoo you hate is symbolic of your deep regrets about something you've done. It could be that you wish you hadn't done whatever it might be, or that you can't seem to rid yourself of certain feelings or effects that have plagued you for a while.

Being covered in lots of Tattoos when you either don't have any, or just don't have that many in real life, mean that you want to be recognised or acknowledged for all the things you've done in your life so far. It may also even indicate excessive pride in your achievements and experiences.

An old faded tattoo symbolises an old memory or experience from your past that you hold dear, or that still carries considerable meaning and gravitas.

Wanting a tattoo can mean you are desperate to do or create something, or for something to happen in your life, that truly means something to you, and will make people really start to sit up and notice you.

Being a Tattoo artist represents you inner longing to impress upon the world your perhaps unusual, strong opinions or views; to make your mark, as it were, on your fellow humans

Taxi

Happy to be taken for a ride, for others to take you somewhere, in a direction you are prepared to go in to achieve a result you want

Tea-break

Temporary relief or respite from something, a fresh, new perspective on a situation is desired, pausing for thought

Teacher

Seeking guidance, learning from past mistakes, having things to learn in life

Teenager

Feeling overwhelmed by responsibility, something needs further development, demands your attention, you possess an immature attitude about something

Teeth - *See **Common Dream Themes**

Telephone - Communication with others, significant messages, confrontations with hidden issues

Telescope

Looking at life through a Telescope? Do you feel far away from where you want to be in your life? Or is there something out of your grasp that you would love to have in your hand right now instead?

Temptation

Difficulty concentrating, envious of others success, external pressures

Tennis

Dealing with someone's aggressive opinions, an exchange of ideas, having a significant conversation with someone, a desire or need to actively prove yourself, repeatedly. Also, a possible lack of commitment to a decision between one thing and another.

Terror/Panic

Sudden changes in your life have unsettled you immensely, intense anxieties, needing to deal with something or calm yourself urgently

Theatre

Searching for dramatic changes, wanting things to be more interesting or eventful, looking for a more challenging role, seeking new aspects to yourself, life seeming dramatic

Throat

Your ability to express your thoughts is strong. A sore throat means you're finding it hard to express your true thoughts

Thunderstorm

Conflict, anger or rage, clash of opinions, turmoil, and potential for violence in the air

Tiara

Attractive feminine qualities, beauty, powerful female influence in your life

Tide

Clarity of purpose, renewal of enthusiasm, spiritual cleansing, emotional ups and downs

Tiger

Abundance of feminine qualities and strengths, extremely sexually powerful, seduction - whether being the seduced or the seducer, dangerous attractions

Times of Day

The different times of the day carry with them plenty of dream symbolism. Pay attention to the time of day it appears to be in your dream - it often means much more than you might realise...

Dawn - *Enlightenment, awakenings of the spirit or soul, realisation*

Twilight (am) - *Uncertain beginnings, lack of clarity, decisions to be made*

Sun rise - *Happiness, positive transformations, renewal of energy or self identity*

Morning - *Starting of a new venture, early stages of development, there is progress to be made somewhere*

Midday/Noon - *Important times or events, a significant point is reached, appointments to be kept*

Afternoon - *Good time to pause for reflection, gathering energies together, tasks yet to be completed*

Sunset - *Impending completion, a situation is ending, an end is drawing near, the conclusion of a cycle*

Dusk - *Unhappiness, sadness, experiencing a temporary gloomy disposition, negative outlook*

Twilight (pm)- *Uncertain future, indistinct results, a tangible sense of possible failure*

Evening - *Endings, something closing down or stopping for good, or potential in the air, a sense of excitement and anticipation*

Night - *Dark energies, obscured feelings, something has been lost, desperation, helplessness, not knowing what to do, cannot see the reality of a situation*

Midnight - *Powerful spiritual situations, incredibly important decisions or actions, complete change is imminent*

Toast

Appreciation of simple things in life, wholesome pleasures, home comforts

Toaster

Expecting something good to happen quite soon, or that you are seeing two different sides to the same situation, and are eagerly awaiting the results.

Toilet

Expressing your true feelings, releasing emotional blockages, wanting to expel and get rid of negative emotions

Tools - Ever found yourself in B&Q or Homebase, trying to find the right tool for a job that needs doing? Well, even if you haven't, here's what dreaming of one of these handy tools might subconsciously symbolise about what's going on in your life...

Chainsaw - *Big changes happening, severe alterations to plans, cutting through obstacles*

Chisel - *An important point needs to be made, making small im-*

provements, steady progress

Drill - New discoveries, searching for something hidden, getting to the bottom of a situation

Hammer - Forcefulness, great masculine power required, determination, strength

Hoe - Nurturing energies, harmonious conditions for growth, the evening-out of unbalanced situations

Pair of Pliers - Removal of something, extracting information, needing to get a better grip something

Rake - Gathering information together, examining all the details you can find, trying to make clear a way or path forwards

Saw - Making deliberate decisions to change, dividing something up amongst many, breaking down a larger problem to ease coping with it

Screwdriver - Careful action, security, securing something in its place

Shovel - Coping with large issues quickly, clearing backlogs, feeling sufficiently equipped to deal with a heavy workload

Spade - Ease of progress, constructive endeavours, working hard to create something according to a plan

Wheelbarrow - Lightening your load, needing help getting rid of things, difficulty handling something

Wrench - Trying to fix something, attempts to forcibly reverse a situation, turning an opinion around

Topaz

Calm wisdom, spiritual warmth and compassion, acceptance, forgiveness and understanding

Torch

The search for truth, to focus or concentrate hard on a particular area or thing, the discovery of that which has been hidden

Towns

Towns represent how you see your social life generally, and

how you interact with those you come into contact with most frequently. If it's busy and feels good there then you're likely to be having a social peak in your life, and if it's busy but feels unpleasant then perhaps you've been going out too much, and need to spend some more time at home. If you feel uncomfortable then it's time to change your social habits a bit and try going somewhere new, or see some different friends to those you've been seeing lately. If it's quiet or even deserted then maybe you need to get out of the house a bit more and see your friends - time to let your hair down!

Toys

Well, we all love toys don't we? (Don't we? Surely it's not just me... or is it?) Unless perhaps your house is choc-full of them, and your kids never seem to put them away so you're sick of the sight of them that is. From children, to the terribly grown-up, or adults who still harbour their 'inner child' so often talked of in the worlds of self-help and psychotherapy, toys usually help make our lives infinitely more enjoyable, fun and playful. And dreaming of them can mean many things...

Dreaming of playing with toys generally speaking symbolises aspects of your childhood, and frequently a particular desire for harmony, joy, fun, even domestic bliss in your life.

The type of toy you dream of can say a lot about the situation you're in at the moment. Ask yourself; what are its main qualities? What do you DO with it? What are YOU doing with it? Does it relate to your life in some way? Is there something you want that you're not getting enough of, or is there something you fear right now?

Broken toys represent damaged, bad, or broken situations. If you broke it, you feel it's your fault things have gone so wrong, if someone else did it, then the blame seems to come from elsewhere, maybe from someone or somewhere unseen or unknowable.

Dreaming of a toybox can mean a thing or two too. If you're putting things into it, maybe you're moving on from old ways, or even literally moving away from childish qualities or things and onto the next stage in your life. Putting things into a toy box though, might symbolise a reticence to let go of your past, or unwillingness to move on.

Train

You want things in a particular area of your life to feel safe and certain, with no hidden surprises. You're single-mindedly going forward in a very specific direction to ensure this is the case

Trampoline

Resilience, ability to cope with life's 'ups and downs', striving for higher and higher goals

Trapeze Artist

Adventurous physical tendencies or desires, undecided between two directions of movement, unusual attractions

Treasure

Reflective of your sense of self-worth, feelings of security, feeling you have much to give to the world

Treasure Chest

Something of value to hide, hidden talents discovered, finding unexpected results, extremely welcome news

Trees

Alder - Secrecy of action, hidden knowledge, deliberate concealment

Ash - Endurance and tenacity, a sense of protection, healing qualities

Beech - Consistency, focus of intentions, practicalities may need consideration

Birch - Renewal, purification, getting rid of old energies or ways, new love, fertility

Elm - Flexibility, significant events or times, darker energies, transitions, the underworld

Hawthorn - Supernatural beliefs, unexplained occurrences, fear of illness or death

Hazel - Creative inspiration, wisdom, self-knowledge, self-defence

Holly - A lifting of spirits, celebration, protection from negativity, control of situations

Juniper - Cures or remedies for problems, getting rid of something unwanted, clairvoyance of the future

Linden - Making something happen, ease of progress, harmonious qualities

Oak - Strength, respect, physical beauty, a large presence in your life

Pine - Clarity of thought or intent, the alleviation of sadness, immortality of spirit or ideas

Rowan - Seeking magical or divine protection, help with mysterious forces, resourcefulness

Willow - Dealing with shocks or surprises well, coping with pain, vitality, positive growth

Yew - Regeneration, longevity, resurrection of old methods, practices or ideas

Triangle

Potential, aspirational activities, spirituality, eternal mysteries, unity between body, mind and spirit

Trishula

Choices or decisions need to be made, awareness of own personal powers, cause and effect

Tupperware container

Saving valuable information for future use, keeping a situation under control, preventing the loss of something important

Turquoise

Lucky events and situations, good fortune around you, willingness to see the best in someone or something

TV (ie. watching it)

Content to coast along with things as they are, without any wish to change how you view things, despite the fact that you might not be 100% happy, taking an objective viewpoint on things, absorbing many different influences, the nature of your overall state of mind - consider what's actually on your dream telly as a reflection of this.

TV Shows

We all watch TV shows all the time, but what does it mean if specific types of shows 'show up' in our dreams? More than you might think. And not just that you might perhaps need to find a few other things to do, rather than just sit there watching the telly every evening either...

Chat Show - Are you the interviewer or the interviewee? Perhaps you have something you'd like to talk to someone about, or there's something you'd love to get off your chest, but can't seem to find an outlet or person to talk to about whatever it is that's troubling you.

Comedy - Are you lacking in fun and frolics in your life? Do you need cheering up a bit? Or even a lot?! It might be that an aspect of your life is causing you to feel somewhat sad or unhappy, and you could do with a bit less seriousness and a good deal more jollity.

The News - Do you have important information you feel a need to tell others? Maybe you have an announcement you'd like to make to people around you, but haven't found the right moment yet. It could be that you've done something significant you would like everyone to know about.

Quiz Show - All about the Questions. Do you have any? Are you searching for answers? Or do you feel you have lots of answers for people, if only they'd ask!

Talent Show - Are you having difficulty expressing your inner desires? Do you feel under-appreciated by those around you? Perhaps you could be in need of a little affirmation or praise of your talents or abilities!

Shopping Show - What is it you need? Is there something you want to help you or lift your spirits? Has something or someone outlived their useful purpose, and you'd possibly like a replacement?

Soap Opera - Do you have a desire for more drama or entertain-

ment in your world these days? Is your everyday routine getting you down? Perhaps you're feeling lonely, and harbour a deep longing to be able to interact with more people on a day to day basis.

Twilight - *See **Times Of Day**

U FO

U FO
Unconventional thinking, unaccepted points of view, desire of living a different life, spiritual desires, the search for meaning regarding existence, a higher purpose, looking for more than just the mundane in your life. Escape from reality, and the yearning for total change

Underwater

Overwhelmed by strong emotions, coping with major personal upheavals, at the mercy of your emotions

Unicorn

Gentle influences and energies, kindness, warm hearted activities, desire to do good

V acuum Cleaner

Old habits or ways need changing, concern over outward appearances, dealing effectively with many small issues

Valentine's Day

Your feelings of love are growing, a strong potential for romance is in your life, emotional excitement

Vampire

Seductive characters, those with dangerous charms, people that are a drain on your energies or emotions

Vase

Seeking attention, inviting criticism, pride over your achievements

Vegetables

Lacking in emotional or spiritual nourishment, desire for a healthier perspective on things, needing more self discipline

Velvet

Smooth transitions, self-indulgent behaviour or circumstances, satisfaction with a situation, lofty ideals, noble achievements

Video Games

Wanting to control life and those around you to your own

ends - but what's happening in the game? This reflects your desires, motives and perspective on life, also escaping from reality, avoiding a particular problem...

First Person Shooter - *Feelings of oppression, frustration, aggression directed towards you, aggression towards others*

Platform - *Fascination with a situation, hunger for knowledge, desire to make important achievements*

Role Play - *Unhappiness with yourself, external limitations of self-expression, dissatisfaction with everyday life*

Racing - *Limited time to achieve something, wanting to be better than everyone else, feeling that others are competing against you in a personal way*

Virginity (ie. still intact!)

Feelings of potential in yourself or a given situation, purity of spirit and intent, high ideals, emotional honesty

Volcano

Uncontrollable anger, volatile energies, something negatively affecting people near you

VR Headset

Seeing things through a Virtual Reality Headset instead of what's really there might mean that perhaps the way you're looking at reality could benefit from a completely different approach or perspective entirely. Are you unhappy with your World as you see it normally?

W alking

Reflecting thoughtfully on your current position in the world, how you fit in to the grand scheme of things, knowing that you're on the path you want or need to be on, Confidence, easy going attitude, steady progress being made

Wall

Barriers, obstructions, impeded progress, limitations to experience, unable to move away from a situation, old habits or beliefs

War

Conflicting elements in life, huge differences of opinion, trying to get your own way, big arguments with someone, standing up for your rights, feeling oppressed or attacked, defending yourself

Warship

Warships can mean you're feeling aggressive about something which is affecting your emotions quite negatively, and you really want to finally deal with it, once and for all.

Wardrobe

You have many aspects to yourself and you need to feel you can pick and choose which ones you want to show to each different person or social situation.

Washing

Ever dreamt of washing a specific part of your body? From scrubbing your toes to sponging your nose, cleaning bits of yourself comes with hidden meaning regarding the different parts of our bodies in the world of dreams...

Is your Back being loofahed? Old attitudes, burdens or responsibilities might need to be jettisoned, and fast too. You might well need a new source of emotional strength around you.

Scrubbing your Bum like there's no tomorrow? Nothing less than your very sense of security and/or comfort in life is being regenerated.

Washing your Chest means you have a new found confidence

that you're just bursting to show off to people. Alternatively, you may feel a large amount of pride in something you've done lately.

Exfoliating your Face? You want to work on improving how you are seen, perceived or thought of by others. It might also literally mean you have been working on bettering your physical image or have a new beauty regime.

If your Feet are being cleaned, your sense of direction in life is being empowered, or you find yourself headed towards a much more positive and happier path.

Hand-washing is symbolic of you letting go or getting rid of people and situations that no longer please you.

Scrubbing your own Stomach represents new appetites being discovered, and that you are developing better methods of coping with life, too.

Wasp

You're experiencing a lot of anger about something, or, if you're being stung by wasps in your dream, there could be a lot of anger being directed towards you

Water

When we have dreams involving water, this symbolises different aspects of our emotional state of being at the time of having them. Seeing as our bodies are 80% water and it's almost impossible to 'switch off' our emotions for any length of time, perhaps our subconscious minds are already programmed to associate our emotions with water, as both things are so important in our lives that they practically rule our very existence...

Generally, Water in our dreams represents our emotional lives, our unconscious, and our spiritual, psychic states of mind.

Calm, smooth surfaced water shows that you're feeling serene, that your life is on a very even keel, and you are experiencing a wonderful peace of mind about things. Spiritually, this signifies that you're feeling absolutely 'at one' with life and your inner psychic processes are aligned well with your desires.

The more movement in the water in your dream, then the more 'movement' there also is in these areas of your life. If it really starts seeming like quite a 'choppy' scene then this indicates you're feeling emotionally unbalanced, and that things are definitely suffering from a degree of upset in your life somehow.

Boiling water means that previously hidden feelings and thoughts from our unconscious are coming to the forefront of our minds and need your attention.

Dirty water represents clouded thoughts or feelings, and even negative emotions about a situation or person close to you. It's time to start clearing out these murky, negative thoughts and issues, to clear your psychic and spiritual 'waters' again.

When it's raining in your dreams this signifies fertile situations. If you dream of seeing rain fall around you, then this symbolises your own feelings of forgiveness towards someone. If you're getting raining upon yourself specifically, then your forgiveness is being directed towards yourself instead.

Watercolour

Idealistic views, having one's head in the clouds, vagueness, uncertainty

Weather

It's certainly this nation's favourite subject - no wonder, really, because we get so bloody *much* of it in Britain don't we? And wherever you are in the world, you can't avoid it, nor avoid talking about it at some point with somebody or other. We engage in small talk about it with total strangers, make all kinds of 'insightful' observations about it, and of course, in the UK our most favourite thing of all is to constantly *complain* about it - whatever the weather! If it's not too cold, it's too darn hot, or too wet, or too windy, or too 'close'... good grief, find something more constructive and interesting to say or do somebody please!

Anyway, given the enormous obsession people have with it, you'd think that dreaming about the weather, in any of its myriad forms, might hide a veritable wealth of hidden meanings wouldn't you? And you'd be right; read on...

Rain - *Feeling emotionally upset, sadness, even depression, but also rather than the frequently rather negative viewpoint we so often have, rain in our dreams can signify fertile conditions in our lives too. It can bring a sense of renewal and a cleansing of the soul or spirit, enlightenment, and even liberation, as well as moments of clarity*

Showers - *Moments of clarity, erratic progress, emotionally uncommitted*

Fog/Mist - *Vagueness, indistinctness, uncertainty, complete lack of clarity, confusion*

Overcast - *Negativity, misery, tendency towards self-pity, depression, darkness*

Thunderstorm - *Conflict, anger or rage, clash of opinions, turmoil, potential for violence in the air*

Lightning - *Sudden insights or revelations, acute awareness, alarming events, recklessness*

Windy - *Wildness, tempestuous, fluctuating emotions, change, willful actions. Alterations in your life direction, possible unforeseen turmoil around you, and strong winds mean especially troublesome upsets. Gentler breezes suggest more idealistic and thoughtful times, or that you're having some rather fanciful notions or daydreamy tendencies lately*

Blue Skies - *Calm, comfortable, gentle acceptance, freedom from past troubles*

Sunny - *Joy, happiness, bliss, emotional warmth, positivity. Also, energy and power, even peace and success. It's generally an extremely positive and very strong sign you're on the right path. Dreams involving sunrise, in particular, symbolise new beginnings, new life to your aims, sudden breakthroughs, and feeling full of new purpose.*

Heatwave - *Creativity, abundance of energy, powerful energies around you, heightened desires*

Freezing - *Hard attitudes, lack of emotion, bitterness, inhibited self-expression, rejection*

Snow - *Life seems tough, hard or difficult to deal with truths are emerging, and may be causing you problems. Feeling under attack, ungrounded, or that something in your world seems particularly unpleasant, emotional coldness, feeling overwhelmed by something*

Weather Vane

Unpredictable behaviour patterns, perhaps there are some choices to be made, or you could be experiencing indecisiveness, or somewhat changeable conditions around you

Wedding

Deep true love, commitment, promises, beginning of a new partnership or venture

Weightlifting

Hidden strengths, serious effort to make something happen, under/overestimating how much hard work might be required

Werewolf

Being wary of sudden change, violent mood swings, temper tantrums, anger management issues

Whale

Deep emotional experiences, extraordinary depth of thought, and intuition, intensely spiritual connections with others of similar minds and viewpoints

Wheel

Circles in life, recognising the existence of a regularly repeating cycle, progressing forwards

Wheelbarrow

Lightening your load, needing help getting rid of things, difficulty handling something

Wig/Hair Extensions

Giving an impression of yourself which is different to usual, pretentiousness, taking credit for other's achievements or abilities

Wind

Changes in your life direction, possible unforeseen turmoil or troublesome upsets, idealistic thoughts, fanciful notions

Windy

Fluctuating emotions, wilful actions, wildness of spirit, tempestuousness, strong life force, the strength of the wind reflects the intensity of these aspects

Wind chimes

Hearing Wind chimes symbolises a more harmonious sort of change happening, one that you are really going to benefit from and are happy to have happen to you

Windmill

If it's turning slowly then you're finding things hard to understand, and the faster it turns then the more capable you feel you are at dealing with things. If it's not working properly or broken completely, you are making no progress with the thing that is troubling you and don't know what to do to get around the problem

Window

Insight, introspection, perspective, hope, new ideas or thoughts. Opening a window signifies your positive outlook, and openness to life, whatever it has in store for you. It represents a willingness to live life to the full

Winter - *See **Seasons**

Wishbone

Strong family connection, a family celebration is imminent, a decision needs to be made one way or the other

Witch

Strong feminine presences, sensing of female qualities, compassionate, nurturing energies, deep understanding, gentle yet powerful action, or manipulative tendencies

Wizard

Overbearingly masculinity, dominating energies, awareness of male qualities,

independence, ambitious plans, assertive action, forceful nature, aggressive tendencies

Wolf

Fascination with the mysterious, dark power, strange behaviour, unusual events, fear of the unknown

Wooden Leg

(Have crutch) Having or finding the support you require. (No crutch) lacking support from others, having lost or desiring something very specific to your needs

Wool

Traditional values, practical approaches, reliability, natural feelings or interests

Work

At some point most of us will have had a dream or several about being in work. Such dreams are very common to most of us, and we can even experience what seems like an entire day at work in our dreams, only then to wake up and finds ourselves having to actually go and do it all over again for real- not often an especially favourite dream memory for some people, that one! To have dreams involving work in some way can suggest other things to us too, aside from the fact that it features so much in all our lives...

The most common reason we dream of our jobs or being at work somehow, is simply that we're working a lot, maybe even too much or too hard. If you find yourself having dreams of being at work very often, perhaps you need to consider whether you're working more overtime than you can cope with comfortably, or that you're maybe taking on too much during your working day. If any of this is the case, try to aim to be more realistic with your workload somehow, and take a well earned break or holiday as soon as you can.

All work and no play can really have a negative effect on you and your life, and will of course affect the quality of your work in the end, too, so you end up becoming less productive by stressing yourself trying to do so much! If we aren't happy in our work, then most of us end up dreaming about our current jobs an awful lot, which certainly would suggest that it's time to start looking at what it is that you might be happier doing for a job.

We dream about doing work that isn't what we normally do for a living too. It's quite interesting to look at the nature of the work you are doing in your dream when it's something other than your usual job, to see what the differences are between them, and then think about whether there is some aspect of your real-life job that you perhaps might want to change or could improve upon, that your dream-life job is showing you in some way.

Sometimes we dream about being in an old job, or doing some kind of work that we used to do a long time ago. What this suggests is that there's an old lesson or approach we once learned that we may have perhaps forgotten, which we need to apply to our life or a current situation somehow. It could be helpful to you, if you have a dream like this, to think back to the time when you were doing that particular job. Think about what abilities or qualities you discovered, learned or found in yourself back then, whether regarding work or other aspects of life, to see if doing this could have any kind of positive use to you now – it may trigger off a memory or two that could be just the thing to help you on your way!

We can sometimes even find ourselves dreaming of doing the dreaded housework, with a duster in one hand and the Hoover in the other, frantically making the place all spick and span! This can actually represent to us that we are making some significant changes in our lifestyle, perhaps breaking with old habits, doing away with a previous way of thinking or living, and moving on to better ways that will serve us much better.

Although it could also possibly be a very literal kind of a dream, and that you really do need to get scrubbing and polishing at home very soon indeed, but surely that couldn't be the case at all... or could it?

World

Ability to 'see the bigger picture', appreciation of many aspects contributing to one overall thing, wholeness, unity

Worm

You don't regard yourself very highly for a reason you really don't want to tell anyone about, you want to hide part of yourself from others

Worry

Feeling tormented by something, consistent irrational fear of something bad happening, awareness of an insidious situation

Wrench

Trying to fix something, attempts to forcibly reverse a situation, turning an opinion around

Wrestling

Dealing with something hard to control, fighting to make a point, struggling with another person's ideas or personality

Writing

Writing symbolises communication and connection, with your inner self, your subconscious, and with others too. Often it's particularly the very thing which you are writing in your dream, which carries further clues to what your dream might concern or be about, bringing with it even more specific messages from your subconscious mind. Handwriting represents your sense of, or desire for, effective self-expression, your creative tendencies, and a desire to express something in your own way. The kind of writing implement carries with it its own qualities too. For example writing with a pencil suggests more ideas-based or temporary circumstances, nothing is really set in stone yet. Writing with a pen represent more definitive messages, more certainty in what you feel, think or wish to express.Typewriting, on a computer or other device, can represent a desire for more swift or effective communications, perhaps with more business-like intentions.

X **-Ray**
Unusual viewpoints, being able to 'see through' someone's motives or intentions, uncanny insight into something

Xylophone

Several differing aspects coming together in harmony, many small elements to a problem or situation that needs structure or solidity

Y **acht** (ie. the luxury type)
Luxury Yachts are symbolic of a desire for the finer things in life, or maybe you want or need some rest and relaxation. Do you feel some kind of boost to your status in the world is required? Perhaps you want more money or some sort of visible evidence of your achievements in life.

Yellow

Positive feelings, joy, happiness, new life coming into being

Yin Yang (symbol)

Balance, actions and reactions taking place, accepting the natural flow of things

Z **ombie**
Emotional detachment, acting without thinking, overwhelmed by forces beyond your control

Zoo

Prevented from being you, held back by something, fear of

others opinions, lacking a sense of liberty or freedom, feeling prevented by others from expressing yourself as you wish, instinctual drives or urges need to be acknowledged

Dear Roi De Lune...

REAL dreams from REAL people (and what they might mean)

Having been a dream analyst and written on and about the subject of dream analysis for the British magazines Chat It's Fate and Chat for over 13 years now, as you might well imagine, I've had to analyse many, *many* dreams. Thousands of them, in fact. Possibly even yours. This section of the book is dedicated to real dreams, from real people.

It contains a selection of dreams upon which I've been asked to give my two penneth worth regarding their meaning, as well as some hopefully helpful advice from me to said real people. Some of these dreams have appeared in Its Fate or Chat, albeit in shorter, less detailed form, due to the practical constraints of having only limited precious print space available in such publications.

I'm always frustrated by the fact that this is something a lot of books written by ever so eminent and worthy dream analysts usually either miss out on including altogether, or seldom seem to pay much attention to; bar a handful of examples they use merely to illustrate their frequently long-winded, dreadfully erudite and supposedly 'learned', but usually rather boring, point. Which is kind of a bit weird of them really isn't it.

I've included the names of the people who were kind and lovely enough to send me their precious dreams to analyse, unless they've requested that they remain anonymous, in which case I've respectfully omitted such sensitive, nay damning information.

Often, people tell me they're afraid that they have such crazy dreams 'there must be something wrong with them' mentally speaking, or that they feel embarrassed about the content or nature of their dreams. If you're one of those people, then I hope reading a selection of *actual* people's really real dreams here will help show you you're not bonkers, strange, mad or odd at all (well, certainly not because of what happens in your dreams anyway - ho-ho yes Roi aren't you *funny), that you're in no way alone in such experiences or thoughts, and that it's utterly needless to go around worrying about these things.

*No.

Actually, REALLY TRULY, the reality is this: everyone has all kinds of crazy, weird stuff happening in their dreams all the time. So just relax, and enjoy reading these examples of real people's dreams, and my interpretations of them.

Toodle-pip. x Roi

*D*ear Roi de Lune,

I had a very strange dream a few nights ago in which I was working late shifts in a pub/bar (never worked in one in my life) & every evening one of the other bar staff would give me a cd explaining that a man had left it for me at the bar. This happened over the course of a few nights & every time it was the same cd with the same title 'Interlude.' Then one night after my shift at the bar and while in bed asleep (still dreaming) I woke to a Chinese man just outside my door. I knew instinctively that this was the man that had left me the cd's at the pub and that he was going to harm me and I woke up at the point that he was trying to strangle me! I would love to know what that all means as have been worrying about it for last few days!

Emma, Leicestershire

Dear Emma,

It seems to me that you've been searching for some sort of relief, rest, holiday or break from things, albeit subconsciously. Your dream suggests that, despite you finding such times away from the stresses of normal, usual, routine daily existence, you've felt you had to work for it, and work pretty hard too. It also appears from your dream that in some way you secretly might like someone else to intervene, and take you away from it all, to give you that well deserved break.

There's something else you also subconsciously recognise here, in that there's a sense of potential danger regarding the situation you might find yourself in, one way or another, if you're not careful. Is it that you might do yourself some harm, should you continue to work so hard without adequate rest and recuperation periods? Or possibly conversely, that you should make sure you don't take too many breaks, or rest so long, that you could endanger your livelihood? It could even be that you should be careful not to let a stranger, or someone you don't know very well, help you in some way with your situation, in case it goes disastrously wrong as a result!

Only you can really know the finer details of what that might be about, deep down, but your dream does suggest trepidation on your part regarding such matters. It's my job to try to relate such information to you, to try to help you see the larger picture of what's happening around you psycho-spiritually, literally, and on a pretty mundane level too, it's all relevant to you, and your life after all.

I 've been having this dream on and off for about 3 years now. I start by walking through a park, and then I have to cross a railway. When I look for trains coming there's nothing in either direction. But as I start to cross, all of a sudden a train is right next to me, and the ground opens up and I fall in, but before I hit the bottom I wake up. Please help me to work out this dream, as I wake up panicking every time.

Kerri, London

Dear Kerri,

Your dream says something about your approach to life in general. In many ways, you love to live freely, naturally, and to do things exactly how you want to - but you sometimes find yourself going against the grain somewhat in the eyes of others. This can happen when you least expect, like the trains in your dream, and catches you off guard. The way that others can unexpectedly mistreat you, or interfere in your life without invitation, is something you really don't like at all! This dream more than likely reoccurs at times when you either anticipate such things happening to you, or are currently being subjected to circumstances of this nature.

*T*he other night I dreamt I was the only person who could see these black shadows/grim reaper type figures, who would follow people that were going to die shortly. I made the mistake of looking into a mirror and seeing the pulse in my neck beat so fast it bulged out, it was disgusting, and then the dream got horribly distorted, with one of the figures trying to attack me.

Alex, Facebook

Dear Alex,

Your dream could well symbolise that you currently see a particularly unpleasant situation is about to change, and possibly quite dramatically... but no one else seems to be aware of the fact. You're worried that this apparent situation change, and other's general ignorance of it, could affect you quite negatively in some way. You're also concerned about something unpleasant happening to you, if you go around trying to inform people about what you can so plainly see happening in the future. I hope it all works out for the best for you and everyone in the end.

I have had two dreams recently about bringing kittens home. I live in a tiny flat where I have a bit of a mouse problem (which is getting sorted out) but I would like to move to a bigger place. In the first, a friend who lives in an equally small flat said "Yes, get a kitten!" So I had a lovely little kitten that was living with me, protecting me from mice and spiders! The second, I was living with a friend's mother in a country house in America, with a huge garden. I saw a kitten at a shop and said I wanted to buy it. The Mother said "Is is a pink and grey one with blue eyes?" I said yes and she said "Buy it!" What could these dreams mean?

Susannah, London

Dear Susannah,

Whilst I'm sure you do want your living circumstances to improve, in more ways than one, this dream is about certain *self-improvements* you subconsciously desire. You want to expand your world somehow, to encourage new aspects of yourself to emerge, and to introduce new energies and happiness. You see this self-expansion as the route to really making the most of things, and feeling way more positive about life too.

I keep dreaming that I'm running through the Woods near where I live, as a white Wolf. I then see a male black wolf, and I say to him 'catch me if you can' and we run off together. It seems there's just us at first, but then we hear another Wolf howl. He says 'we have got to get you out of here' then howls, then the rest of our pack come and we start running. Some other wolves run after us, but they're Red, like they have fire for fur. I jump up a tree with the rest of our pack, and we watch as the red wolves run under us.

Clare, Bristol

Dear Clare,

You appearing as a white wolf symbolises your awareness of your own beauty, together with your more mysterious, attractive qualities, and the power that these aspects of you wield when it comes to captivating the interest of others! You value the attentions of those you're attracted to, and especially those of a very particular, strong person around you - but when it comes to the other, less desirable, attention you also receive, you see the people giving you such attention as dangerous and threatening. You sense that this strong person in your life, represented as the black wolf, will protect you from them though.

I dreamt a bird was flying towards me surrounded by an aura of purple, pink and blue. It touched my mouth, so I put my hand out and it landed on my finger. It was so beautiful.
Rae, Newcastle

Dear Rae
Birds in dreams are associated strongly with the more 'spiritual' side to life. Your beautiful dream bird symbolises feelings of happiness and liberation, possibly from a specific situation that's been preventing you from fully expressing yourself. It's showing you that, now, you feel you can express yourself in any way you want, and that subconsciously you realise you're going to be much happier as a result.

E *ver since childhood I've had recurring dreams of elevators.*
Although they aren't all the same; sometimes the door will
open to find no landing to step out onto, or the lift door
opens and I see just the lift-shaft and cables, and other times the lift
will fall down or shoot up, and it even spins and tumbles in some
dreams. It can really scare me, and sticks in my mind all day.
Donna, Essex

Dear Donna,

Elevators most commonly represent quite literally the 'ups and downs' of our lives; successes, failures, things increasing or diminishing and so on. The thing is of course, that in your dreams the elevator does all kinds of things, except act like a normal elevator should. The main reason for this is likely to be because you tend to find that life often behaves or treats you in ways quite contrary to how you think it's supposed to, and this unsettles and worries you. The best thing you can do is try to remember this - however we think life 'should' go, life always has its own ideas about how it wants things to be, whatever you might have to say about it, so it's beneficial to learn to go with the flow a bit more, and try to relax. It's very likely to make life quite a bit easier on your nerves.

*W*hen I was at school, I used to have a massive crush on my form teacher. But recently I keep having dreams that we're going to end up being together! I left school over 25 years ago, and haven't even seen him in all that time. What do these dreams mean?

Sharon, Brighouse

Dear Sharon,

Your dream reflects a subconscious awareness of your development as a woman that you don't fully realise you possess... at least not quite yet! When you were in school, you never used to believe it was really a possibility that you could end up being with the grown man who was the subject of your teacher crush, largely due to your age at the time. Being such a young and relatively inexperienced girl, what you sensed you lacked in potential 'partner material' is what helped you keep a real sense of perspective on things romantically speaking. Your subconscious is sending you a message - it's time it dawned upon you that you are now a very different person from whom you once were. You once were a girl. But you are now a grown woman, and have so much more going for you now in many ways, not least of all being romantically I'm sure. It's time for you to acknowledge these more mature aspects of yourself fully, and really go for it. Live your love-life however you choose, and don't ever feel that you're inadequate or incapable of being loved by your heart's true desire.

*O*nce I dreamt I had a fight in the pub I work in, and then I ran away with friends, through water, and down some stairs with a trolley towards an airport check-in. Then I

fall over and am looking for my friends but can't find them!
Carla, Basingstoke

Dear Carla,

You feel that things are changing and want to leave your current job for something better- it's just you don't know what direction your work life is going to move in, which is proving emotionally frustrating for you. You know it's possible the direction your job takes you in may mean you won't be able to see certain friends so often, or that you may even lose contact with them. Try to remember that although we always move on in life for one reason or another, the friends really worth their salt stay friends wherever life takes you, even if you aren't physically near them.

3 *O years ago I dreamt very vividly that I saw an Alien spacecraft in the clear blue daylight sky. They took me inside my bedroom in my parent's council house and connected me to a strange looking device with tubes coming out of it, attached to a control panel. I don't remember what they did, but I remember seeing the light from their spaceship streaking away from me through the night sky. I've always wondered if this was just a dream or did I really experience an 'Alien visitation'?!*
Alison, Bridgend

Dear Alison,

Whilst I'm no expert on Alien visitations, Alien experiments or Alien abductions, reports of phenomena such as this usually come from people who either remember the whole experience in vivid 'detail', or those who've allegedly 'disappeared' for a certain amount of time, but don't remember anything about it at all. So by my 'powers of deduction' I would say that in all likelihood it was actually a dream you had rather than a full on Alien visitation. In this case, your dream symbolises your feelings of unfamiliarity and anxiety regarding a major change in your circumstances at the time, something that you felt you had no choice but to go through, due to no fault of your own. Hopefully, you've dealt with whatever change you were going through by now though.

I *dreamt my 16 year old son burnt all my clothes in the back garden of the house my family and I once lived in. I looked through the clothes to see if any of them were undamaged, packed what I could find in a suitcase and fled from the house as quickly as I could. It was a very sad and distressing dream, particularly as the time I lived in that house was really awful for me because my son and my now ex-partner made my life a living hell at the time.*

Susan, Birmingham

Dear Susan,

This dream represents an emotional issue that you are unable to ignore any longer, which is really demanding your attention. Also, this is in particular relation to how negatively you feel others see you. You feel that your son has played a large part in creating this through his behaviour during the period when you all lived in this house. Try changing an old attitude, previous method or behaviour pattern that doesn't seem to be serving you very well anymore regarding your relationship with your son. It may help more than you think!

I *n my dream, I'm lying in bed and then my bed starts shaking very violently. I tried to get off the bed, but I couldn't move, like I was stuck in treacle. There seemed to be a presence of some kind, and I was so scared I shouted out 'leave me alone'. Suddenly all became calm and I was able to get up and leave it. By this time I had woken up and done that very thing too! My dream was very frightening and has left me sleeping with my bedroom light on permanently.*

Tracey, Liverpool

Dear Tracey,

Ooh, that sounds like a dreadful nightmare you had there I must say, no wonder it made you feel so anxious. Dreaming of your own bed normally represents the sense of security you feel within yourself, and how secure your life appears to be to you in general. Your dream suggests very strongly that you were experiencing a distinct lack of secure feelings at that time in particular. Maybe something was happening or had happened to seriously disturb your equilibrium and your peace of mind. The fact that you shouted out, that you did something, and it actually changed the situation positively, represents you needing to take more responsibility for your own security to really be happy.

I *have a disturbing dream where I open the fridge door and there's a large frog sitting there inside that looks really menacing. I'm too embarrassed to tell anyone about it, but it was so scary at the time! Help!*

Nicola, Staines

Dear Nicola,

I think that if a large frog was menacing me from within my fridge, I might be quite scared too. This dream symbolises your feelings of apprehension and fear of 'the unexpected' happening. When things feel like they're completely beyond your control, or appear to take you by surprise in ways that you're unprepared for - just like your large frog in the fridge does - it can feel disconcerting at best, and downright frightening at worst. It's completely natural to be wary of such situations occurring, but ultimately it's good to remember that whatever happens in life, despite our initial reactions to 'unexpected' or potentially 'frightening' circumstances, we don't really have any choice but to just 'get on with things' and, basically, to deal with whatever it is we have to deal with, don't we? Even if it does turn out to be a giant, chilled amphibian!

M *y family and I are moving back to our last house, 55 miles from where we live now, and in every dream we are decorating a different room very differently to how it was when we lived there. My best friend, who still lives back there, is in every dream, but I never tell her about the move until we've moved in. I've had this dream 9 times!*

Sarah, Sheffield

Dear Sarah,

Dreaming of moving home symbolizes a desire or need for big changes in your life. Seeing as you are dreaming of moving back where you used to live, this could mean that you perhaps would like things to be a bit more like they were back then, when you had your best friend near you. As you're dreaming of decorating the place in a different way, this suggests that although you'd prefer certain things to be how they once were, there's still a few things you'd wish to change about how life could be in the future, rather than just have it all exactly like it was.

I was making pancakes, cracked 3 eggs and each was filled with blood, then 1 of the cooked pancakes was pink. I always dream in high technicolour, hear talk, music, sounds, experience emotions – I awake tired and never get any restful sleep! Can you explain why?
Dimi, Chelmsford

Dear Dimi,

You are highly sensitive and currently have a very emotional state of mind, which together are responsible for all your vivid and detailed dreams! The cracked eggs could represent you feeling extra vulnerable lately, although the blood signifies life, love and passion, and the pancakes symbolise pleasure and satisfaction with your current situation in life. It sounds very much to me like although you may be feeling a lot more sensitive of late, there's so much life that you have the potential to be to living right now, which is rather wonderful.

When I last saw my daughter Anna when she was a toddler, before I gave her up for adoption. I dreamt of her around that time and she was about 7 years old in the dream, wearing a red ribbon in her hair and I was looking down from the ceiling at her. She placed something in my hand which felt so real, but then I woke up. Will I ever see her again?

Elizabeth, Sheffield

Dear Elizabeth,

The red ribbon represents the undeniable emotional and spiritual connection you feel with your daughter. The fact she was giving you something which felt so significant symbolizes your hope that one day, when she's older, she will want to know who her natural mother is and want to see you again, which you feel would be a wonderful gift to receive from her. It's a dream of your own hopes, rather than indicative of whether you will see her again or not I'm afraid.

*F*requently as I drop off to sleep, I feel an overwhelming terror and dream an invisible force drags me from my bed throwing me from one wall to the other. I can't see what is hurting me, it's so real, and now my daughter has the same dream. I can sense when I'm going to be attacked, and I'm very nervous about going to sleep.

Dawn, Cardiff

Dear Dawn,

This sounds like a very frightening experience that you and your daughter are both having. Dreams can be so vivid that they just seem to be completely real to the point that we are as affected by them as you both have been by this awful nightmare. The sense of terror is likely to be representative of a very real unresolved fear or doubt in your lives, that you may feel helpless and powerless to do anything about. You are certainly being subjected to a good deal of stress or change one way or another, aside from your reactions to this terrible dream, and I'd seriously recommend finding ways of genuinely relaxing yourselves before bedtime, which will certainly help at least a bit.

*I*n my dream I'm living at my Gran's house, lying on her bed, and I'm with a man who seems very special to me although I don't know who he is. He loves me and cares for me a lot, and my Gran, who I don't get on with all that well in real life, is happy for me and him to be together. I tell him I love him, but then he says 'I'm not here for you' and he goes! Then a Pop star I like comes into the room and kisses me and then he disappears too!

Julianna, Cornwall

Dear Rachel,

It would certainly seem that your Gran has certain ideas about who you should be with! This dream is all about you wanting to do what you want in your life regardless of what your Gran thinks you should, and that you can be with whomsoever you want, whatever she thinks about the people you have been, or are, seeing. Only you can decide what's best for you in matters of the heart, so maybe it's time for you to gently but firmly make this clear to her, otherwise you're both going to start moving further apart from each other in the end.

I've been plagued by dreams of hearing a loud knock on my front door or window which then wakes me up from a deep sleep. I always get up and look outside my window to see but there's never anyone there.

Emily, Shropshire

Dear Emily,

This is a classic example of something significant imminently about to happen in your life, and a sign of a big change in the air for you in some way. Knockings of this nature are often dreamt of, and sometimes even actually occur, when these times are upon us. It's nothing to be afraid of, but rather just a time where you need to have your wits about you and make sure you're prepared for a bit of change potentially coming your way very soon.

I dreamt I was in a really posh, big hotel room. I was just locking door thinking how lovely, only people like Madonna have this kind of privacy, when all of a sudden a band knock the door asking me if I would swap my room for their smaller one, as there's about ten of them and my room would be perfect for them! I go and see their room which turns out to be really small and not very nice at all, but I still swap with them!

Miranda, Nottingham

Dear Miranda,

This dream reflects the fact that you will readily do what's best for the many rather than the few, or even the one. You often find yourself either compromising in order to either keep the peace, or benefit others. This is a lovely quality to possess, even though sometimes it can feel a little like it back-fires slightly, but in fact you are someone who is truly giving and caring about others in this world, and puts others first more often than not. Good for you – I think the world would be a vastly better place for us all to live in if more people thought and behaved like you!

I *was in my family home in my Mother's bedroom, and had*
spent a long time sorting through my Mother's belongings al-
though this should only have taken a short time to deal with. I
felt I was taking three steps forward and two steps back, and crying
as a result, that I'd been there for days not seeing anyone or leaving
at all and completely alone. I wanted to leave but felt that I couldn't
as I had to finish what I was doing.

Pauline, Norwich

Dear Pauline,

You're feeling a lot of pressure to devote your time to something, and worried that you are neglecting yourself in the process too. It seems that you should try to treat life with a more even hand, balance out your duties against those things which you'd like to do for your own pleasure and own happiness. If we spend too much of our time and energy on others, no matter how important they are to us, we'll find that we end up sacrificing ourselves beyond points which we are comfortable with, and when this happens, we're less able to be any help to them or indeed ourselves.

I *was at Uni when Prince William came to visit, to check out*
the horse riding facilities as he was thinking of studying
there. Then I got on a horse in front of him but the hat didn't
fit and I couldn't get my feet in the stirrups, I rode into an arena
really fast and then I fell off! Prince William came running over to
help me, but no one else even noticed.

Briony, Cork

Dear Briony,

Your romantic ideals are blinding you to the truth where your heart is concerned right now. Prince William's appearance in your dream represents the almost 'fairy tale' vision you have of what you want to see and experience in your love life, but you feel that you aren't receiving such wonderful attention and love, and perhaps also that no one else understands or appreciates your rose-tinted view either. It's not a question of lowering your ideals at all, but be careful you don't miss out on a romantic opportunity as a result of having your head in the clouds too often.

T here's a reoccurring dream I have where I am asleep but can't wake up. I try to spin around in my bed to knock something off my bedside table to make a noise to wake me up, but can't, and then it feels like a person or force is squeezing me really tightly and won't let me go, which is very frightening.

Diane, Canterbury

Dear Diane,

Sleep paralysis can actually happen to many people in life, and although it's quite common, and usually nothing to worry too much about, it is nonetheless very alarming indeed when it occurs. When we dream of being paralyzed like this in our sleep, it represents us feeling an inability to do something know we need to do in life. The added restriction you feel in this dream means that it's more because of your feelings about another person or their influence on you that makes you feel helpless in this way.

M y brother passed away a couple of years ago. I keep hav-ing dreams about him standing over me, laughing while cutting me right down the middle and taking all my organs out and throwing them over his shoulder. I beg him to stop, but he just carries on. I don't understand why would my brother do this to me in death, when in life he was such a lovely person?

Lindsay, Isle of Man

Dear Lindsay,

Your dream represents how distraught and greatly upset you

were and still are about your brother's death. You could almost feel like it's his fault he's not with you anymore somehow, that he's 'done this' to you... but you know that really it's just that you're still grieving for him an awful lot. When we lose those we care so much for it's totally natural to feel as you are, and to have upsetting dreams like this. Try to understand that time will eventually help you heal what must be a terrible wound for you. I hope it does so sooner than later.

I *'m in a place where there are 2 swimming pools. The first one I go to feels dangerous, and then I realise there's a crocodile in it! I run to the second one, and this one is safe so I dive in, have a great time, then I wake up!*
Ruth, Carlisle

Dear Ruth,

Water broadly represents our emotions. When it's a more 'controlled' body of water we dream about, as in your swimming pools, and it not being a wild, stormy sea for example, it's a sign of you having a fairly good understanding of your emotions at that time. This dream means that you are being faced with a choice in your emotional life, and must decide whether to risk taking a chance, or perhaps to go for the safer option.

I *n my dream, I'm a car factory, in the offices upstairs. There are a few boxes of cigars on a desk. I had one from each box, smoked one of them, and was then offered more as I left but I said no. My father is dying, is this anything to do with him maybe?*

You're feeling like life is a bit ordinary right now, perhaps even a little bored and no doubt emotional in regards to your father's situation of course. This dream symbolises concern over an important financial decision you are going to have to make, and the fact you smoked only one cigar, although you had many offered to you, means that you simply want to make sure that when you choose, you make the right choice and stick with it.

I dreamt that I was going to go away somewhere to do a huge bungee jump with my old boss, who I loved working for. I was packing to go on the trip and couldn't find my trainers, but I thought oh well, I can do without them anyway. However, when we got there the organizers of the jump wouldn't let me do it without them!

Helen, Swansea

Dear Helen,

This is all about your work life. You felt stable and comfortable working for your old boss and happy about the future prospects you had ahead of you. Your dream shows that since you stopped working for him you're feeling unsure about your future, and that you wish you felt like you used to about your working life, particularly who you work for. Maybe have a chat with your current employers and tell them how you feel about working there, because if there's something that could be improved or changed they might be able to do something about it, which could help you to really enjoy your job.

I n my dream a Falcon lands on my head and wraps its wings around me. It doesn't feel uncomfortable or threatening, in fact if anything it feels quite protective. I'm walking around with this Bird of Prey, and then someone tries to pull it off me and the bird gets injured so I try to heal the bird and as I'm holding it in my hands it transforms into a really beautiful hand-held Victorian type mirror that says 'look in me'. Then I wake up!

Falcons symbolise a longing for freedom and excitement, often accompanied by feelings of impatience, and a desire to be in a position of leadership or authority too. Your dream is telling you that you need to be careful you don't end up letting others prevent you from progressing or doing what you'd like to do in life. Although you need to concentrate on such aspects, try to also go with the flow, whilst staying true to all your desires and goals, so you can eventually become the person you're meant to be – which is probably a good lesson to remember for us all too.

I *dreamt that my best male friend and Tommy Lee Jones, who's his absolute hero, were 'freefall' sky-diving together. They were performing all kinds of tricks and stunts, and just kept on falling and falling, laughing all the while as they were so happy! The very next morning, he called me to tell me that his wife is pregnant for the first time, which is something he's wanted to happen desperately for years, so he's over the moon about it. Is the dream anything to do with this happy event?*
Toni, New Zealand

Dear Toni,

Yes, this dream is certainly related to your friend's wonderful news. It's quite a psychic dream in fact, you're obviously very close to your friend, and you 'tuned in' to his feelings of joy about it in your dream. His hero being with him represents the fact that he's likely becoming more of the man he wants to be, which being a father is a big part of. The constant free falling through the sky without landing, whilst having such fun at the same time, symbolises his happiness and new 'lust for life' as a result, too.

*H*ere's a vivid dream I had where I dreamt I was in a holiday resort set in lush, green fields surrounded by forest. I walked into a wooden lodge surrounded next to a vast lake in the middle of the fields and had a chat to some of the people there. At that point it arose that I was looking around to decide whether I wanted to work there. The lodge then moved onto the lake and it turned out it was a plane and could fly like a bird! It took off and flew to another part of the park, which was next to a beach by the sea. I couldn't decide whether or not to work there either, as it was a long way from home.

Charlotte, London

Dear Charlotte,

You're not totally happy with your work life at the moment, and you're thinking about moving on at some point soon to a job where you'll be happier, and also about your long-term job prospects too. You're feeling quite positive and ambitious though, which is great, although you suspect subconsciously that you may have to move away somewhere else in order to get that 'dream job'.

*I*had a dream that I was in the bedroom with my ex-boyfriend and for some reason we'd decided to have a threesome with some other girl. When we were on the bed with the other girl, sometimes my ex would turn into another ex of mine instead. I decided I needed to go the toilet and left the room. When I was out of the room I decided I didn't really want to go back in and be involved, *feeling*

sad and hurt by the involvement of the other girl – when I had been in the room I hadn't really cared the she was involved. So I just left them to it. Then I woke up. My last boyfriend and I have only recently split up, and I'm not sure if we've done the right thing.

Cathy, Edinburgh

Dear Cathy,

This dream reflects the fact that you wonder if you could or should have done anything which would've helped you and the partners you've had stay together, instead of splitting up. The truth is though, that if you had compromised your true feelings in order to do this, it's you who would've paid the price for it in the end. You'd have ended up really unhappy with the situation you were in, much more so than you have felt after splitting up with them, and what's more, you'd have most likely ended up eventually splitting up anyway as a result.

I *'m on my way home on a train with my sister and niece (of which I have neither). We don't live in the same place, and they live further on but because we're having such a nice time I decide to stay on a few stops past my own. When I get off I realise I've gone much further than expected and I feel panicked. I ask a lady member of staff for help but I can't hear what she's saying apart from 'I can't help you anymore, I'm busy'! I begin asking the same questions to the man behind the desk but the same thing happens and he writes something down but it's just scribble so I can't read it. I go to a ticket machine and there are loads of them, so I go to one with no queue but then it's too expensive.*

Camilla, Brighton

Dear Camilla,

This is about your path in life. You know that something must change and you're worried you might waste time ending up doing things you don't want to do. You don't feel that anyone else can help you decide what you should or shouldn't do anymore, and you know deep down that only you can really decide what's best for you in the end. Be determined but also careful that you don't make an over ambitious decision at the moment, too.

*S*ometimes I dream about the school I went to that had a staircase with windows the whole way up, and as I'm walking up the stairs with my friends, a helicopter with armed soldiers appears outside the window and starts shooting at us. We're still school children in the dream. I take cover as best as I can away from the window, and I always wake up in a cold sweat as the shooting continues. I'm not hurt in the dream but just have an incredible sense of fear.

Amanda, Edinburgh

Dear Amanda,

This represents your own unresolved feelings of insecurity from when you were a child. You have some anxiety still about your own abilities in life and feel you still have much to learn, especially when you feel confronted about them either at work or amongst friends, and it's at these times you're more likely to have this dream. Try to develop your self confidence more and you should find you have this dream less and less frequently, and that it maybe even stops altogether.

O *ften I dream that I'm sleeping naked on top of the Empire State Building in New York! My bed is at the very top instead of the pointed bit, and I always feel afraid I'm going to fall off and that everyone will see me in the nude.*
Cynthia, Wolverhampton

Dear Cynthia,

You sometimes feel very aware that you're quite separate from others in a particular way, and you aren't always too happy about these feelings when they occur. You're very sensitive about how you relate to people around you, and it can get quite disconcerting because you place a lot of value in others opinions of you. It's only natural to feel like this from time to time, but try not to worry as much about how people might judge you. Remember that you're totally entitled to be exactly who you are whatever others may think of you.

I *have this dream where I have to keep changing all the light-bulbs in a house. Also, it always seems really important to me in this dream that wherever there is a dark area in the house, I absolutely have to put more and more bright lights up, to make the whole place shine. The thing is, I quite like low lights at home in real life!*

You're at a stage in life where your perceptive abilities are on the increase, which is great. You have a strong yearning for the truth, and want to know as much as you can about both the world around you, and your own inner world too. Now is a perfect time for you to start a new course of education in some way, or to explore different areas of life to those you're used to, or even just to get out and about and meet some new people and see what or who comes your way.

*M*y son is 6, and has bad dreams every night. It's always things like he's in a nice sunny place and then a crocodile appears and bites him, or he's in his room playing and then a big bear smashes through the window and attacks him – always him being attacked by fierce animals. I even swapped bedrooms with him to see if it would help, but he still keeps on having them. What should I do?

Although it is perfectly normal for children to have very vivid, frightening dreams or nightmares, sometimes known as 'night terrors', it doesn't make it any easier on them or their parents to know this. Children don't understand a lot of the thoughts and feelings they experience in their dreams and the sheer intensity of their nightmares is quite hard for adults to comprehend, especially when they're particularly curious and imaginative children, and their nightmares can become quite an issue. The most important thing for you to do is to make sure that you continue doing all you can to reassure and comfort your child, and make them feel safe as much as you can during this period of intensive brain development and activity for them. It may be helpful to try and gently talk with them during the daytime about their dreams, as this may shed some light on some of the reasons they're having so much trouble sleeping at night.

I dreamt I was walking in the snow and found a frozen baby,
the mother was frozen as well. I took the baby into a nearby
hot pool with me to try to defrost it. I remember feeling the
baby slowly defrosting - for some reason I thought it would live.
I was dribbling the water directly onto its face but then I think I
became more conscious of what I was dreaming because I started
worrying if it would be brain damaged! I didn't feel like the only one
doing it and I think maybe a friend was in the pool too with another
baby. As it defrosted it was more like I was defrosting meat because
I was squishing its arm lightly to see if it was still frozen all the way
through. It was all very odd!

Lucy, New Zealand

The frozen baby symbolises something about your inner nature that you've realised has now changed, come to an end
and gone forever. You've been feeling emotional about this, almost like you'd rather this change hadn't happened at all, but
really you do understand subconsciously that this change had
to come one day. You also realise that it's best to accept it in
order to move onwards and upwards in life.

I dreamt that I was sitting by a river with my partner on a
sunny day. As I opened my eyes I caught sight of a long snake
leaping in the air to catch a fly. I said to my partner 'did you
see that?' and when I looked the river was full of snakes, which
made me feel threatened. When I looked around me at the grass I
could also see holes where snakes could come from.

My partner then walked over to a cat sitting on the wall. He leaned
down to put his face right in front of the cat's face and I knew it was
going to bite him. It then turned into a snake and I was worried it

was going to bite his nose. I felt very uncomfortable.

You're afraid of something disturbing the happy emotional relationship you have with your partner. The snakes represent worries that you may very well be unaware of, about hidden or unknown dangers that may lurk as yet undetected in the 'long grass' of life, waiting to pounce! The cat turning into a snake and almost biting your partner's nose represents your fears about your own sense of femininity, symbolising a subconscious worry that he might one day not find you 'womanly enough' for him perhaps.

I 'm getting recurring dreams about water. Often it starts off calm then changes to gushing waterfalls or white water. I'm never in the water or even in any danger from it. People around me don't seem concerned, but I feel real fear and have even woken myself up screaming. It'd be good if you could help me, as I'm starting to get nervous about water when I'm awake!

Don't worry this is nothing to do with you being in any danger - water represents our emotional state, and that's precisely what your dream is about. You're extremely sensitive to your emotions, but you tend to keep the effects of this hidden from others. When all your feelings start getting on top of you, and you aren't letting anyone know about it, or talking about how you feel with someone, it's no wonder you're being so troubled. Try to find someone you can talk to about how you feel sometimes, it sounds like it'd do you the world of good.

M *y dead Grandad keeps coming to me in a horrible repetitive dream. I dream I'm lying in bed when he comes into the bedroom and tries to frighten me, laughing scarily, and tries to kiss me in a sexual way. At this point I try to escape, and find my partner, but then I 'wake up' still in my dream and I'm so scared I can't even look around the room.*

Although this is undoubtedly a very upsetting dream, it isn't about your Grandad at all. You feel the need for a lot of love and affection in your life, and you aren't feeling like you're getting enough of this, you're becoming more insecure and almost childlike in your desire for attention in these ways. It may even be that you're in fact the recipient of the opposite, and are actively being treated poorly in some way from time to time, and just need to feel like everything is OK again. Whichever it is, and I hope it's the former not the latter, I hope you get more love and attention than you know what to do with very soon indeed.

I *n my dream I'm on a plane with my family, and my Mum is standing up, folding clothes into piles. Then the pilot shouts 'everybody sit down, we need air!' and a big window in the top of the plane opens up letting a strong wind in. As the plane drops quickly I look for Mum but she's now miles away in the distance running to me, and when she gets to me at last, the plane hits the ground and breaks into pieces.*

You're looking beyond your home-life and your boundaries these days, you want more than you've experienced of life to date, and are beginning to 'spread your wings' - you've either 'left the nest' and are thinking about moving your life on even further, or are thinking about doing so soon. The thing is though, you're worried that your relationship with your Mum is going to change in a negative way, that you're going to lose the closeness you feel to her as a result. When this is the case, it's good to remember that whilst the nature of all relationships changes with time, when people are as important and close to each other as you are with your Mum, you'll always be there for each other in whatever capacity you both can even when you're far apart - and it works both ways, so don't forget to talk to Mum about how she might be feeling too.

I had a dream my house was covered in scaffolding. I went to lean on it and it all started collapsing, so I ran into the house scared and crying. When I tried to tell my family what happened, no one seemed interested in my story. I then went back outside, only to find the scaffolding was back up again, and I felt so happy! As I opened my front door though, to go back inside, I felt a big sense of dread and fear, and then I saw a large pair of glowing eyes looking at me from the top of the stairs - I was petrified!

The house in your dream represents the way you perceive yourself, and how you see yourself in relation to others in life in general. You've been feeling a distinct lack of emotional and maybe even physical support from one or more of your family members of late, although this is something that only you have begun to notice. It seems to happen very much 'behind closed doors' as it were... not 'in public' so that most people would be able to notice. From the outside, things appear fine and dandy to others. Only you know the truth about your home life, and it's making you feel really horrible and afraid. Try speaking to those that you feel this lack of support is coming from, tell them about how you truly feel, and about your fears that have arisen as a result of how they're treating you. It could really help you and them too.

I dreamt I was in a really huge Toy shop, looking around at all the cuddly toys, dolls and teddy bears there. I noticed that amongst them was a cuddly toy that looks really familiar for some reason, so I go for a closer look - and then I suddenly realise it's actually my own child! And then it turned it's head and looked at me, blinking, but then I woke up. I don't even have a child, what can it mean?

You're feeling that your life lacks domesticity, that you require the luxury of a few more home comforts than you're getting, or even just a bit of TLC. It's easy for this to happen to us in life from time to time - whether we're working too hard, or too much, or perhaps the demands of others are taking up more of our time than usual, leaving us less energy to look after ourselves as much as we might need, or would like. You want to enjoy life more than you are at the moment, so try to do something about it to redress the balance a bit, and give yourself a break where you can.

M y dreams have been getting, well, extremely 'sexy' lately and I'm worried. It's almost every single time I have a dream that I seem to be having one like this. I enjoy them, don't get me wrong, it's just that that's the problem really. I'm enjoying the sex I'm having in my dreams a lot - it's usually really wild, whether it's with my boyfriend, or with strangers, famous people, or people I don't know very well. I feel like I get more 'turned on' and excited in the dreams than I do by my 'real' sex life with my boyfriend! Is there something wrong with me?

Jessica, Ipswich

Dear Jessica,

Having erotic dreams, especially frequent ones, can often indicate, quite simply, the desire for a more interesting physical sex life. In our dreams we're often less inhibited than we are in waking life, so maybe it's an idea to try to inject a bit more 'adventure' into proceedings with your boyfriend - I'm sure he won't mind if you do, as long as you both agree on what to try together! Although, conversely, this can sometimes be a rather obvious conclusion, and not always the point our subconscious may be trying to get across - but to be frank, in your case, I think it's fairly plain to see that you and your partner could very well stand to benefit from taking a bit of inspiration from your rather insistent subconscious mind's suggestions.

*W*hat's the significance of this dream I had recently? In it, I'm in my kitchen with a little black kitten curled around my shoulders, purring and kissing me, and, though I'm very scared of them in real life, a large black Alsatian dog is there too. Then I looked out of the window and saw a pack of wolves, all growling and running towards the open back door! My Alsatian starts barking and baring his teeth at them, and I run to the door and just about manage to lock it as the 'leader' of the wolf pack is putting his nose inside the doorway.

Briony, Suffolk

Dear Briony,

Black animals, birds and other creatures are a really positive sign when they appear in our dreams. They're often seen as being strongly symbolic of being protected in some way, particularly in Native Indian and Ancient Egyptian culture. You've been feeling that you need to stand up for yourself lately, in spite of an oppressive or disagreeable force that seems to be trying to prevent you being how you want or doing what you want to do. Deep down though, you know and feel instinctively that you can be exactly how you are and do just what you want - even if for the moment it seems you have to try harder than normal - but you certainly have the protection and strength you need around you to be able to do so.

I always have dreams where I'm going about my daily life what seems like perfectly normally, only... I'm completely made of plastic like I'm a big Barbie Doll! No one treats me any differently, but I'm very aware of the fact that I can't do things like others do because I'm really only a doll version of myself, and it makes me feel sadder and sadder as the dreams go on.
Paulina, Birmingham

Dear Paulina,

Your dream reflects the way you perceive how you are around others, and that you aren't really being how you want to be in life generally. You seem to think you should behave or live in the particular 'perfect' way that you think that others expect you to, instead of just being brave and being your true self, and this is what's upsetting you. The thing for you to learn from these dreams is this: if you compromise how you want to live for the sake of trying to keep others happy, you only harm yourself in the end. You can't please all the people all the time, and there's no point running around trying to be something you're not in order to try and do so either.

*W*hen I was a child, I had a recurring dream. I'd go to the bathroom in the night, only to find a figure of a lady in a wedding dress and veil coming out of there. I turn to run to my parents room but an old man in a suit stood in the doorway, and as I ran downstairs and outside to get away, they would be calling my name saying they needed me. When I got outside I look back at the house and all the lights are flashing on and off and the figures are floating above it. So frightening...
Stephen, London

Dear Stephen,

It certainly sounds like you had a difficult time of it at some point during your childhood - which happens to most of us of course, to varying degrees. These upsetting or insecure moments in our young lives can be extremely disruptive to our subconscious minds, and this often manifests in our dreams albeit sometimes not in very easy to decipher ways. Whatever it was that was so upsetting for you back then, it made you feel very unhappy at the time, and your dream would suggest that it was strongly related to your views at the time on 'adult relationships' in some way, most probably your own parents. Typically, children have dreams of a nature similar to yours at times when their parents were having difficulties in their marriage or relationship with each other.

*L*ying in bed with the blinds open looking at the sky, I dropped off to sleep, when suddenly a beautiful light appeared and turned into an Angel dropping lots of little white feathers from her hands into my garden. I call my 10 year old granddaughter to come with me downstairs to collect the feathers, some of which *have stuck to a bush (which I don't actually have) - only when I picked them off they turned black in my hand. Then my grand-daughter looked up at the sky and said 'that's where I'm going when I'm 12'. This dream really worries me - does it mean something bad is going to happen to her?*

Sarah, Belfast

Dear Sarah,

Your dream is all about your hopes and fears for your grand-daughter. You see how relatively innocent and pure she is, and how happy, warm and easy-going life is for her. However you also see that, as life goes on and she gets older, how you fear what may happen to her, and that she'll need protecting from the world in many ways. This is a totally natural, understand-able concern though, and I'm sure that if you're there for her as much as you can be when she needs your advice, help or pro-tection, she couldn't ask for more.

I'm in a room in my dream, completely naked, and the walls all have 'peep-holes' in them. I look into one of them and see a couple having sex. The man sees me looking at them, and he stops and comes into my room and starts touching my breasts - and before anything else can happen, I wake up! I don't understand what it's supposed to mean, but it certainly felt very frustrating at the time!*

Natalie, St Albans

It definitely looks like you're feeling that you aren't experien-cing as much sexual adventure and excitement as you want in life - particularly not as much as you think other people seem to be having! The peep-holes represent the limited views you get of what your sex-life could be like, if only your situation was different in some way. Perhaps this is in relation to your partner, the people you might be seeing, or even the lack of either of these... whatever the reality is for you, it sounds like you are in dire need of some 'stimulation' in this department!

I dreamt that my father presented me with a huge leather-bound old book of poetry which he'd written - although as far as i know he doesn't write poems, or even particularly like reading them either! It felt incredibly important to me that I never let anyone ever take it away from me too, like it would have been totally disastrous to let that happen. What do you think it means?

Robert, Leeds

Dear Robert,

This dream is all about your relationship with your father, and in particular regarding his experience and perspective on the world and how much you value and treasure his words... which appears to be quite a lot! You're very protective, maybe even defensive, about him in many ways, which is understandable of course seeing as he's your father, but family ties aside, you have a wonderfully close psychological affiliation with each other. His words are a great source of inspiration to you, and you both share a strong sense of idealism about life, much as we might find in the words of poets and indeed all those with such 'romantic dispositions' - just like the one you and your father seem to share with each other.

I dreamt that I was packing all my things up into an old suit-case, and I mean EVERYTHING - my clothes, records, orna-ments, hi-fi, telly, furniture, the lot! Then, I ran out of my front door and onto a bus, which took me to the beach somewhere very hot and tropical. Then I ran off the bus, threw my suitcase down and lay on the beach, laughing hysterically but totally relieved - so much so that I actually woke myself up by laughing so hard! I don't really even like hot beachy places, so that's all quite bizarre really.

Violet, Liverpool

Dear Violet,

You may not want to go away for an exotic holiday, but it's fairly indicative of the fact that, outside of your home life, you'd like a complete change from things as they are right now in other areas! You packed absolutely everything with you, which shows that you value and are happy with a lot about your domestic situation at least. Maybe you need to take a break to evaluate your life, work and friends situations, see what conclusions you come to away from the everyday pressure and expectations these things can put on you.

I *found a huge Raven in my dream, badly injured. Although he was really heavy, I managed somehow to pick him up and hold him in my arms and talk to him with comforting words, gently stroking him all the while. Then the dream skipped to him being all well again, flying around me and we were even playing together. It was a lovely dream in the end, but so sad to begin with.*

Ravens do represent the darker sides to things, and especially things relating to - though not literally representing - death, so I'm not surprised to hear that you felt sad during the initial stage of this dream. This is about you coming to terms with this darker side to life, perhaps even the death of someone near to you. What's happening here, is that you're beginning to understand that if you can live with these darker, but nonetheless, very real and present aspects of life more easily, your own existence becomes lighter and an altogether more pleasant and rounded experience over-all, too. It's nothing less than the eternal dance of the Yin and Yang of life.

M *y dream takes place in a Medieval town, the kind with a market square and where the houses are all white with black beams. I'm asking people if they know where my husband is, but no one knows, until a couple say he's at the top of a white tower. I went there, and climbed up the long staircase to the top, then drew back a curtain to a room and saw my husband, who I called to - he turned around only for me to find he now had a balding, flaky scalp and some sort of disease on the right hand of his face. It was horrible!*

Lorna, Aberdeen

Dear Lorna,

This reflects an old way of thinking about your husband you've had, that's no longer relevant to either of you. In fact,

350

it would even do him harm if you were to continue thinking this way about him. Whatever this particular issue is, I'd say it seems to be something to do with the way he looks to you or perhaps how you think he's perceived by others around you. Try and be objective about your thoughts and this might lead you to discover exactly where you've been going wrong here. I'm sure it'll do the both of you the world of good in your relationship together.

I had the strangest dream ever a couple of nights ago. I'm in my Granddaughter's room when a white dog appears and goes to the toilet in the corner - and there was LOADS of it, all pure white too! The next thing I know, I'm trying to find my Granddaughter's house but I can't remember the name of the road or even the number of the door. P.S. I'm not a young person, but I can assure you, I'm not round the bend!

Iris, Cardiff

Of course you aren't 'round the bend' my dear! You feel fiercely protective over your Granddaughter, naturally enough, though you're concerned that maybe you might be being too protective occasionally, and that you worry too much about her. You don't want to adversely affect your Granddaughter by stifling her at all, especially as you might feel that you ruin things between you, and potentially lose the close relationship you have with each other as a result. So long as you remain aware of the potentially negative effects this kind of unnecessary over-protectiveness would have, I think you'll remain a perfectly wonderful Grandmother to her as she grows older.

I keep dreaming that I die - which is horrible enough to 'experience' - but I then find myself talking with a nurse, as she
prepares my 'body' for embalming and burial, and she was
showing me how she was draining the fluids from me and so on. As
she does more things to me, I found myself gradually feeling, seeing,
and hearing less until I felt like I really was really dead and there
was nothing more I could do about it. It was really vivid too, which
made me feel horrible all day afterwards. I'm worried it means I'm
going to die soon or something.
Olive Winmore, Manchester

Dear Olive,

Don't worry, this is nothing to do with you dying - this is
all about transformation in your life. A particular episode is
coming to a close, you're changing as a result and your subconscious is only too aware of it. It can be alarming and
even frightening sometimes, when things or situations we are
used to being a certain way start to change, alter and morph
into something unfamiliar, especially if it happens suddenly.
It sounds like you're going through a major upheaval of some
sort, but these times are soon gradually, and sometimes
quickly, replaced by their energetic opposites in life sooner or
later.

I was 'hanging out' with Kate Moss in my dream and we were
walking down the street in the rain, when we see a nice garden
with a lovely 'outhouse' in it, so we sneaked in to smoke some
cigarettes. We were sitting on the comfy, dry seats in there when
suddenly an angry man appears at the window, shouting and shaking his fist at us - we run off, out and down the road, and then I lose

sight of Kate, finding that the only way to escape is to run through a Leisure Center, dodging past the security guards - weird. I don't even fancy Kate Moss really either!

Scott, Edinburgh

Dear Scott,

You feel that you aren't getting enough space or time to do the things you enjoy in life, certainly not as much as you'd like to anyway, and that there's always something or someone 'spoiling your fun' as it were. Perhaps Ms Moss isn't quite the actual object of your desires or affections in real life, but what she symbolises here is the desire for female energies near you, maybe your partner, or perhaps just a yearning for a bit of a 'change from the norm' somehow in this respect.

I *n my dream I'm in a forest when I come to a clearing where there is a beautiful white stag being attacked by a mangy grey wolf, unable to defend itself. I ran toward it, throwing sticks, telling it to try picking in something that fights back, ie. me. It does so, but just as I'm thinking I might well lose but at least the stag was safely away, 2 beautiful wolves - one pure black, one pure white - come and chase the mangy one away. They then started licking and cuddling me, and then I woke up feeling refreshed and with a deep sense of awe and wonder at what happened.*

Gene, Peterborough

Dear Gene,

The mangy wolf attacking the white stag represents some kind of uncontrollable situation in your life that concerns you a lot. However, the white and black wolves symbolize your own valiant efforts to confidentially deal with whatever this is and your abilities to successfully do so, which enable you to protect those around you from it with ease and grace. Wonderful, almost 'classic' dream imagery.

I never have a nice dream. Each night my dreams involve me being chased, held hostage, and people I know being seriously hurt; I often shout out in my sleep "Leave me alone!" and "Help me!" and wake up crying and scared. It puts me off even trying to sleep, it's like starring in the film 'A Nightmare on Elm Street'! Any advice would be helpful to my problem
Melissa, Bath

Dear Melissa,

This sounds like a case of you being at a highly emotional, troublesome stage in your life, and that things around you are causing you to feel insecure and afraid. Your energies and thoughts are pretty much 'all over the place' aren't they? Try to relax as much as you can, aside from the time when you go to sleep at night, and if you can, try to do something to alleviate some of the external events causing you concern. Regarding the more 'internal' events - I'm absolutely sure that given a little more time, you'll begin to find things easing up in your fraught subconscious mind. Don't forget that we're always changing internally and externally, even if we sometimes can't see it and are convinced otherwise.

I *was staying in a fancy high rise apartment block and had a crazy party with lots of beautiful people and models staying over in the flat, friends of mine, people I work with and hangers on. It felt like it was where I belonged, hanging out with them all, but also it felt like the real me was observing me and the party and thinking they were all conceited, and I didn't really want to be there.*

Sam, Portsmouth

Dear Sam,

This is about how you see yourself in the role you currently inhabit in the world, in your work life, social and personal life. Although you find yourself behaving in certain ways and hanging out with certain people, you aren't happy about the position you're in. Something is lacking or wanting in your world, and though you've recognised this fact, you don't know what to do about it yet. Identifying the problem in the first place is the main thing though, and now you're aware of this 'imbalance' in your life you'll soon see that ways of changing things for the better will soon present themselves to you.

E *ver since I was a small child I've had this recurring dream. I'm tied to an Altar, and 'The Devil' appears, who then performs rituals with me. I can feel the effects of them strongly, both inwardly and outwardly, and for days after I've had the dream these sensations remain with me. What is this and why do I dream this?*

You've often found yourself to be afraid of the darker, negative aspects of your own mind, to the point that you almost 'obsess' about it. You feel that you are limited or even prevented from being how you would ideally like to be in life because of these 'negative' traits you find so distasteful. The thing is, you'll find if you try to accept this side to life a bit more that we in fact need it to balance out the lighter side to things and to give contrast and dynamics, and that it's nothing to be afraid of really.

Q uite often I dream that I go into a telephone box and there's money on the shelf. I don't actually phone anyone but I always know I will get money if I go in it. Last night I dreamt that I still got money but there was so much it was spilling out of the edges of the phone box underneath the phone. Although it's a nice dream, I don't understand it.

You have no problems when it comes to effectively communicating to others what it is that you actually need or want in life, and you know it too which is great. As you become more and more experienced and you refine your 'skills' as it were, you're finding that you're becoming more and more effective too. Long may it continue - who knows where it'll all lead?

I dreamt I was walking around the rooms of a lovely big house which was mine, but my belongings were stacked here and there, and it didn't have the 'lived in' look. Suddenly drops of blood started dripping from the ceiling onto the floor. I said 'we've got to get out, the house is going to collapse!' and I began picking important items to take with me. I looked in a back bedroom and there was a lovely fabric Rocking Horse in a storage box. What do you make of that?

You've gone through some major changes recently in your personal life, and you feel very strongly that it's time you moved on from how you and your life used to be. You know that the way you were is no longer of as much help or use to you as it once was, but that there are still some aspects to yourself that are worth holding on to - it's not about getting rid of every-thing from the past, more just holding on to and cherishing character traits that you feel are relevant to your life now.

*H*oping you will be able to explain this dual dream as it's puzzling my whole family. My daughter dreamt that she had to take her 12 year old son to hospital to have his right eyelid stitched up as there was a hole in it. The following morning while on the school run, my Grandson said to her 'Mum, I had a strange dream last night. I dreamt I had to go to hospital as I had a hook stuck in my eyelid'. When she asked which eye he said 'my right'. None of the 'Dream solutions' books I've read explain this.

As mother and child, they must have a very strong link with each other, but it certainly seems that they have an even deeper connection than what might normally be expected between such close relations. Unfortunately though, there seems to have been some kind of obstacle impairing your Grandson's understanding or knowledge of the world in some regard that both he and his mother are both unconsciously, and simultaneously, aware of. Tell your daughter about this, and encourage her to sit down and have a chat with her son to see if she can shed some light on the predicament he finds him-self in here - it could prove to be very illuminating as well as helpful to both of them.

I dreamt I was a rock star, performing a concert on the ocean, with no clothes on, and my audience were holding up sparkled fringed tiny clothes against me so I wasn't naked, but it made dancing awkward. I remember feeling that I really wanted to have a baby but had no one to have it with. Then my ex-hubby and an old

friend left me stranded there by nicking my helicopter ride home!
Danielle, London

Dear Danielle,

You're being almost extravagantly emotionally honest about yourself with the world these days, and you feel somehow let down by your ex, and your old friend. It's almost as though they've got in between you and a sense of stability, of being grounded, which you felt you had more of a sense of before you became this new, more open and more emotionally honest *you.* Many people seem to be finding this candidness of yours in some way uncomfortable, or disconcerting, but it's the way you feel you want to be, it's how you *have* to be, whatever anyone thinks or says about it.

My parents died last year, and I had a dream that I had to view my dead father in an open coffin, when he suddenly opened his eyes, started talking, and got out of the coffin. Then my Mum appeared too, and they started following me about like they wanted to come home with me, but I tried to get away from them, as they both smelled terribly of decomposing bodies. It was very upsetting to me though because I miss them so much.
Jayne, Hull

Dear Jayne,

The memories you have of your parents deaths, and the fact that they've passed away so recently, are things you'd like to distance yourself from more. This dream is your subconscious showing you that despite your willingness to make the most of your life, you still understandably have very strong and overpowering feelings about them and about the fact they're no longer here. It's not that you don't wish to remember them or want to forget them, it's just that you want to move on with your life, in whatever the best way for you might be, going forwards.

I *dreamt my son and Granddaughter were talking in German together, and when I asked them why they were talking in a foreign language, they said 'why are you talking in English?'* *Then somebody else in my dream told me that I had bird's mess on my jacket! I woke up, and when I checked my jacket - there WAS bird's mess on it! I was shocked that my dream came true - is this dream trying to tell me something?!*

Rose, Basingstoke

Dear Rose,

Your dream represents the fact that you're having difficulty understanding something relating to your son and granddaughter's lives. It could be their opinions or viewpoint on something, or perhaps they way they choose to live which you cannot get to grips with. Whatever it is, it's certainly proving somewhat vexing for you to say the least, and you feel very negatively towards yourself in relation to this. The bird's mess must have landed on you previously, and you were subconsciously aware of it happening at the time, but for some reason you simply didn't consciously acknowledge it until after your subconscious 'prompted' you about it in your dream.

I *dreamt I am at my ex-neighbour's home, alone, talking on an old black phone with my sister. It was set some time in the past, but my body was my present self. Suddenly a light bulb explodes on the ceiling with a big 'puff', and I have to put the phone down because my hands are covered with glass shards, which are also all over the floor. There's no blood, but the hundreds of shards clearly pass all the way through my hands. I know I have to clear the whole place, as if somehow it was my fault or I shouldn't have been there from the beginning; but to do anything I need to pluck the shards out of my hands first... but even though there's no pain, just a tingling feeling, I just don't know where to start. There's too many shards, and it might hurt. There's also a trail of nuts and bolts and other toolbox stuff from the main door to the kitchen, and the kitchen is a building site, which I find curious but do nothing about, as I've got other concerns 'at hand'!*

There has been a time (or times) at a previous point in your life when you've found that something has seriously affected communications between you and your sister. It's an issue that has proved difficult, hurtful or impossible to discuss, and although some other factors are involved it certainly seems that you yourself feel somehow responsible for the situation as it is or was. It's related to protection, specifically the protection of your sister, and also to important changes that have taken place in your life. The home life you grew up with seems to be of much less relevance to you these days, especially in relation to this situation, to the point that it essentially doesn't exist in a way that you are happy with anymore. I hope that in the future you can eventually move on to a more positive relationship with each other as brother and sister, without so much emphasis on who might to blame for any old troubles or regrets.

M *y dream is always the same, although I mainly had this vivid dream as a child. I am a young male, about eight years old and in the dream my clothes are always identical. I was in the bowels of a very old schooner, I can really smell the ship's wood. I know I either live on this ship, or I am at least on this ship a lot of the time. We are in a battle of some sort, I can hear shouting and gunfire and I know that the ship is sinking, and that I'm on a wooden bed that has a sack filled with straw as a mattress. I am kneeling on the bed and hitting my fist on the side of the ship, trying as I might to somehow hit my way out. When I wake up I am physically hitting the bedroom wall in fear.*

Sophia, Cirencester

Dear Sophia,

You are obviously a very emotional, sensitive person. When we are younger, especially, our emotions are new, fascinating and a particularly potent source of all manner of alarming highs, lows and general turmoil, but you seem to still feel greatly affected by your emotions to the point that you feel quite at the mercy of them. No wonder then, when you're travelling in your 'em-ocean' going vessel in your dreams, it can feel like you're in the middle of a battle. Sometimes you feel as if you really would rather just escape your emotional storms completely, to 'hit your way out' of whatever situation is troubling you... and I think most of us can appreciate just how you must be feeling at these times. Let's hope there will be plenty of smoother waters and some emotional 'plain sailing' ahead.

A bout a month ago I had a huge argument with my boyfriend's mother and we have not spoken since. I keep having dreams nearly every night that she and I are either having a row or not speaking, and in other dreams she talks away to me like normal. What does this mean? I'd really like it if we could get talking again.

Emilia, Salford

Dear Emilia,

The huge argument you and your boyfriend's mother have had has obviously affected you very much indeed. Your subconscious mind is replaying events in your dreams in this way, going over and over all the tumultuous feelings you must have had at the time. This is because you don't know what to do to resolve the situation, which you would clearly love to sort out. I think that if you try and make the effort to make the first move towards talking about things again with her in a calm and sincere way, you'll at least find you make some headway and you'll both begin to feel better about it all. And, your dreams will soon start to become less troubled as a result.

I recently had a dream where my flat was infested by mice. Not ordinary mice, but mice wearing tiny little knitted jackets, trousers and hats, all pastel colours. I caught one and fed it to my cat! Now THAT I would love to have interpreted, Monsieur de Lune.
Guri, London

Dear Guri,

You've been feeling slightly overwhelmed by many somewhat lesser, but by no means insignificant, issues or problems caused by the people around you in general. They're not huge great big problems, but more like slightly irksome or annoying ones! You're dealing with these things suitably well enough though, but this dream is also a little subconscious reminder to you, to keep making sure you don't allow others to interfere in your life.

I dreamt that it was night, and very dark outside. All I can remember was me drowning in a river under a bridge, and although I can swim, I was really struggling to come back up. As
I was going down, deeper and deeper into the water, I looked up and
saw a man looking down on me, and he had a knife in his hand. I
couldn't make out his face as it was blurry under the water. Ever
since that dream, I've been feeling edgy and anxious about walking
under bridges at night.

Kerry, Chesterfield

Dear Kerry,

Don't take it literally... this dream symbolises the fact that
you're struggling to cope with something very important in
your life, which is negatively affecting your emotional life.
Your subconscious is telling you to acknowledge and utilise
your authoritative, more forceful side, to help you deal with
this situation. Although you normally find this unpleasant,
and really dislike behaving this way, you must try not to be
too afraid to do so, for your own sake.

I keep dreaming I'm at the weddings of people I don't know.
There's sometimes more than one wedding per dream, and at
each one, I'm always having a lovely time, and dressed in the
same pale coloured summer dress. We've recently had three deaths
in the family, and I seem to be constantly grieving for them - yet
I keep having these really happy dreams at night. Why is this happening?

from Doreen, Alderly Edge

Dear Doreen,

Right now you are in dire need of a more harmonious time of it in life, generally. You've obviously had a trying time in many ways due to these deaths in the family, and they've really affected you a lot. Your subconscious is attempting to find you some relief from all the sorrow and grief you've recently been experiencing so pertinently, and so painfully.

I *dreamt a gentleman who I see on the school run was taking me somewhere. We were walking through a derelict village, when a hairless cat started talking to us! She said to the gentleman 'I've been waiting for her', suddenly transformed into a beautiful young woman, and the next thing I know myself, her and this gentleman were having a 'bedroom liaison' together! She said her name was Bastet, and she was in love with me. I looked her up and discovered she was an Egyptian goddess; anything else you can tell me?*

Nikki ,Penrith

Dear Nikki,

This is all about your own personal feminine power and sensuality. Lately your powers of attraction and womanly wiles have been on the increase, and your subconscious is letting you know that it's about time you did something more with them, one way or the other. Bastet, or Bast, is the Egyptian Goddess of Cats and symbolic of fabulously feminine strength - what better symbol could you want to represent the grace, allure and sheer sexual energy of a woman at the peak of her powers?

I had a completely bonkers dream last night where I saved a baby from drowning, then travelled back in time to 1981 where I bumped into Princess Diana, and wanted to warn her of her early death, but chickened out and let her walk away. I would love to know your thoughts on this - which are probably 'stay off the cheese sandwiches before bedtime'!

from Dawn, London

Dear Dawn,

There's something about you or your life which had been making you feel particularly emotionally vulnerable, and even threatened in some way. The good news is though, that although you were unsure quite what to do about it, somehow you've managed to turn this situation around. This dream was your subconscious telling you that in an ideal world, you might have benefited even more from doing what you've finally managed to do, if only you'd done so in your earlier life.

I dreamt I was standing by a derelict building surrounded by overgrown grass, and nettles taller than me. I cut them down but they kept growing back, and I was scared. I knew I could leave the area but didn't want to until I'd cut down all the nettles. It felt like I was going to be there forever, and I was sad as it meant I'd be forgotten and no-one would remember me. What does it mean?

Lyndsey, Yorkshire

Dear Lyndsey,

An old approach to life, bad habit, or undesirable character trait of yours is in dire need of changing or getting rid of, and your subconscious knows it. But there's something about this thing that you feel reluctant to give up or lose, despite the fact that you know it'd be bad for you to continue along your life path in this way. You feel protected by the familiarity of it, and afraid of what might happen if you step away and go forth into 'uncharted territory'. I hope you find the strength to change.

I had a funny dream last night. We went to the zoo and somehow we came back with a black monkey with eight eyes! We forgot we had it until our [actual] cat, which is also black, got off the floor, where she had been using it as a cushion to sleep on - and when she got off it, the monkey was purring. We rang the zoo and took it back. What does that mean?

from Clare, Caerphilly

Dear Clare,

Somewhat inexplicably, to you, there's quite a bit more mischief and oddness in your life than usual of late. This is symbolised in your dream by your acquiring of the strange 8-eyed black monkey creature... but, however odd or unexpected these mischievous influences may be, at least your dream indicates that it's not an entirely unpleasant experience. You're quite calmly accepting of these recent developments in your life for now, but if and when things get too troublesome or out of hand, you'll deal with them just as calmly too.

Last night I dreamt I was running fast, in the semi-wild under the moonlight with my two cats - like a sort of 'Secret Garden' halfway through it's make-over! When I awoke, my cats were as usual tightly cuddled up to me, but it seemed like they knew what I'd been dreaming, because they had been in the same

situation in their dreams. Is it possible?
Nicky, London

Dear Nicky,

Actually, it IS possible that more than one person, very often couples, siblings, and people who share a strong emotional and psychic bond with each other, can experience what is essentially the same, or at least a very similar, dream. I'm sorry to say it's impossible to find out for sure if there had been any similarity between the dream you had, and the dreams your cats had! However, you've obviously grown very close to your cats, and you have have a strong psychic connection between you and them, so it's entirely possible in theory this could have lead to such a shared dream experience.

I *had this dream the day before my girlfriend Nina passed away. I was in a big old house trying to find her, I knew she was in there. I came to 2 big doors, and felt a presence in the room beyond. I had no idea what, but knew it was bad. I was afraid but also felt that she was in this room, so I opened them and walked inside. As soon as I was in the door slammed shut and everything went pitch black. I froze and called out to Nina - no reply - but then felt this presence getting closer. I hyperventilated, and as I felt the presence right over me, I woke up, breathing heavily. Nina passed away the following the night. I have always believed that it was my subconscious telling me I was about to lose her, and that the presence was death itself.*
Richy, Skelton

Dear Richy,

Yes, I agree, this dream of yours was certainly your subconscious mind showing you what you instinctively knew was about to happen. Also, it shows how you were already sub-consciously attempting to come to terms with the imminent loss of her from your life. The effects this tragic turn of events would have on you, personally, are symbolised in your dream by you trying to find your way around the unfamiliar, scary old house, the house representing you as you anticipated you would see yourself, and your life, after she was gone.

*R*ecently *I keep dreaming I'm sleeping with my best friend's husband, but when we're about to 'do it' I wake up! Also, I dream about a stranger making love to me, so vividly I can actually sense everything that's going on, and I dream that I keep 'going to the toilet' whilst I am in bed. I suffer with my health and from depression, and work has been hard for my hubby lately. Are my dreams related to any of this?*

Zoe, Devon

Dear Zoe,

Your dream represents your subconscious dissatisfaction with the 'physical' side of your life, but not simply alluding to 'just' your sex life, although that is of course a very significant part to all our lives, and I'm sure including yours too! You are in fact finding it hard to come to terms with something which has happened or changed in your life, something which you feel powerless to exert any real control over. It is quite likely, as you mentioned, this is something to do with your own ill health, or perhaps even the stress your husband is feeling through finding work to be so hard for him lately is taking it's toll on both of you, and affecting your love lives together. Try talking about these dreams with him, it may help both of you, ultimately, to move onwards.

I was wondering, what does it mean when you dream about the Aurora Borealis (the northern lights)? In my dream, I'm basically there myself, looking up and feeling totally amazed. It was a lovely dream!

Leanne, Glasgow

Dear Leanne,

It is indeed a very interesting sign to find yourself dreaming about the Aurora Borealis, Leanne. They are a beautiful, amazing, and fascinating phenomenon, and when they appear in our dreams they signify much to feel similarly about happening in our lives. Your dream symbolises that you've had a new kind of insight into your life, as though something in you has 'woken up', that something previously obscured or hidden has suddenly been illuminated.

J ust wondering if you could help interpret a rather weird dream I had. I felt like I was waking up but when I 'woke up' I was lying in a 4 poster bed in a white room. I'd travelled back in time and I had a husband and 3 kids! Strangely though, I never saw the kids faces. I lived there for 3 months and my husband was a horrible man who used to get very drunk. Then, one day, I was leading my horse along the lane. I looked down at the rein and it had morphed into my dog's lead, and I was back in 'present day' again. Any idea what this means?

Anna, Falmouth

Dear Anna,

There's are things regarding your past, which your subconscious mind is telling you you need to be wary of, although you can't quite see what they are. Think of this dream as an indication that you need to be careful where you tread currently, so that you don't repeat the mistakes of an earlier stage or time in your life, because to do so could well prove to be detrimental to you now. It also symbolises the potency of your own personal power and innate strength, and that you should simply let your 'animal instincts' guide you forwards to success and happiness.

I had a strange dream where I was standing on the grounds of my old school, with my best friend, and we had both been shot! But then we both walked calmly to our French lesson together, only to find ourselves alone in a dark, empty school. Can you help me understand it?

Jennifer, Swadlincote

Dear Jennifer,

You obviously feel an empathetic connection with your friend. Your dream represents your current perspective on both your own life, your state of mind and general being, and that of your best friend. Recently, whether you were actually in school with them or not, you've come to realise that you and your best friend have both come a long way since your childhood. Literally, you sense that many of the lessons you were taught back then have since lost much, if not all, of their relevance to your lives. It's all good though, it means you're developing and growing as people, as one ideally should.

Since January this year, my 'Angel Oracle cards' have led me to start writing my dreams down a lot, and there's a theme that seems to run through all my dreams lately - 'famous' people, both living and deceased, in everyday situations. In my dreams I am aware of their celebrity status, but I am not overtly 'star struck' - although I must admit it was nice to once find myself going for a walk in the park with John Lennon in one of them! Some of the stars I like, and others not at all... what does it all mean?

Elizabeth, Glasgow

Dear Elizabeth,

Keeping a dream diary gives you a fascinating insight into your subconscious, and it certainly sounds like your cards were telling you that it would be especially beneficial to you to do so recently. The fact that your dreams have centered around celebrities and such like, whether you like these characters not, is symbolic of there being qualities these people possess which you respect, and subconsciously identify with - albeit on a very real and 'everyday' non-celeb type of level. Ask yourself what it is that they have about them that you might have in common with them, or whatever it might be which affects you so much. These are the aspects of yourself that your subconscious mind is telling you to focus on and develop, and maybe even improve upon too.

I dreamt I saved a tribe of people from danger. As they were cheering and I was leaving, I briefly looked like an eagle. This was obviously some predicted sign for them, as the whole tribe gasped and their leader said "It's true, then I am dead." Even though there was nothing visibly wrong with her, she slumped to the floor. I ran back and picked her up sobbing and then a grim reaper type person appeared and the tribe all hid. The leader made me promise to take her to him, and hold open her mouth so her *spirit could escape into the afterlife. This was the most important thing I had to do and I wasn't sure I could do it because I didn't want her to go.*

Zoe, Bristol

Dear Zoe,

There's a situation which you're unsure about being involved in, although you feel that it's something you should try to help with. You're exercising considerable personal strength and courage by continuing to let yourself be in this situation, because you know that it's the right thing to do, for the good of others around you, as well as your own spiritual growth. There is also a certain person who particularly stands to benefit from your presence and assistance, a person in a position of some authority or higher standing, so you realise it's important that you ensure you stick at it, especially for their sake.

I had a dream I was in a huge metal container which had been converted into living spaces with 10 beds, there was a real live crocodile in there, some water on the floor and a tarantula fell on my back and my bf got it off for me. What does this mean? I did not eat any cheese before bed!

Lucy, London

Dear Lucy,

Lately, you're feeling more protective than usual towards yourself, your way of life, maybe even your personal beliefs, as well as those nearest and dearest to you, such as your boyfriend. There's something, or someone, around in your life which you're sensing could pose a serious threat to you and all these things in some way, which is why you're, subconsciously at least, in 'extra protective' mode.

I keep having the same type of dream, where I'm always on an aeroplane but never find out where I'm going Can you help please?
Marjorie, Telford

Dear Marjorie,

Your dream symbolises an inner desire to escape your normal life, to break free and 'fly away' from those mundane, ordinary aspects of life which seem troublesome to you. The thing is though, that although the desire to escape might be there, practically speaking, you don't really know how on earth you're going to make this happen, nor where you would go, or what you might do with yourself if you did.

I often dream that my spirit leaves my body, flies to the ceiling, and I see myself asleep. It swoops around for a few minutes, whooshes into the sky, and flies to my Dad's house - who died 9 years ago - and enters his back door. I know in the dream that my dad is dead and I'm scared of what I will find in his house. Sometimes I find him sitting in his favourite chair and I swoop over, hug him and cry, and he cries too. We tell each other how much we love each other, and he tells me other things too, a lot of which come true in real life. I love seeing my dad but this leaves me quite distressed when I wake up.
Catherine, Newcastle-Upon-Tyne

Dear Catherine,

I'm not surprised you're feeling distressed after having that dream repeatedly. It can feel so real seeing deceased loved ones apparently 'alive again' in your dreams. Houses in dreams often symbolise how we, or others, see ourselves, our true inner selves. Aside from obviously loving and missing him, your dream in fact represents those positive qualities in him which you aspire to, or indeed do, possess yourself. You find these qualities a source of strength, and comfort - it's likely you're experiencing these dreams at times of stress or pressure in your waking life, where you subconsciously turn to them for guidance or help.

I dreamt I was walking through the streets when fireballs started falling from the sky, destroying part of the city I live in. I ran, and found a beautiful Japanese place with people sitting on cushions, drinking tea serenely. They beckoned me in and showed me to an underground place where I would be safe. When I emerged after the fire storm, I was a little Japanese girl, the city had been taken over by Germans in old WWII planes and cars! They caught me and took me to a concentration camp with lots of others, but treated us very well.

Jayne, Sunderland

Dear Jayne,

You've been having a tricky time of it lately. Other people and events surrounding you have seemed out of control, destructive and harmful to you and your life. But all is not so bleak, you're doing something about it, breaking ties with previous ways somehow, in order to liberate yourself from these troublesome elements, to find your personal 'nirvana', a happier state of being. There are clearly some things in your life which you still feel dictated to and controlled by, but I feel they're transforming into something more beneficial to you. I hope you get there sooner rather than later.

I *n my dream I was shopping at my local supermarket with my partner. He was in a different isle, when I suddenly got an itch and I lifted my top up, to see a baby growing in my fallopian tube on the right-hand side, but at the bottom. I tried to move the baby into my womb but with little success.*

Stacie, Portsmouth

Dear Stacie,

Your dream is symbolic of something which you subconsciously feel is lacking in your life with your partner. It could be an emotional need, or perhaps even something more practical and tangible, but there is definitely a desire for something which you feel would have a hopefully transformative effect on your lives. You're aware that you might have the solution to this situation yourself, but for some reason you don't know how to make it happen, or can't seem to work it out. Why not try talking to your partner about how you feel regarding whatever it is that you're attempting to make happen? He may be able to help if he's more aware of what you're trying to do.

I *found a plastic tupperware box on the windowsill of a house, that was full of tiny baby kittens. After a week or so nobody had taken them out of the box, and they'd got bigger and bigger, til they were all squashed inside and couldn't breath. They were scratching at the side so I bought a box ten times bigger and carefully opened the small box but one of the kittens jumped out and ran away over a fence. I tried putting the kittens in the new box but they were squirming and I kept getting their ears and tails trapped in the lid.*

Roi de Lune

Ella, London

Dear Ella,
Sounds like there are many new things coming into your life recently; new projects, people, ideas, maybe even new job prospects too. Whilst this is all very exciting and stimulating for you, at the same time, your dream tells me that you're feeling a little stressed by it all. It's clear though that you're trying your best to keep on top of things, to manage all these delicate new situations as carefully as you can, to give them chance to develop, so as not to spoil them before they've really got underway.

F ive years ago my Grandad died. We were extremely close and I miss him dearly, but I dreamt I was keeping his corpse on my bed. Two of my brothers came to visit, and one said 'no wonder people get freaked out seeing my Grandad's corpse there', then pushed him to the floor. I started screaming at my brother "get out" and that I wish my brother was dead, and as they left, and I cuddled up to my grandad saying how sorry I was. Then he opened his eyes! I was in shock - he started to say he wasn't dead but in a deep coma, and his heart was in a lot of pain. My family came to visit, telling him how much we missed him, and I was showing him a photo of my boyfriend, and he seemed to approve - but then I woke up.
Hannah, Carlisle

Dear Hannah,
Clearly you miss your Grandad a huge amount, understandably enough. Your dream symbolises how much you valued his presence in your life, which you feel, subconsciously, was in some ways even more than how much you think your family valued him whilst he was alive, perhaps especially regarding your brothers. You also hope that he's not suffering, wherever he is. You are keeping part of his spirit alive through your own actions and thoughts, after all, and I'm sure he wouldn't

want you to suffer as a result of your grief for him.

I keep having a strange dream that I hope you can explain to me. I dream about the witches in "hocus pocus"! I've had it three nights running, and I am dressed in a white dress hiding in a cupboard and I always wake up when they find me. Please help me!
Teri-Anne, Oldham

Dear Teri-Anne,

You have obviously attributed certain negative emotional associations with these three trouble-making main characters. From your dream, seeing as they're attempting to find you, and given their characteristically 'terrorising' nature in the film, it appears that you've been feeling similarly victimised by someone, or something, in your life, and it's starting to really get to you. I hope you can start to identify what or who it might be, and do something about it.

I dreamt I saw someone with a huge, sleek, black, and what seemed to be very wild Panther, walking along the road I live on. I went up to them to see them both more closely, and we somehow ended up sitting down together, me in the super strong paws/arms of the panther, holding hands with my fingers locked in between one of his paws' 'fingers', looking into its eyes and feeling totally safe and full of love for it! What can it mean?
Francis, Glasgow

Dear Francis,

Panthers are usually seen to be symbolic of powerful, dark and dangerous elements lying in wait, ready to 'pounce' and cause a person untold troubles and problems. However, your dream is suggesting something very different. You've recently come to terms with, and 'tamed' if you will, an element in your life which until now has been causing you major issues. Now, though, you've found the personal power to be able to not only deal with whatever this is, but learned to completely accept it with grace, and have transformed it into something truly beautiful.

S o lately I've been having dreams about my stepmom. In the dreams she usually has fallen over though, and I can't help her up. What does it mean?

Summer, Santa Monica

Dear Summer,

It seems to me that it's highly likely you find your step-mother to be someone whom you feel needs support and help with the problems in her life. They may not necessarily be very serious or overwhelming problems, but your dreams are telling you that you feel somewhat unable to make too much real difference to her waking life and this situation in general. It's quite clearly, perhaps unsurprisingly, frustrating to you, and this is why the subject keeps appearing in your dreams.

M y partner had a dream that really bothered him. There was a TV show with lots of evil clowns in, which only aired for 2 mins as it was so intense and scary. Then the dream changed to black and white, and a little boy dressed in victorian clothing appeared. My partner asked if he was OK, but he looked up and wet himself! Then it skipped to Blackpool tower, and a man

in a black miners jacket and black hat was standing there, but never spoke, then they were both surrounded by more Victoriana people walking around. He took some photos of it all, but when he looked at them, all the shops were modern. Then his dad appeared as his younger self, who went to touch my partner but then he woke up.
Gem, Lancashire

Dear Gem,

Well! There's plenty going on there, my goodness. There is someone around him who he's discovered really isn't what they pretend to be, and they've been making him, and maybe others too, feel threatened, unsafe and significantly repressed. This is very likely to have something do with people at work in some way. There's some particular aspect of his Father that he feels he needs to get back in touch with, within himself, as his subconscious mind suspects it might hold the key to the solution to this unpleasant situation.

*I*n my youth I thought Cancer was like an infected yellow pus which spread around your body. In my late teens I dreamt I was on a train travelling to Coventry, but couldn't get off as I was connected by tubes to a giant pus-filled onion shaped sack, taking up the whole carriage. And when I was 19 I ended up being sent to that very city, for a scan which diagnosed that I had cancer. What a coincidence! I never had any connection to Coventry before that either. Was my dream some kind of premonition?
Carol, Shrewsbury

Dear Carol,

It most certainly sounds like it yes! Wow, that was quite a detailed precognitive dream you had back then, I have to say. No one can explain how or why precognitive dreams occur, they are one of life's truly great, unexplained mysteries, and a source of endless fascination to dream researchers, and of course people everywhere. What a shame it was regarding such a dreadful condition that befell you, but given that you're writing to me now, I will take this as an indication that you have coped with it well and are very much alive and kicking!

I dreamt a huge Dragonfly landed on my face and started laying its eggs in my cheek! It was a beautiful creature, but so horrifying that it was doing such an awful thing to me. What can it mean?
Caroline, London

Dragonflies have all kinds of symbolism for people, across the whole world. This being the case, and there not being any especially significant aspect to them for you personally, it makes it more difficult to see what that dream of a dragonfly laying it's eggs in your face might truly mean, but that said: I still think that there has been something, or indeed several somethings, happen lately which you've felt were unwanted, and quite possibly invasive to you, and negatively affected how you feel others perceive you to be, how they see you. Personally, I get a sense that Dragonflies are more representative of protective qualities. In Japanese culture they symbolise strength, courage, and happiness even. It may be that despite you exercising such aspects of your psyche and personality, there were or are still things which have been getting to you and affecting you as I mentioned. Could it even be *because* of such traits in you perhaps? Perhaps they are related more directly to your upsetting experiences in a way I can't tell from your dream though.

I *had a really scary dream. I'm picking my kids up from the park from my Mum, and we are crossing the bridge from the park when I notice an old coin, which I bend over to pick up to show them. Suddenly I hear an enormous sound - a roaring jet engine, of what turns out to be a passenger jet plane, coming right at me! I dived off the bridge moments before it took off my head, then scrambled around for my kids and Mum, who are all fine, and then I woke up, petrified!*
Denise, London

Dear Denise,
There's been a valuable opportunity for you and your family that's come your way, which really caught your attention. However you've been afraid of the consequences of taking this opportunity up, in case something awful happens if things don't go according to plan, or even just how you would prefer them to. The thing to think about here is, are you just worrying too much about the potential risks involved, or are your concerns truly justified? Once you know the answer, you'll be able to act.

A *vivid dream I had was where I was walking outside in the middle of the night, and was surprised to see lots of people taking photos of the sky, which was flashing with all sorts of colours. I joined in with them, but somehow I couldn't manage to get a clear photo on my phone, they just kept coming out black. Suddenly a huge red hologram appeared in the sky with a 3D Jesus in it! And I knew it meant it was the end of the world, and I was kind of glad but also frightened. I grew up a Catholic but I lost my faith as an adult, and I was worrying in my dream that I might get sent to hell now! What can it mean?*

Agatha, Bratislava

Dear Agatha,
Something has seriously disillusioned you, and recently dashed your somewhat romanticised hopes about something important to you on the hard rocks of reality. You fear the consequences of the predicament or situation you find yourself in, and even suspect that perhaps there might be significant dangers waiting in the wings ahead of you! Let's hope not, eh; I don't think this dream really reflects any religious leanings you may have had to any great degree, but it's possible you are fearing some sort of judgement or retribution might be coming your way.

I had a dream that started off great, but soon went bad. In the dream I was with my boyfriend in our bed. We were kissing and having fun, but when I came back up from under the sheets my boyfriend had turned into my dad. What can this mean? Angie, Sunderland

Dear Angie,
It's likely that there's something about your relationship with your boyfriend which has changed lately. It may be that you feel him to be a stronger, perhaps more domineering presence in your life than he used to be, or that he's become more dependable and nurturing towards you - much like a father figure would typically be. Or are there other qualities which your father possesses that your boyfriend is echoing in some ways?

I had a weird dream that I was inside a Pinball machine! I was trying to get out, but was having to dodge loads of balls flying at me, avoid huge flapping things everywhere, and try not to fall down the holes... it was pretty terrifying, but quite exhilarating too. I was glad to wake up but it made me laugh when I thought about the experience really.
Imogen, Canterbury

Dear Imogen,
I'd say that your dream represents how your life seems to you right now, principally that you're having to deal with a lot of trying, tricky and troublesome things currently. Perhaps these things are all within your expectations in a way though, rather than just utterly random, bizarre challenges coming your way - everything that happens in a pinball machine happens within the physical limits of its shape, size and design, after all. So although things are testing your metal of late, it would seem to me, from your dream, that you're handling things very effectively indeed.

46666663R00215

Printed in Poland
by Amazon Fulfillment
Poland Sp. z o.o., Wrocław